THE ISLAND ON AN ISLAND

CULTURAL HISTORY OF COSTA SMERALDA

FRANCESCO BUSCEMI

COMMON GROUND

First published in 2025
as part of the **Tourism and Leisure Studies Book Imprint**
doi: 10.18848/978-1-963049-37-4/CGP (Full Book)

Common Ground Research Networks
2001 South First Street, Suite 202
University of Illinois Research Park
Champaign, IL
61820

Library of Congress Cataloging-in-Publication Data

Names: Buscemi, Francesco, author.
Title: The island on an island : cultural history of Costa Smeralda /
    Francesco Buscemi.
Other titles: Cultural history of Costa Smeralda
Description: Champaign, IL : Common Ground Research Networks, 2025. |
    Includes bibliographical references and index.
Identifiers: LCCN 2024055875 (print) | LCCN 2024055876 (ebook) | ISBN
    9781966214007 (hbk) | ISBN 9781966214014 (pbk) | ISBN 9781966214021
    (pdf)
Subjects: LCSH: Smeralda Coast (Italy)--Description and travel. | Smeralda
    Coast (Italy)--Social life and customs. | Smeralda Coast
    (Italy)--History. | Tourism--Italy--Smeralda Coast. | Sardinia
    (Italy)--History.
Classification: LCC DG975.S3 B88 2025 (print) | LCC DG975.S3 (ebook) |
    DDC 945/.9--dc23/eng/20250121
LC record available at https://lccn.loc.gov/2024055875

LC ebook record available at https://lccn.loc.gov/2024055876

TABLE OF CONTENTS

INTRODUCTION

This book is a trip. Its topic is tourism but this is not the reason the book was written. Actually, many studies about traveling and the visitor experience do not suggest any idea of an itinerary. However, conceiving a book as a trip was the first idea that I had when I decided to write a history of Costa Smeralda. I have never been a tour operator, I thought, but this time I will be one—kind of. Like any tour operator, what I ask of the reader is to trust me and follow the line that I trace. It starts from what was in Sardinia before Costa Smeralda and arrives at what this place is today and probably will be in a few years.

Costa Smeralda is particularly suitable for this diachronic analysis. Its development over the years is a fascinating adventure, where good and evil collide or combine, and sometimes combine and collide simultaneously. Walking alongside the history of this place, dwelling on its key moments, trying to interpret them, and to reach some conclusion is what I do in this book; however, it may also be a fruitful exercise for the reader in order to relativize opposite concepts such as "good" and "evil" and things in general.

In this sense, this book owes much to Maria Cristina Addis (2016) and her semiotic analysis of Costa Smeralda, seen as a land of opposition that all together create a fascinating system of signs. Relevantly, Addis, in some parts of her book, tries to understand whether or not the invention of an artificial tourist destination, which however gave good environmental regulations to a place where they did not exist, should be considered good or bad, and she confesses that she is not able to answer. I immediately felt familiar with her uncertainty, as this is exactly what I have witnessed since my first stay in Costa Smeralda. This uncertainty in jumping to a neat conclusion has probably been one of the reasons why investigating Costa Smeralda is so appealing to a researcher, to the point of making them become a particular kind of tour operator.

Moreover, this trip has a historical structure. In it, the reader will find the chronological development and the physical and social construction of a holiday site from scratch; and its transformation into, in turn, an exclusive paradise, a political headquarters, a TV channel and, in the end, a big question mark.

Narrating in chronological sequence the antecedent, construction, development, success, crisis, second life, and today's uncertainty of Costa Smeralda holds together both "history" and "story." Costa Smeralda means history, specifically cultural history, as by writing about it (and I also hope by reading this book) one flies over the glory and vicissitudes of various ages, in Sardinia and more generally in Italy and in the world, seen through the lenses of tourism. Cultural values have very frequently interacted with Costa Smeralda, starting a dialogue that has ended up in changing both: Costa Smeralda has changed thanks to new cultural trends, and cultural trends sometimes have taken from Costa Smeralda (for example the concept of sustainability). In addition, social structures and even political ideologies have sometimes participated in the evolution or involution of Costa Smeralda, as in the years of Berlusconism, which marked twenty years of this history.

What is more, this book is also a "story," and what a story: an exciting series of narrative plots animated by contrasting sentiments and emotions, fueled by great dreams, hope, and abilities, and at other times, moved by equally big mediocrity and pittances. The human spectrum is, in large part, represented in Costa Smeralda, and thus in the following pages of this book.

Moreover, this is also a semiotic analysis of all of this. Semiotics is a theory stating that our world is in the end a system of signs, which waits to be interpreted for us to better understand what is around us. Semiotics is an analytical tool that has been often accused of being too theoretical and poorly practical. This may be true in some cases but never when semiotics has become social semiotics and has connected the systems of symbols to cultural values, social structures, and the actual people's lives. This is exactly what this book does, relying on social semiotics and its continuous reference to reality.

To put the reader at ease, the historical account of Costa Smeralda is situated in each chapter at the beginning, while the semiotic analysis occupies the final part of it. If someone is only interested in one of the two, they now know what part to read and what to discard. However, I suggest reading both. On the one hand, the semiotic analysis will help the reader understand history. On the other hand, the historical part contains information and details that render the reading of the semiotic analysis much more complete and enjoyable, with narrative plots included.

Semiotic analysis is a frequent companion of my media and cultural investigations. However, this time, one of the most important semiotic theories, Baudrillard's map of the territory, came up abruptly during my first visit to Costa Smeralda, immediately after COVID-19 restrictions. Baudrillard assumes that the postmodern society adds representative maps to the territory, rendering the real land invisible and giving the public only representations about it.

During my first visit to Costa Smeralda, I had another impression: many shops, hotels, and restaurants were closed, the beaches were almost deserted, and only a few tourists walked through the towns. The just-finished lockdown seemed to have canceled the many postmodern maps that the media added to the territory. What was emerging was actually Monti di Mola, the real toponym of the geographic area of Costa Smeralda before the imposition of the new, commercial name. Did reality win over the fairy tale? My romantic impression lasted a couple of days. Later, I realized that Monti di Mola was probably a map too, a mythical representation based on our dreams of a pristine, untouched, and unspoiled place able to heal our postmodern discomfort.

Instead of discouraging me, that contradiction persuaded me to write this book. The questions were more than the answers and this made the topic exciting to me.

To sum up, I have chosen this topic for three reasons. Firstly, I love contradictions, and Costa Smeralda provides a vast array of them. Secondly, Costa Smeralda is a clear example of how deep Baudrillard's theory of hyperreality was, where the media are able to construct new forms of reality and to superimpose them onto the original one. Thirdly, Costa Smeralda has been built on an idea of tourism that disappeared in the 1980s; it thus adapted to a new concept of tourism in the 1990s and 2000s; and now that even this concept is over, it produces sentiments of nostalgia for a world that is fading, but also relevant questions on what this place might become in the near future, which I try to answer.

More specifically, Chapter 1 provides the readers with basic information about Costa Smeralda. Moreover, it reviews existing literature about the relationships between Italy and Sardinia, the construction of Costa Smeralda, and the type of tourism that it has attracted over the years.

The chapter also designs a framework based on three theoretical standpoints: the first is Jean Baudrillard's hyperrealism, his concept of simulacrum, and the theory about the map of the territory, which he drew from a short story by the Argentinian writer Jorge Luis Borges; the second theoretical model descends from Roland Barthes's conception of mythologies as media creations aiming at promoting dominant political ideologies, and from the relatively new ideas of the relationships between nature and culture carried out by biosemiotics. The third theory is Michel Foucault's differentiation between utopia and heterotopia, where the first is an idealized non-existing place and the second, a worrying, existing site placing humans in a state of suspension. Finally, this initial chapter also touches upon the methodology adopted to investigate Costa Smeralda, which is a combination of historical analysis, an ethnographic observation, and social semiotic multimodal analysis.

Chapter 2 looks at Sardinia before Costa Smeralda. It could be taken for a presumptuous chapter, as it spans a massive time period, from the Neolithic era to the 1950s. It is certainly superficial, but I hope it gives the reader basic notions about what Sardinia was and how many of its old characteristics are still there, while also exploring tourism in general and Costa Smeralda specifically. After the mythological aspects of prehistory, the chapter investigates the culturally rich Sardinian Middle Ages, the Spanish dominion, the creation of the Reign of Sardinia and its giving birth to the Italian State.

This part of the book does not hide the contrasts between Sardinia and the central State, which led to a sort of isolation of the island. Finally, a Sardinian problem such as banditry and a cultural element such as matriarchy are demonstrated to be certainly more than superficial components of Sardinian life. Rather, they are cultural values informing the way in which the Sardinians have looked at themselves and the others and have searched for their position in the world.

The adventure of Costa Smeralda starts with Chapter 3, the rise of "The Age of Hope." It in fact gathers data, documents, and information about the people who constructed Costa Smeralda and the way they were perceived by Sardinians. The chapter starts by developing a portrait of the Aga Khan, the person who made Costa Smeralda possible. However, in Italy, the Aga Khan was mainly a social and media construction, as newspapers, magazines, and TV channels gave the Italians a precise version of him. The Aga Khan was not alone; along with him, other men and one woman collaborated on the project according to their expertise and personal characters, and therefore even these people are described, although more briefly.

The Aga Khan and his collaborators were animated by a spirit that combined a romantic search for an untouched place and the commercial wish to transform it into a fruitful enterprise. Understandably, this second component implied buying lands from the locals at the best possible price, and this led to justifiable accusations of exploiting the Sardinian owners. After taking possession of the land, the group formed a Consortium, which became, soon, a sort of government of Costa Smeralda, the political (in the sense that it fixed the rules) and commercial arm of the group. The chapter ends with a semiotic account combining all the three theories mentioned above in order to better understand this constructive process.

If the previous chapter focuses on the social and media construction of Costa Smeralda, Chapter 4 centers on its material construction. Architects, buildings, hotels, architectural styles, and material issues are the protagonists of this part of the book and open the way to "The Age of Enthusiasm." Behind it, there is a never-solved issue: the negotiation between the new and the old owners of the land. The locals agreed to sell for little money as they had no idea of the huge value of that land, and even when they were aware of it, they could not construct Costa Smeralda. So they sold useless lots of land, used only for grazing animals. Those who bought, instead, acquired a potentially golden area, very valuable pieces of land, but at a very low price.

This uneven negotiation had a great absentee, the Italian State, which did not intervene, because it was convenient for the Italian governors that Costa Smeralda was soon commercially active. This is also why the Sardinian and Italian politicians left to the Consortium, the responsibility for making the regulations, only leaving to the State the duty of checking it out. Portraits of the main architects of Costa Smeralda and of what they built (plus an alternative village) occupy the central part of the chapter. This was a straightforwardly creative adventure, which produced some of the best architectural gems of the second part of the twentieth century in Italy. Finally, all of this is seen through Barthes's lenses, as, actually, we can consider the material construction of Costa Smeralda a great holiday mythology.

Chapter 5 delves into the first period of Costa Smeralda taking over Monti di Mola, the original toponym of the area, its successful "Age of Inaccessibility" when high-class tourists enjoyed their holidays far from journalists and photographers, and the magic atmosphere of those years, with princesses, fashion models, and international entrepreneurs. Unfortunately, it lasted only for a few years. Drugs, banditry, accidents, and the start of the long period of kidnapping suddenly turned paradise into hell and utopia into heterotopia, to say it with Foucault.

Even the Aga Khan changed his approach to his creation: if in the first years it was a mixture of adventure and commerce, in the 1970s he proposed Phase 2, which meant the abandonment of any romantic aim and a concrete pour that would destroy the beauty of that place forever. Thankfully, the Sardinian and Italian institutions rejected the plan, but the long night of Costa Smeralda began. Socially ruined by crime, attended by less fashionable tourists, depending on an uncertain future, the destination seemed not to have an exit strategy. All of this is also seen through the lenses of narratology and the theory of the narrator.

Chapter 6 focuses on the earthquake that woke up Costa Smeralda after the long night: Berlusconism. Berlusconism means not only Silvio Berlusconi, the powerful tycoon who, since 1994, was Prime Minister three times, ruling in Italy for about twenty years; but also his collaborators, tourists having him as a model, and, above all, a lifestyle. On a theoretical level, it means the passage from modernism to postmodernism.

When Phase 2 was rejected, the Aga Khan sold his commercial dream to the US entrepreneur Tom Barrack, who, at least at the beginning, left things as they were. However, life in Costa Smeralda totally changed, as those years can be called "The Age of Showing off." Berlusconi interpreted the island on an island as the perfect mix of entertainment and politics. In his luxury Villa Certosa, he was the protagonist of many discussed photographs and questionable parties, but also official meetings with Tony Blair, Vladimir Putin, and other international leaders. Berlusconism became thus the new narrator in Costa Smeralda, telling a different story from the previous narrative, which was narrated by the Aga Khan. The Berlusconization of Costa Smeralda would only finish with the end of the political trajectory of its leader. At that point, another night began.

Chapter 7 concerns the present and the future of Costa Smeralda, the night that is still there, and what might happen upon awakening. However, first of all, the chapter adjourns the reader about another change in ownership: Costa Smeralda is today part of the huge patrimony of the Emir of Qatar, who bought from Tom Barrack the whole enterprise. Barrack left for the same reason as the Aga Khan, complaining that the Sardinian and Italian politicians did not allow him to "innovate" Costa Smeralda, in a similar way as the Aga Khan's Phase 2. The new owner seems not to want to change things. Costa Smeralda, however, is still in its second break between one model and another. Berlusconism is over and no new groups appear to emerge as the next narrator. This state of suspension is well explained by a documentary, which the chapter analyzes in depth. The lack of new perspectives is instead underlined by a brief analysis of social media messages about Costa Smeralda.

To break this state of indecision, I have reviewed the new global trends in tourism and seen if some of them may fit in the case of the island on an island. The results are positive, as Costa Smeralda seems to be suitable for many forms of cultural, experiential, and sustainable tourism that are tourism hot topics around the world.

CHAPTER 1

Contexts

Introduction

This chapter helps the reader orientate before delving into the very center of this book, that is, the history of Costa Smeralda. To fully put at ease the reader, it is necessary in fact to give them three elements before starting the trip: an account and review of similar trips that have already been carried out, discussing the same topics as those that I will discuss below; a theoretical guide on how not to lose their sense of direction; and some methodological lenses through which I have already looked at Costa Smeralda, so they can see it the same way.

As regards the previous trips, the first section reviews literature concerning the general history and culture of Sardinia, the construction of Costa Smeralda, and the perception of tourism flourishing in that area. The theoretical framework is explained in the second section, in the form of theories connecting reality to the media, sociology, and philosophy. Finally, the third section concerns the methodological apparatus that I have applied to Costa Smeralda, its history, and its impact on the local and the national scale.

What Is Costa Smeralda?

Costa Smeralda is a tourist invention dating back to the early 1960s and still existing as one of the principal destinations in Italy. It is a coastal area, 55 kilometers long, spanning from Capo Ferro to Porto Rotondo, in northeast Sardinia, the site of many luxury resorts, restaurants, and bars.

At the end of the 1950s, the British tycoon John Duncan Miller went back to London after a trip to Sardinia (La Stampa 2022). He was astonished by the beautiful places he saw in the northeast, in particular an area called Monti di Mola, only inhabited by farmers and shepherds taking animals to graze on beautiful white sand beaches in enchanting coves. A business club goer, Miller spread the word about this beautiful place among London's richest groups of financial investors, to arouse their envy and admiration. Among Miller's audience was Prince Karim Aga Khan IV, the forty-ninth and current Imam of the Nizari Ismailis. Born in Geneva in 1936 and having succeeded his father when he was 20, he was also a businessman, well acquainted with the London financial environment of those times. The Aga Khan and his affluent friends started going to Monti di Mola in the summer, and lived there for some weeks adventurously, without electric power and other comforts they usually had in London. The Aga Khan started buying the first lots of land, and was followed by his friends and business partners (Barone and Di Francisca 2015). After a couple of years, the hobby took the form of a business. The Aga Khan and his friends bought many lots of land from shepherds and farmers, very often for little money, as those lands were not inhabited and only used for animal grazing. On March 14, 1962, the group formed by the Aga Khan, comprising the discoverer John Duncan Miller, the businessmen Patrick Guinness, Felix Bigio, Andrè, and René Podbielski, formed the Consorzio Costa Smeralda (Consortium Costa Smeralda), following a previous formal act in September 1961 where the group established norms and regulations of the new tourist area.

In a few years, in that untouched and depressed area of Monti di Mola, renamed Costa Smeralda, a sort of gold rush saw not only hotels and restaurants spring up, but also social services nonexistent earlier: roads, harbors, hospitals, an airport, a specially-made airline company, golf courses, heliports, etc. Costa Smeralda was ready to cater to the highest class of international tourists.

Research Context

First of all, it must be said that there are no studies about the focus of this book, that is, Costa Smeralda as it has been constructed by the media and how it has become, in itself, a medium. That is why this section reviews the literature regarding more general issues: firstly, Sardinia in the Italian context; secondly, the construction of Costa Smeralda; and thirdly, its successful transformation into a tourist destination and its current state of decline. This literature review takes into account both positive views on the topic and the studies that have highlighted the contrasts between those who invented and realized the project and the Sardinian people who opposed it, in a social, economic, and cultural sense.

Sardinia and Italy

Bua (2013) tells the entire history of the human presence in Sardinia and observes that a difference in development between the coastal part (more advanced) and the inner one (in difficulty) dates back to Roman times. Colavitti (2022) finds this disparity still decisive to this day if one wants to understand the many contradictions of the island. Sorge (2015) analyzes violence and crime in Sardinia and advances that they descend from the relationships between the Sardinians and the central State: actually, Sorge (2015) insists that Sardinians have always been split into two parts, one living in the mountains and other remote areas, who avoided the coercive presence of the State; and the others, the peasants, very often subjugated by Italy.

Moreover, another difference that emerged in the Middle Ages was between the north and the south of the island, the first centered on the city of Sassari, and the second on Cagliari. After the Italian unification in the second half of the nineteenth century, Cannaos (2013) points out that the only places that acquired inhabitants and social benefits were those by the sea.

In terms of tourism, Onni (2013) recognizes that Sardinia had its early tourism infrastructure in place shortly after the end of WWII, but that it has become a real tourist destination since the realization of Costa Smeralda.

The Construction of Costa Smeralda

Some studies analyze the process of construction of Costa Smeralda. Cappai (2014, 2015) describes the birth of the project and its first stage in the 1960s and 1970s. She investigates the architectural work behind the construction of Costa Smeralda, arguing that Vietti, the most important architect among those hired by the Aga Khan, found inspiration in the Mediterranean style in general rather than in the Sardinian one and that he built an illusory world but coherently and was aware of what he was doing, without the superficiality that some critics saw in his work (Cappai 2014, 2015).

Trillo (2003) underlines that the work of the entrepreneurs establishing Costa Smeralda was, at the beginning, an act of creation of a new tourist place ex-nihilo; but that, once founded, it became a work of control of the environment. These

people, in fact, decided architectural standards, the material to be used to build
the houses, and even the company that was chosen for the security service. No
one could build a house in Costa Smeralda with other architectural styles or
materials, and they could not hire another security company. Decandia (2017)
advances that all that work actually represented the process of urbanization of a
part of Italy where cities did not exist previously. Paolinelli and Salierno (1988)
describe Monti di Mola, the name of the area where Costa Smeralda would be
built, as a poor area where people did not recognize the potential value of the
land by the sea. In fact, when a farmer died, those who inherited the part of the
countryside by the sea were considered the unlucky heirs. Incidentally, the less
valuable land, that by the sea, was very frequently left to daughters, while the
more precious stretch for grazing animals, the inner one, to sons.

Posocco (2017) thinks that the architectural effort in the construction of Costa
Smeralda was the actual result of much modern architectural theory. In this regard,
its mixture of different styles and conceptions is relevant on a global scale. For
this reason, she pays tribute to two of the many architects who were employed to
contribute to the construction of Costa Smeralda: Antonio Simon Mossa (Posocco
2018) and Luigi Vietti (Posocco 2019), who was the leader of the architects hired
by the Aga Khan. Riccardi (2010) is a memoir written by a man who was part of
the team, working on the birth of the new villages, where nostalgia for the good
old days and sincere admiration for the Aga Khan, confidentially called Prince
Karim, contribute to framing the enterprise in a positive way.

On a journalistic level, Barone and Di Francisca (2015) interview a woman,
Giselle Podblieski, who was a part of the first group of the Aga Khan's friends
and whose husband, René Podbielski, participated in the construction of Costa
Smeralda (he is mentioned among the group of the Aga Khan's friends and as
one of the founders of the Consortium at the beginning of this chapter); and many
farmers and peasants who sold their land to the Prince. The documentary also delves
into the architectural style of the buildings conceived by the architects working
with Prince Karim and their supposed similarity to the traditional Sardinian style.

The anthropologist Bandinu (1980) has dedicated a relevant part of his life to
studying the transformation of Monti di Mola into Costa Smeralda and finds it
as an example of the wider global transformation from the industrial world to
the consumer society. In *Narciso in vacanza* (Narcissus on Holidays) (Bandinu
1994), he goes back to the mythical past of Sardinia and connects it to Costa
Smeralda. To further delve into the transformation of an entire human community,
Bandinu even turns into a novelist (Bandinu 2011) to emotionally tell the story

of a Sardinian family in the 1960s and the impact that the construction of Costa Smeralda had on all of its members. Finally, Scano (1986) analyzes the impact of a similar experiment to Costa Smeralda, Porto Rafael, close to the town of Palau, to reflect on the advantages and disadvantages of consumerist tourism.

Tourism in Costa Smeralda

Addis (2016) analyzes the contrast between Costa Smeralda and the rest of Sardinia. She finds that if you are out of Costa Smeralda and enter it as a citizen, you feel you are in an empty space or a disabled world, while if you are in it as a tourist, you feel you are on a film set in the middle of nowhere. Even Cannas and Giudici (2015) shed light on the relationships between Costa Smeralda and the rest of Sardinia and find that the inhabitants of the two areas have never shared a common point of view in terms of considering each other as citizens of the same place. Analogously, Del Chiappa et al. (2018) investigate the locals' perception of tourists and find that they would prefer forms of tourism more concerned with localities and traditions and allowing the locals to grow. They also discover that the Sardinians expressing these ideas do not differ in terms of gender or age; rather, their answers are guided by common cultural values, independent of age or gender. They conclude that all of this has a more general meaning: local people in tourist destinations are affected by cultural values more than by socio-demographic belongings.

Cannas (2018) focuses on today's Costa Smeralda and its environmental problems linked to global warming. She finds that some political and cultural obstacles still prevent one of the most popular tourist destinations in Europe from offering new tourists what they expect. Moreover, she finds that in comparison to the rest of Italy, Sardinia has excessively seasonal tourism, which prevents the entire region from growing economically, and Costa Smeralda with it.

Critically, Colavitti (2018) sustains that, in the end, Costa Smeralda resembles the rest of Sardinia. Even in this place, that is designed to provide a luxurious experience, tourism has not improved the lives of the locals, exactly like in the other tourist destinations in the other parts of the island.

As for the future, Cannas and Giudici (2015) put forward two suggestions in order to improve tourism in Sardinia, both economically and environmentally: firstly, as Sardinia has many small islands around it, they believe that it should be promoted as an archipelago rather than as a single island, to diversify its market and find new tourists; secondly, they suggest a strong turn toward sustainability and the involvement, in this new trend, of the inner parts of both the main island and the small ones close to it.

Del Chiappa and Presenza (2013) identify the problem as the lack of a robust network among the various stakeholders, both public and private. In summary, Costa Smeralda needs a new marketing strategy to improve collaboration and integration, as the present system results in poor consensus among people working in it. Conversely, Fiori (2015) believes that Costa Smeralda is a working system that has turned one of the poorest areas in Italy into one of the richest. Moreover, this winning model has become an example for the rest of Sardinia. This demonstrates that tourism may be relevant in improving the status of a local community (Fiori 2015).

For Longhi Javarini (1992), this success has been achieved thanks to the visual impact of Costa Smeralda. Certainly, the architectural inventions of the Aga Khan and his architects played a winning role in this, but also the outstanding shapes of its rocks and other natural elements, which have inspired the class of creatives working on the Aga Khan's project, had relevance. The author describes the visual upsides of Costa Smeralda in detail and with overt admiration. One of the most illuminating examples, for him, is the series of stone pillars used in many villas. Made up of the natural stone of Sardinia, and left in their original forms, they take nature inside human constructions coherently and homogeneously, connecting nature to culture.

What has been reviewed so far highlights that there are not many studies on Costa Smeralda and that only a few of them are in English. Moreover, the existing studies analyze this tourist destination from partial and specific perspectives, while a more general, historical study has not been carried out yet. What is more, a study sustaining the media perspective adopted by this book has never been published. This is why it is worth investigating Costa Smeralda from this unusual perspective. In this regard, the next section explains the theoretical framework underpinning this study.

Costa Smeralda, Theoretically

The Medium: Costa Smeralda as a Baudrillard's Simulacrum

After staying in Costa Smeralda for some months and reading the studies about it mentioned above, the first assumption that came to my mind was that Costa Smeralda is a medium like TV channels, social media, or magazines. Is this possible? Undoubtedly, Costa Smeralda is also a place. May a place be a medium?

Jean Baudrillard (1994) spent much of his life overlapping places and media, looking for the communicative power that places can have and the system of symbols that they semiotically create. The ability of places to communicate was a part of his wider theory called hyperreality, an explanation of the increasingly invasive role that the media play in postmodern society, which he witnessed from the late 1970s until he died in 2007.

Put simply, Baudrillard's standpoint is that the media substitute reality with their continuous and almost obsessively detailed representations. Unfortunately, this abundant quantity of representations does not result in information or clarification for the public. In fact, the more the media represent reality in detail, Baudrillard (1994) substantially says, the more they hide it from the audience's eyes. The media do not show reality; rather, they create simulacra of it. Simulacra are "models or signs that simulate reality and thus conceal the fact that the real is not real" (Lahusen 1996, 266).

To better explain all of this, Baudrillard (1994) refers to a short story by Jorge Luis Borges, in which an emperor asked a group of cartographers to prepare the perfect map of the empire. The cartographers prepared the first map but the emperor was unsatisfied, as the map did not represent the land exactly. Gradually, the cartographers projected other maps more in detail, but the emperor always found that they did not represent the territory exactly. Eventually, the last map satisfied the emperor, as it represented the land perfectly. However, the map covered the land in its totality. Thus, people were not able to see the real territory anymore and could only see the map, that is, its representation.

Baudrillard (1994) says that this is exactly what happens in the age of hyperreality with the media, which today cover reality with the multitudes of their representations. As a result, people cannot see actual things anymore, but only their media images, believing that they are real. Baudrillard found in Disneyland a clear example of hyperreality. Disneyland in fact overtly represents an unreal world, but gives the people the idea that it is a real one. Moreover, simulacra connect to and shape society. Baudrillard in fact says that Disneyland is certainly a totally invented world; however, this suggests that the United States is a version of that nonexistent world. Only in that specific kind of society could Disneyland have been possible.

Similarly, this book advances that Costa Smeralda may be seen as an interesting case of media hyperreality, the construction of an unreal world that is given a connotation of reality. Moreover, in this case, by investigating the various historical stages of Costa Smeralda, we can see the various maps that have covered the real territory over the years, and the cultural and social changes which that imaginary place has undergone over the years. Finally, I also suggest that Costa Smeralda did not come about by chance , but that it reflects something that has happened to Italian society over the years, or better, that each stage of its history connects to Italian society of the corresponding years, as found by Baudrillard with Disneyland and the U.S.

Specifically on tourism, Stringfellow et al. (2013) argue that consumers do not consume destinations, but simulacra through the fruition of celebrities. We can thus imagine Costa Smeralda perfectly fitting into this theory: it is a part of this hyperreal world created by the media. More specifically, Costa Smeralda is, in this book, a medium that creates simulacra of itself to be sold to the tourists.

The Content: Costa Smeralda as a Barthes's Mythologies Factory

If Costa Smeralda may be considered as a medium, we should now ask what it communicates. To better understand this, the present book also draws on Roland Barthes' (2013) *Mythologies*. In this book, Barthes analyzes a series of what he calls myths of the consumerist society. Among them are the Eiffel Tower, popular advertisements, and even wrestling. Barthes finds all of them as elements appearing as if they were natural or ever existing but actually being socially and culturally constructed by capitalism. Just for this reason, he points out that they are precious containers of symbols that, if decoded, may be useful in understanding how the consumerist world works. What renders these messages so strong, Barthes says, is the fact that they are part of people's daily lives.

The mechanism that constructs a myth is linear: a real product, object or element, for example French wine, is represented as an aesthetic form, while its content and the information about it are eliminated. What remains is an image, "which can then be repackaged as part of specific ideology (that is, roughly, a system of beliefs)" (Gòmez 2017, 2). In this constructive process, elements lose any historical and real reference to acquire ideological meaning. French wine, for example, becomes a symbol of French refinement and drinking it allows people to participate in this cultural (constructed) value. Refinement, incidentally, has nothing to do with wine, but the construction of the myth connects the product to the feeling for ideological reasons.

In this book, Costa Smeralda is thus analyzed as a hyperreal place like Baudrillard's Disneyland, producing and transmitting (like a TV channel) Barthes's myths. The tourist destination in Sardinia is considered a map, or a series of

maps, that the system of the hyperreal media has put on the real Sardinian territory to cover it and to represent something else, persuading people that the map
was the territory. Costa Smeralda has thus produced mythologies in Barthes's
sense, elements deprived of their history and truth and turned into ideological
weapons, changing according to the years. That is why this book tells the history
of Costa Smeralda in chronological order: each chapter focuses on a period and
describes the map of that period and the mythologies that this tourist destination
has produced.

Finally, Barthes's notion of mythology here needs to be accompanied by studies
about the relationship between nature and culture. Biosemiotics is the branch
of semiotics that analyses the systems of signs pertaining to living elements,
from animals to plants. Its view of the relationship between nature and culture
is important for this book. Biosemiotics points out that there is a traditional view
of the relationship between nature and culture and aims to challenge it. This
traditional view says that nature and culture are separate and in contrast with
each other. Barbieri (2008) contests it and advances that the semiosis of cultural
elements is a part of the broader biological semiosis. This may be explained by
the fact that, for the biosemioticians, analyzing culture means analyzing a part
of the natural environment, as nature and culture are not separated, but the first
contains the second.

This idea was first put forward by Sebeok (1977, 1991, 2001), the founder of
biosemiotics, and also explained by Martinelli (2010). They have constructed a
more holistic paradigm in which culture, that is, human intervention, is seen as
a part of nature. Human beings are a part of nature like any living being on this
planet, but their cultural abilities allow them to play a different role. As a result,
nature involves everything, even what humans produce (culture), as it is made
by the brain, an organ given to humans by nature. All of this also reduces the
difference, for example, between a beehive and a building created by an architect, as they are both forms of expression created by living beings inhabiting
the same realm.

What is more, if nature and culture are not separated or in contrast, this new
biosemiotic vision does not justify pollution or animal killing, as humans and
non-humans live in the same area, and damaging the planet or killing non-human
animals for humans would mean damaging themselves and their realm. The
biosemiotic view of nature and culture will help us understand how mythologies
have been built in Costa Smeralda over the years.

The Audience: Costa Smeralda Between Foucault's Utopia and Heterotopia

I am thus conceiving a theoretical framework where Costa Smeralda is a medium acting as a simulacrum (or more simulacra according to the historical stage) of reality and communicating mythologies in Barthes's sense. The last aspect I want to understand theoretically is what the reaction of the people in front of all of this consists of. First of all, I must say that "people" is too generic a word, as the review of the existing literature on Costa Smeralda has clearly demonstrated that there are two kinds of "people" acting on that stage: the tourists and the local inhabitants of the area. We have also seen in the literature review that the two groups have different points of view of Costa Smeralda: locals feel it is a disabled world, while tourists view it as a film setting (Addis 2016). For this reason, I think that the two groups deserve two different theoretical assumptions or, better, a unique one considering the two different views of the phenomenon.

In the previous section, among other studies, I have also reviewed Maria Cristina Addis's (2016) semiotic analysis of Costa Smeralda. In it, there is also the idea that Costa Smeralda has to do with Michel Foucault's (1966, 1986) categories of utopia and heterotopia, and I think that this intuition may be useful for my investigation. Foucault (1986, 24) writes that heterotopias are "counter-sites, a kind of effectively enacted utopia in which the real sites…are simultaneously represented, contested, and inverted. Places of this kind are outside of all places…I shall call them, by way of contrast to utopias, heterotopias." Thus, heterotopias subvert utopias and the usual notion of space. While utopias do not exist in reality, heterotopias are existing sites that have precise regulations. They are places where people enter a kind of suspenseful time, separated from everyday lives. Trains, cinema halls, and swimming pools are examples of heterotopias.

Interestingly for this research, Foucault (1966, 1986) says that utopias and heterotopias have different effects on people. Utopias console us, while heterotopias worry us. Utopias suggest a pleasant, serene, and better place to us, even though that place does not exist. On the contrary, heterotopias, originating from the Greek words heteros (other) and topia (place), are real sites that mark a separation from our everyday lives, suspend our status, and create a sense of threat in us.

To Addis (2016), heterotopias are relevant to Costa Smeralda, as they constitute real places that somehow are necessary to each society, hosting its contradictions, silenced truths, and omitted characteristics. They suspend usual laws and regulations to activate other rules and allow people to experience things in a way that society usually forbids in the other areas of its domain. Addis (2016) thus underlines that holiday locations may be seen as heterotopias, as in those sites people interrupt their everyday lives, forget usual laws, and adopt other rules. In this work, utopia and heterotopia are two categories able to frame people's experience in Costa Smeralda. In the next sections, in fact, I will examine how consolations and worry play their roles when people experience Costa Smeralda.

In the end, in this section I have developed the theories that sustain my research. This implies that I want to develop the history of Costa Smeralda through Baudrillard, Barthes, and Foucault's lenses. To carry out my research, the study needs a set of coherent and effective methods of investigation, which are developed in the next section.

Methodology

Constructing Costa Smeralda as a Research Paradigm

This book emerges from a personal experience that later activated a historical, social, and textual analysis. In terms of methodology, this means that various techniques of investigation have contributed to the final result. All of these layers, however, have not gone messily. In this research, they are in fact coherently conveyed under the common umbrella of constructivism. Each method that the reader will find in the following chapters assumes that the analyzed reality—Costa Smeralda in its historical, discursive, and visual semiotic development—is not an objective truth to be investigated from the outside, but a continually changing flux that is constructed every day by the people participating in its life and discursive existence and even by the researcher, that is, me, with my direct testimony and personal interpretations.

Constructivism is a philosophical paradigm that originated at the end of the eighteenth century from the sociological work of Emile Durkheim (1982), Max Weber (2012), Marcel Mauss (1990), and other scholars. Durkheim sustains that societies are affected by culture rather than by natural laws, and that they create multiple "socially constructed identities and beliefs" (Parsons 2022, 76). In line with this, Weber (2012) finds, for example, that capitalism emerged from Protestantism, a further demonstration that culture, in this case religion, affects society more than any other element. Finally, Mauss (1990) investigated the human social practice of the gift as a means to understand how societies work.

Constructivism is based on the idea that "realities are multiple, constructed, and holistic. If this is so, then construction of reality must depend on some forms of consensual language. Meaning is determined through…negotiation with the environment and the individuals" (Rodwell 1998, 26). This implies that reality is not out there, external to the researcher; rather, the researcher is a part of it and of its inner area, along with the other people inhabiting it and is able to change it continuously.

More elaborately, in constructivism "the researcher attempts to reach understanding about the phenomena under investigation by understanding the internal and intangible process of the minds of the inquiry participants" (Rodwell 1998, 27). Costa Smeralda, thus, is a phenomenon that is continuously changing thanks to what people or the media do, think, or say about it, and each method adopted in this research has tried to clarify these mental processes and outputs (such as the media articles or photos about this island on an island). Costa Smeralda will be, thus, not a static phenomenon, but "the composite picture of how people think" (Rodwell 1998, 27) about it.

As a result, this book applies four methods, all of them under the constructivist umbrella. Firstly, what people in Costa Smeralda say and think about the island on an island has been investigated through my ethnography, which has been explained above. Secondly, the history of Costa Smeralda has been reported, thanks to historical analysis of first and second-hand documents. Thirdly, media discourse and images representing the island on an island have been studied according to the principles of social semiotic multimodal analysis.

An Ethnographer on Holiday

The initial part of this research was achieved through the ethnography that I have mentioned at the beginning of this section. Ethnography is a research method based on the direct participation of the researcher in the research field. According to Stewart (1998), ethnography has four relevant characteristics: the first is participant observation, that is, the researcher is present in the field, immersed for some time in the everyday setting of the place along with local people; the second aspect is holism, meant as the fact that the researcher puts together various, wide-ranging, and disparate phenomena which together form a coherent version of culture or society; the third element is the concern for the context and the frequent links connecting what has been observed and its contextualization;

the fourth characteristic, finally, "is the detailed depiction and analysis of social relations and culture" (Stewart 1998, 7). Finally, Stewart (1998) also mentions another important element of ethnology, which however is seen differently from the previous four: the connection of what has been observed to sociological or anthropological theories. It seems clear that this research also draws on this last point, as demonstrated in the previous subsections about constructionism and media theories.

The three periods of time that I have spent in Costa Smeralda were fundamental in lighting up my interest in this issue. The first time I went to this island on an island was between the two periods of restriction due to the COVID-19 pandemic. Costa Smeralda was almost totally tourist-free, apart from some worried Italians. Visitors from abroad were banned at those times and the entire landscape of the area seemed to change because of this. Beaches and bars were almost deserted, many hotels closed, and the great majority of the houses had their doors and windows barred. It was in those days that I had the impression that Monti di Mola, the original name of the area, later renamed Costa Smeralda, was striving to reemerge after about half a century. In those days, I mainly talked to Sardinian people inhabiting the area and started knowing the mindset of local people and their perspective of Costa Smeralda.

The second time was about one year later, when limitations were abolished and tourists partially came back to the island. The tourism machine was fully restarted and hotels and resorts, still partially empty, seemed to retrieve their usual rhythm. The lack of visitors was evident in Porto Cervo, the most important city of Costa Smeralda, entirely built from scratch by the Aga Khan and his architects. There, the extra-luxury shops were empty apart from the salespersons, who spent entire days alone and were enthusiastic about chatting with me, a strange figure between a tourist and a researcher, to sum up, an ethnographer on holiday. The chats I had in those days were principally with people working in the tourist industry and worrying about their future.

The third period, finally, occurred more recently, when tourists were back to the point that I saw Costa Smeralda again overwhelming Monti di Mola and the tourism realm restored and reminding the many habitues of the good old days. It was in that period, however, that I felt that Costa Smeralda had some difficulty in coming back to its past and was shown to be a bit out of fashion. I saw this feeling in the disappointment of many "new" tourists, especially young ones, coming from abroad and asking me and themselves: Is this Costa Smeralda? It was at that stage that I started writing my book proposal.

Historical Analysis

As said above, this book also investigates laws, institutional documents, and private regulations that have led to the constitution, management, and modification of the statute of Costa Smeralda. This part of the study applies historical analysis, which is a big umbrella comprehending various kinds of investigation. In fact, it "is a method analyzing and interpreting what has happened using records and accounts" (Marshall and Rossman 2011, 185). Interestingly for this book, "it is particularly useful in qualitative studies for establishing a baseline or background prior to participant observation or interviewing" (Marshall and Rossman 2011, 185). Actually, in this book, participant observation (ethnology) has come earlier than historical analysis, as it has fueled my wish to delve into the analysis of Costa Smeralda.

What is more, historical analysis is very often based on the investigation of primary sources, such as testimonies, records, documents of various types, etc., that is, sources directly and originally coming from the past that the researcher is studying. Primary-source documents have always been of pivotal importance in historical analysis, as they "are mainly primary source or eyewitness accounts provided by people who were actually 'making history' or witnessing the events being examined" (Noonan 1999, iv). Supported by primary sources, this part of the study aims to give the book an in-depth insight on the construction of this tourist destination. However, historical analysis does not underrate secondary sources, which are already-existing studies on the same issue or reports of people on the same event, or referring indirectly to it (Marshall and Rossman 2011, 185). In this study, I have analyzed both of them, original documents regarding Costa Smeralda (primary sources) and historical accounts of it (secondary sources), in order to clarify how Costa Smeralda was created and with what aims, how its regulations and governance have changed over the years, and who were the people participating in its management.

A Semiotic Journey to Costa Smeralda

This work also investigates discourses and visual items representing Costa Smeralda in the media. Costa Smeralda media items have been analyzed more in depth, thanks to semiotics and social semiotic multimodal analysis.

Semiotics is frequently defined as the science of signs. It is certainly a theory stating that the entire world, in both its natural and cultural manifestations, is a system of signs that humans can comprehend through specific categories and oppositions. However, if we accept that cultural artifacts are also systems of signs, we must accept that semiotics is also a methodological tool to open each system and discover how it works. In this sense, any form of expression may be considered as formed by signs, which are organized in codes in order to produce meaning. Semiotics is "concerned with how meaning is made and the various ways in which language, here broadly intended, can be used to represent reality" (Aiello 2020, 367). As a method of insight, semiotic analysis investigates "texts" which can be visual, written, musical, sculptured, painted, drawn, and so on, and also places, buildings, cities, and every product of nature and culture. Specifically, semiotic analysis "aims to make the hidden structures, underlying cultural codes, and dominant meanings of such texts both visible and intelligible" (Aiello 2020, 368).

To decode any system of signs (and thus everything), many semioticians have created specific tools and categories. In this book, I draw on Charles S. Peirce, who was one of the two founders of semiotics, and specifically of the American branch (while the European section was founded by Ferdinand de Saussure). Peirce (1960) theorizes that a sign may have three different relations to reality. It may be an icon, an index, or a symbol, according to how the signifier and the signified relate to each other. When it is an icon, it means that the signifier physically looks like what it represents, for example in the case of a portrait depicting a person. The sign is instead an index when the signifier is linked to something else through causality or contiguity; for instance, the presence of smoke tells us that there is a fire somewhere close to us. Finally, a sign is a symbol when the signifier and the signified are connected arbitrarily, in a relationship that is acknowledged within a community or a group, as in the case of the red roses holding a romantic meaning, a connection that is recognized in some groups but not in every part of the planet (Jenks 1998) and that does not have any logical reason. Importantly, a sign usually has all these characteristics, but it contains them in various quantities. Frequently, one of the three categories is the dominant one, while the other two are secondary, or one of them is not present within that specific sign.

Semiotics has long been accused of being a rigid and abstract discipline, totally detached from the social fluxes and the unpredictable winds of change that sometimes affect societies. This could be true only if we did not take into account social semiotics, the branch of semiotics that combines the severe science of signs with the more flexible cultural and social contexts. Even social semiotics has its methodological tools. Social semiotic multimodal analysis is the method of inquiry chosen in this book when it comes to analyzing images and texts published by TV programs, magazines, newspapers, and social media depicting the Aga Khan, Costa Smeralda, the debate about the legitimacy of the project, the various stages of the dolce vita in the area, or discussing the future of the island on an island.

Social semiotic multimodal analysis investigates both "the material resources of communication and the way their uses are socially regulated" (Van Leeuwen 2005, 93). Multimodal analysis allows the researcher to break up any media message into different modes (audio, moving image, drawing, etc.), to analyze each mode separately and finally to gather them in a conclusive reading (Taylor 2014). This is what this book does, analyzing drawings, photos, and texts regarding Costa Smeralda, its history, and representations. Bezemer (2012) advances that multimodal analysis is particularly fruitful when one must investigate forms of communication developed through many modes, coming from sources that are socially, culturally, and politically shared within a society, and with which people may interact. That is why this method seems to me really relevant to analyze Costa Smeralda in many of its expressions.

Importantly, multimodal analysis has also been recommended for studies that aim to analyze historical developments and changes, as it can highlight processes and reframing of meanings over the years, also taking into account changes produced by new cultural beliefs and social values (Maiorani and Christie 2014).

Finally, the last semiotic tool that I use in this book is the stratified idea of signification according to the categories of denotation and connotation. Barthes (1977, 45–51, 2013) adds that a text has two levels of signification: denotation, which is the literal or more evident meaning; and connotation, which is a more hidden sense, influenced by ideology, cultural context, interpretation, and so on. Connotation very frequently helps unveil myths, the construction of ideological elements profoundly rooted within society, and symbolical meaning. In this sense, connotation intertwines with Barthes's mythologies and with the social semiotic's ability to connect texts to the correspondent society and cultural values.

Conclusion

This chapter has established the aims and the boundaries of this book by focusing on three elements. Firstly, it has reviewed the existing literature concerning Costa Smeralda. It is not a wide scope of studies, as the complete history of

Costa Smeralda and its unclear future have never been developed in depth apart from a very small quantity of studies. Rather, the existing analyses of this tourist destination have regarded really specific perspectives and topics. In answering the research questions, this book aims to bridge this gap and to provide the reader with a complete account of the history, media construction, and uncertain future of Costa Smeralda.

Secondly, this chapter has developed the theoretical framework stating that if we take Costa Smeralda as a medium, this medium must have its status, content, and audience. Its status is coherent with the theory of hyperreal simulacra by Jean Baudrillard (1994). In brief, this book considers Costa Smeralda as a simulacrum in Baudrillard's sense, that is, a whole of media representations fictitiously depicting reality but hiding it. In so doing, the media substitute reality and, as a result, people are not able to distinguish one from the other anymore. As regards the content transmitted by this medium, this book assumes that it is composed of Roland Barthes's (2013) mythologies, which are real elements deprived of their history and truth and re-constructed as images containing powerful ideological symbols. Finally, the audience of Costa Smeralda has been analyzed through Foucault's (1966, 1986) opposition between utopia and heterotopia, constructed places able to give their participants hope and worry respectively.

Thirdly, this chapter has also designed the methodological apparatus required to investigate Costa Smeralda. Starting from constructivism, the tools that this book adopts are three: firstly, ethnography, concerning my stays in Costa Smeralda; secondly, historical analysis, based on primary and secondary sources: original documents are cited along with already published works which have shed light on some of the aspects I treat in this book; thirdly, social semiotic and multimodal analysis of various documents and representations. It is necessary to underline that for semioticians, buildings, places, hotels, etc. are to be fully considered as representations, and thus items to be analyzed as a media text or a painting.

The next chapter introduces the topic of Costa Smeralda, telling the story of its territory before the rise of the tourist industry.

.

CHAPTER 2

The Age of Unawareness: Sardinia Before Costa Smeralda

Introduction

This chapter focuses on Sardinia as a geographic entity before Costa Smeralda. Starting from the Neolithic era, it developed through the centuries until the 1950s. The chapter aims to orientate the reader before delving into the subject matter of the book. Put simply, to fully understand Costa Smeralda, it is necessary to comprehend Sardinia, and what follows is the part of the book devoted to this not-easy task.

What the reader finds in the next sections is Sardinia in its age of unawareness. From the Middle Ages to the 1950s in fact, the island was, for a long time, neglected by the central powers, which exploited it and did not take care of its inhabitants. To sum up, the Romans, the Spaniards, the Italians, and in turn those who governed Sardinia, with different degrees of flexibility, ignored the potentialities of the island and mistreated it. The Sardinians resisted, and in doing so grew that sense of annoyance toward people coming from abroad that would also affect every stage of the history of Costa Smeralda.

To complete the picture, the last section analyses some Sardinian cultural elements that have had a great echo in Italian culture, banditry, and matriarchy, which have shaped the idea of Sardinia that has become dominant in Italy.

Sardinia, Geographically

Sardinia is the largest island of the Mediterranean Sea, apart from Sicily, having an area of almost 25,000 square kilometers. It is positioned in the western part of the Mediterranean, north of Tunisia and south of Corsica. It is thus placed west of the Italian peninsula and east of Spain, specifically of the Spanish islands of Maiorca and Minorca. Its population is one million, six hundred thousand; this makes Sardinia the most populated Mediterranean island, again after Sicily (Sardegna Statistiche 2023).

The island is made up of rocks dating back to 500 million years ago and has fascinated geologists from all over the world for the age, typology, and characteristics of its conformation (Funedda and Cocco 2019).

Sardinia is one of the twenty Italian regions. The Italian Constitution, designing the political structure of the State that was promulgated in 1948, states that Sardinia is one of the five regions that have a special statute, guaranteeing a major degree of autonomy in comparison to the others. The other regions benefiting from special statutes are Friuli Venezia Giulia, Sicily, Trentino Alto Adige, and Valle d'Aosta. All of them are situated at the borders of the Italian nation and have always been places with strong political movements asking for independence from the central State.

Sardinia's largest city is the regional capital Cagliari, in the south of the island, which has around one hundred fifty-eight thousand inhabitants, followed by Sassari (about one hundred twenty-nine thousand), Quartu Sant'Elena (nearly seventy-one thousand), and Olbia, the nearest city to Costa Smeralda, which is inhabited by around fifty-two thousand people. Olbia has nearly the same latitude as Naples in Italy and Tarragona in Spain.

Hills occupy about 68 percent of the Sardinian territory, plains account for 18.5 percent, and mountains constitute 13.6 percent of the island. Its highest mountain is Gennargentu, 1,834 meters high. Sardinia has only one natural lake, the Baratz, close to the city of Alghero. Many others have been created by humans in order to fight the endemic lack of water of the island. Ponds and lagoons are frequently close to the coasts, allowing the existence of pink flamingos and other species of birds.

Sardinia's coasts are about 1,897 kilometers long, with alternate rocks and beaches, which are famous for their white color (Oviglia 1987). Actually, there are also yellowish and darker beaches in Sardinia, but the most promoted by the tourism industry today are the white ones, evidently for commercial aims. When one talks about the Sardinian coasts, it would only be fair to mention the many small islands surrounding them. The biggest is Sant'Antioco (about 109 square kilometers), followed by Asinara (52 square kilometers), in the northwest. In 1885, Asinara was expropriated by the Italian State and during WWI, it was adopted as a prison for the Austrian soldiers who were captured by the Italian army.

After WWII, Asinara became a high-security prison where the most dangerous criminals were secluded. From the 1970s to the 1990s, the terrorists of Brigate Rosse (the Red Brigades) and the criminals belonging to the mafia and camorra (the most dangerous criminal organizations in Italy) were jailed in Asinara prison. The jail was called "the Italian Alcatraz" (Lisai 2013) because of the very strict rules it had. For the most dangerous criminals, isolation was continuous, and even rec time was only allowed separate from that of the other prisoners. Among the others, the heads of mafia Totò Riina and Leoluca Bagarella, the head of Camorra Raffaele Cutolo, and the terrorists Renato Curcio, Alberto Franceschini, and Pierluigi Concutelli spent many years in Asinara (Pasqualetto 2019). In 1979, the terrorists of the Brigate Rosse organized a rebellion against the terrible conditions of imprisonment (first of all, the never-ending isolation). Only one inmate managed to escape the prison, the Sardinian bandit Matteo Boe in 1986 (Lisai 2013).

The average maximum temperature in Sardinia is 20.5°C, while the average minimum is 10°C. The hottest month is July, in which the average maximum is 30.5°C. while the coldest is January, when the average minimum temperature is 4.9°C. If we examine the plains , we observe that in August the maximum temperature remains above 34°C. It only snows from 500 meters above sea level. It rains about 780 millimeters of water in one year. In the most humid areas, it rains around eighty days each year, while in the driest this happens about fifty days each year (Motroni 2019). Studies regarding global warming foresee that in 2050 the temperatures will be 2.7°C more, and in 2070 will increase by 4.5°C. Rains will decrease respectively by 7 and 13 percent, encouraging a process of desertification.

Being a windy island, many fires (the majority of which are caused by humans) every year destroy large parts of land. Fires caused by humans were tolerated for centuries. They had the purpose of expanding the land destined to pasture. In the 1980s and 1990s respectively, 1.8 and 1.4 percent of the entire surface of the island each year was destroyed by fires caused by humans. The practice is luckily decreasing, and it has recently been calculated that in the 2010s that this percentage went down by 0.4 percent (Vacca 2019).

Sardinia's underground is extremely rich in carbon, lead, zinc, copper, and silver. This led to the opening of many mines, especially in the south of the island. In the nineteenth century, the MP (and later Prime Minister) Quintino Sella (1871), a mining engineer, wrote a very informed report on Sardinia's mines, which cited historical studies asserting that the first exploiters of Sardinia's underground were the Phoenicians. They extracted silver to make their coins, which were recognized by many people in the Mediterranean and allowed them to make good businesses along its coasts. Carthaginians and Romans continued to exploit the Sardinian mines. When Sardinia was governed by the Republic of Pisa, from 1087, its mines were improved and the activity was extended to new sites. Under Spanish domination, the activity was partially interrupted as minerals, especially silver, arrived from the Spanish dominions in South America.

Only under the Savoy family, from 1726 and over the first half of the nineteenth century, was the mining activity restarted, and new mines opened to extract antimony and graphite, among other minerals (Sella 1871). This also happened thanks to the arrival of experts from abroad, especially Germany, and the use of explosives to improve and fasten the phase of extraction. Miners doubled in a few years and the production rose from 9,400 tons in 1860 to 127 tons in 1868. As a result, being a miner was one of the most widely available job opportunity for Sardinians.

While Fascism continued to rely on Sardinia's mines, since the 1960s the activity has gradually decreased. The mines that are closed are today part of a geo-mining park that was the first of this kind to be recognized by UNESCO.

Agriculturally, in the plain of Campidano, the Sardinians have, for centuries, grown wheat, and later, artichokes, cereals, and tomatoes. Bovines and ovine are raised on the entire island, while close to the coasts there are many fish farms. What is more, many parts of the island are dedicated to the production of cork, which is used to produce bottle caps, insulating material, and handcrafts.

Finally, Sardinia has three national parks: Asinara National Park, La Maddalena Archipelago National Park and Orosei Gulf—Gennargentu National Park; and five protected marine areas: Asinara, Sinis peninsula—Mal di Ventre Island, Capo Caccia-Isola Piana, Tavolara-Punta Coda Cavallo, and Capo Carbonara.

Sardinia in the Old and Middle Ages

According to newer studies, the human presence in Sardinia dates back to around three hundred thousand to five hundred thousand years ago, when specimens of Homo erectus inhabited the areas of the island close to flint deposits (Marrocu 2021). These people probably arrived from central Italy, specifically Tuscany, as it seems that in that era Tuscany and Corsica were almost united and only separated by a small and shallow sea. From Corsica, thus, probably these people made their way to north Sardinia. They carved and somehow worked some stones, leaving us signs of their presence, today evident, for example, close to the River Altana and to Laerru, in the north of the island. Homo sapiens arrived in Sardinia about twenty thousand years ago (Marrocu 2021), firstly inhabiting the caves in the coastal areas and gradually moving to the inner part of the island, in those times composed of dense forests (Tolu 2023). Till date, about 60 percent of Sardinians have a genetic patrimony coming from humans immigrating to Sardinia during the Paleolithic era (Sanna 2006).

From that period on, Sardinia developed an autonomous culture, with only a few influences coming from other places (Mazza 2006). Certainly, its being an island played a role in this; however, other Mediterranean islands such as Sicily were much more affected by other cultures. Sardinia's proud independence is a fact that has permeated its entire history and is present and discussed even today. This issue will feature in this book often, as it is decisive in comprehending the relationship between the Sardinians and Costa Smeralda.

During the Neolithic age, around 4000 BC, humans were established in various areas of Sardinia, as we can see from the archaeological remains found in Bonu Ighinu and Ozieri, in the northwest. These people lived first in caves when involved in hunting and fishing, and later in huts, when engaged in agriculture (Tolu 2023). Sardinia's inhabitants of a subsequent period, around 2500 BC, built instead dolmens, funerary buildings through which they constructed their death rituals.

However, the most important expression of this cultural autonomy was surely the Nuraghic civilization, which occurred in Sardinia from 1800 to 200 BC (Marrocu 2021). The symbol of this civilization is nuraghe (from Sardinian *nur*, English *build-up* or *mound*), the characteristic megalithic buildings still preside over the entire island and attract thousands of tourists every year (Touring Club 2013). Nuraghes had military, residential, or religious purposes. They were made of huge stones sapiently put together to form buildings that are surprisingly complex for that era (Lilliu 2006). On the top, they also feature a kind of dome made with smaller stones and a stab.

The complexity of these buildings has raised questions about the level of civilization achieved by the Nuraghic people, who were divided into tribes, very often waging war on each other, and the architectural techniques that they adopted. Another confirmation of the high cultural level reached by Nuraghic people is the fact that they also developed a complex (for those times) system of writing (Vacca 1990).

Nuraghes can be 20 meters high and have a diameter of 10 meters. They are the highest prehistoric buildings in the Mediterranean area apart from the Egyptian pyramids. Today, there exist about seven thousand nuraghes all over Sardinia, with many tourist tours with guides and experts illustrating their history and architecture.

Around 1000 BC, the Phoenicians, coming from the area they inhabited (in today's Lebanon), arrived in Sardinia with their extraordinarily efficient boats (Marrocu 2021). They established commercial relationships with the Sardinians and founded important cities, such as Olbia and Bosa. Later, the inner cities run by the Sardinians attacked the Phoenicians, who involved the Carthaginians, who, around 500 BC, conquered the entire area apart from today's Barbagia (Tolu 2023).

The Romans took over from the Carthaginians in 238 BC, starting the long Roman domination of Sardinia, which lasted about four hundred fifty years (Vasconi 1998). Officially the Romans controlled the entire area, but the Nuraghic people never gave up and for centuries tried to reconquer parts of the island, unsuccessfully. Under the Romans, there were two geographical regions, also divided politically: Barbaria was the inner eastern part, still Nuraghic; Romania was the rest of the island, controlled by the Romans (Bua 2013). The dominators understood the geographical relevance of Sardinia, a kind of bridge to Africa and Spain (Anatra et al. 1989). They also exploited the mineral resources (silver and lead), cultivated wheat, created new cities, and built roads and infrastructure that improved the Sardinians' daily lives.

After a Vandal parenthesis, in 534, Sardinia was conquered by Justinian and became, for more than three hundred years, a part of the Eastern Roman (or Byzantine) Empire (Marrocu 2021). It was hierarchically organized and became Christian, apart from Barbagia, whose people continued to adore archaic deities linked to nature and old myths. Around 800, the Arabs started their incursions and the empire did not fight back. As a result, the Sardinians left the coastal cities and moved to the inner lands, while the Arabs conquered a part of the island.

Between 800 and 1400, Sardinia was fragmented and each area was governed by local institutions called *Giudicati*. They were organized democratically, each relying on a parliament composed of people's representatives. The head of the State was the Judge, chosen through a half-hereditary and half-elective process. The political organization of *Giudicati* was really innovative in those times and presented dynamics and institutions that no or only a few other states could rely on (Casula 1998).

These independent states, even when independent from each other, constituted a nuisance for the maritime republics of Pisa and Genova and for the Pope (Bua 2013). In 1016, Pisa and Genova together defeated the Arabs and later split up the *Giudicati*: Pisa owned Gallura, Arborea, and Cagliari; Genova annexed Torres.

The Giudicato of Arborea (close to Oristano) was the last one that gave in. Its resistance was principally based on the firm character of its queen, Eleonora d'Arborea (1340–1404), who was King Mariano IV's wife. Eleonora is key to comprehending the proud personality of the Sardinians and matriarchy. She created a system of laws (*Carta de logu*) that specifically contained very strict punishments for rapists (Fiocchetto 2003) and that more generally regulated Sardinian life until 1827. Eleonora became a symbol of the rebellion against the invader in the nineteenth century, when she was utterly idealized as a female warrior, a fearless patriot, and a heroic politician through supposed documents that were recognized as false by historians (Pitzorno 2013). Actually, we know very little about her. However, what was falsely constructed around her, that is, a past golden age of Sardinia where Eleonora ruled without any dependence on foreign states but only relying on local people, tells us much about the desires and the wishes of the inhabitants of the island.

When the Giudicati ended, the various areas were briefly controlled by rich families settled in Pisa or Genova, but later, Sardinia entered the contest between Angevin and the Aragonese. The island was conquered by Alfonso of Aragon in 1326, apart from the Giudicato of Arborea, which was annexed in 1409.

Sardinia Under the Spaniards

What strikes the historians is that the Renaissance as a cultural and artistic movement revolutionized every corner of Italy apart from Sardinia. The island remained extraneous to the most important process of renovation and artistic innovation that ever happened in Italy.

The Spaniards controlled the island for about four centuries, probably the most obscure period in Sardinia's history. The Spaniards established a feudal economy and organization and erased any form of autonomy: as an example, the Sardinian Parliament was convoked every ten years, and this clarifies that it did not influence any aspect of political life. The power was in the hands of the Viceroy, who represented the Spanish government on the island (Tolu 2023). It was divided into two big parts, il Capo di sopra (cape of the top), whose most important city was Sassari, and il Capo di sotto (cape of the bottom), with Cagliari (Bua 2013). Cagliari and Sassari are, even today, the most important Sardinian cities.

This strict and oppressive apparatus had negative effects on the Sardinians' daily lives. The island was knocked out by a series of health calamities such as famines, the continuous spreading of out-of-control malaria, and various plague epidemics. The political atmosphere was exacerbated by many tumults and riots, culminating in the assassination of the Viceroy Marchese di Camarassa in 1668 and in the death sentence for his killers.

Culturally, the Spanish domination caused the detachment from the rest of Italy that we have mentioned above. Not only was Sardinia extraneous to the Renaissance, but it also missed out on the artistic flourishing that other areas of Italy underwent in other periods, such as the Sicilian Baroque of the 1700s. What the Spaniards invested in was the construction of churches that retrieved the styles that were already successful in other areas of Italy.

Also literature lagged: among the contributors to Italian literature from the 1300s to the 1700s, the Sardinian novelists were fewer than those coming from other regions. It was in this period, however, that the Stampace School in Cagliari developed and created beautiful retablos that may still be viewed today (Agus 2016).

Economically, Sardinia was firstly subdued by the Catalan merchants; later, from the second half of the 1500s, they were replaced by the Genoese traders, who gradually occupied the markets of the island. This accentuated the dependence of Sardinia on traders coming from abroad. In 1690, all Sardinian incomes were already pledged until 1692 (Anatra et al. 1989). The few commercial potentialities that the Sardinians had shown in the 1300s were now overpowered by the new occupants. Added to this was the fact that the internal market was of no interest to the entrepreneurs working in other states. Sardinia had 110,000 inhabitants in 1485 (6 people per square kilometer) and 230,267 in 1688 (10 people per square kilometer) (Anatra et al. 1989); it was an almost deserted land without any appeal to entrepreneurs wanting to find new land for their businesses.

The only strength of the island was the export of agricultural products, especially wheat, from the 1500s. The Spaniards exploited Sardinia's countryside, growing what was requested from the European markets, that is, principally wheat and secondarily cheese. The Spaniards also benefited from the very low cost of life in Sardinia. Venetian Ambassador Federico Badoer in 1557 wrote that in Sardinia "one could do with ten ecus what in other places could not with 40 ecus" (Anatra et al. 1989, 18).

In the 1600s, it became evident that the precious position of Sardinia in the center of the Mediterranean had downsides: in 1623, the corsairs invaded Posada beach and there were other incursions of the pirates along the Sardinian coasts in 1640; in 1646 a French invasion seemed close, but it did not happen; other invasions from the Turkish appeared possible some years later, and so on (Anatra et al. 1989). The geographical upside became a political problem. The Spaniards decided to reinforce the fortifications but in the end, Sardinia remained weak, and their enemies knew it. If in 1659 the French and the Spaniards reached an arrangement to split the Mediterranean into two parts and not fight each other, the pirates and the Turkish remained menacing enemies (Anatra et al. 1989).

All of this may explain the isolation that Sardinia has always suffered, not only under the Spaniards. In those times, going to Sicily or other islands was much easier than visiting Sardinia. Unpredictable perils, rough seas, absence of wind, pirates, political fights, and other issues rendered travel to Sardinia a dangerous adventure. In times when navigating was still difficult (it took forty-three days to go from Barcelona to Constantinople), no one was enthusiastic about going to Sardinia, apart from a few businessmen—a sentiment that did not stop when the Spaniards went away and a new, more open, era dawned on the island.

Sardinia and Modernity: 1713 to 1861

Carlos II's death and the contrasts in the succession to the throne led to a chaotic period in Spain. Taking advantage of it, in 1708, the Austrians occupied Sardinia and in 1713, the Hapsburgs were officially in charge of the island. However, it was a short dominion, as in 1718, thanks to the Treaty of London, the Reign of Sardinia was given to the Dukes of Savoy, who wished to take control of the whole of Italy, managing to do it after about one hundred fifty years.

The Savoy dynasty governed in a more enlightened way in comparison to the previous dominators, even though problems were not totally solved and some responsibilities of the new governors arose. From 1799 to 1831, a series of Savoy kings encouraged the development and the modernization of the island: Carlo Emanuele III of Sardinia, Vittorio Emanuele I of Sardinia, and Carlo Felice encouraged huge improvements, especially in Sardinian infrastructure. They funded the making of new roads, new defensive walls, and a new urban organization, with architects and engineers coming from Piedmont, Milan, and Genova to work on the renovation of Sardinia. The road linking Cagliari to Porto Torres is even today named after King Carlo Felice, as he authorized its construction.

What changed under the new kingdom was trade. In the first part of the eighteenth century, merchants operating in Sardinia principally came from Genoa or Corsica. Later, a group of Sardinian traders emerged, as underlined by Sanna (2007). The group gradually developed and grew, forming what Curtin calls a "trade diaspora" (Curtin 1984, 2), that is, a group of traders belonging to the same cultural or national environment going to different cities or places and networking to make their businesses together. Sanna (2017) analyzes how this strategy revived the spirit of the Sardinians after centuries of cultural, political, and economic domination; and how all of this ended when Sardinia passed under the Savoy family.

The new kings, from 1760 onwards, centralized many commercial activities and wanted the state to directly control commerce. Tobacco, coral, mines, and Cagliari's customs stopped being administrated by private entrepreneurs and began to be part of the State's responsibilities. What passed under the control of the State were the most remunerative sectors, while only the less profitable activities were left to the private merchants (Sanna 2017).

Finally, Italian replaced Castilian and Catalan as the official language for acts and documents (Tolu 2023). Sardinia also gained centrality to the Reign when the Savoy court moved from Turin to Cagliari, as Napoleon was conquering substantial parts of northern Italy (Lisai and Maccioni 2021).

However, Piedmont's central government also exploited Sardinia's immense patrimony of wood. The large forests covering the island almost disappeared in a few years and their wood was used to make the ties for the new railway in northern Italy. Commercial companies arrived in Sardinia from other parts of Italy to take the precious material and to make a business that would change the landscape of the island. Moreover, the Savoy Kings' attempt to establish in Sardinia some factories producing paper and glass did not have the expected results (Lisai and Maccioni 2021). In 1836, King Carlo Alberto of Sardinia (1831–1849) abolished the existing feudal system but increased the taxes.

What has been presented so far is the main historical account of what happened to Sardinia during the Savoy government. However, it is also fair to take into account the version of some Sardinian authors, who, on the contrary, consider the Savoy family as the principal disgrace of the island. Among the many, Asunis (2014) sustains that the unbalanced society that the Spaniards built in Sardinia remained untouched under the Savoy family and that their supposed renovation was a fictitious strategy to draw the sympathy of the Sardinians. Marrocu (2021) points out that as the Savoy family took possession of Sardinia, many representatives of the higher classes even longed for the past domination of the Spaniards.

The many critical perspectives of what the Savoy family did in Sardinia may also be associated with the fact that they were the organizers, and later the kings, of unified Italy. In 1861, Italy was united by Garibaldi, who officially consigned it to the hands of the Savoy, who already controlled Piedmont and Sardinia. As a result, the King of Savoy became the King of Italy. Thus, the Reign of Sardinia ceased its existence and the island became only a region of the new State, losing centrality and turning out to be a peripheral part of the new nation.

Sardinia as an Italy's Region

In the last part of the nineteenth century, the Italian monarchy continued to improve Sardinia's infrastructure. The railway unifying the entire island was completed and the precious minerals in the subsoil were extracted, thanks to the opening of many mines. They seemed to be an opportunity for many Sardinians to find a job; however, the working conditions of miners were substandard. This also provoked the rise of the unions and the fight for better conditions, even though miners' lives remained particularly hard.

During WWI, the Sassari Brigade acquired fame for the heroism of its members, but after the war, a really hard economic crisis hit Sardinia. In 1921 the Partito Sardo d'Azione (Sardinian Action Party) was created to ask for more autonomy from the central State. In the same year, Mussolini founded the Partito Nazionale Fascista (National Fascist Party), which took power in 1922 and sometime later closed down all other political organizations, including the just-born Sardinian party.

Mussolini's regime fought against Sardinia *banditismo* (banditry) and reclaimed many lots of land. The island became strategic in WWII and was used as an aircraft carrier in the Mediterranean. Just for this, it was bombed by the US and UK forces: in 1943, Cagliari was almost totally destroyed.

In 1946, after the defeat of Fascism and the end of the war, Italy became a Republic and Sardinia was one of its twenty regions. As mentioned at the beginning of this chapter, in 1948, Sardinia obtained a special statute that, till date, guarantees it a higher level of autonomy in comparison to some other regions.

In 1950, malaria was eventually eliminated, and in the 1960s, the industrialization of Sardinia started, managed by the central State through the so-called *piani di rinascita* (plans of re-birth). New roads, deforestation, dams, industrial plants, petrochemical companies, and oil refineries turned the Sardinians from farmers into builders and industry workers. The change was certainly economic, but also cultural and anthropological. In an illuminating book, the US anthropologist Carole Counihan (1984) examined the Sardinian women's loss of domestic power in the 1960s and 1970s, when they gave up making bread at home and started to buy it at the supermarket.

However, the 1973 oil crisis hit the Sardinians more than the other Italians. The island relied on the oil industry more than other regions and thousands of people lost their jobs in a short time. Unable to come back to agriculture and with industrial jobs gone forever, the majority of those who had been fired resorted to emigration, going to the northern cities like Milan, Turin, or Genova, where other kinds of industry were flourishing.

Another part of the modernization of Sardinia, as the Italian State intended it, was the opening of many military bases. Since the 1960s, the island has become a land of soldiers sent by Italy and NATO. Till date, 60 percent of the Italian and NATO forces in Italy are placed in Sardinia. Related to this, Sardinia also became the land of experimentation with new weapons, with predictable accidents and suspicious deaths of soldiers and local inhabitants.

Sardinia in Italian Culture Until 1970

"I'll send you to Sardinia"!

Mines, high-security prisons ("the Italian Alcatraz"), oil refineries, military bases, and relative weapon experiments: it is not difficult to understand why Sardinia has, for long, been a place subject to negative perceptions, hateful preconceptions, and neat rejection. All of this has its echoes in Italian culture, where Sardinia has always been an island, even symbolically. What pertains to Sardinia very often does not pertain to the rest of Italy. Its being an island geographically has certainly counted, and even another Italian island, Sicily, has followed this path, but to a minor degree.

For a long time, in Italian culture, Sardinia constituted a kind of nowhere: not knowing what there was on that island very often turned into disdain. Today, it is difficult to understand why, in the military language, the worst threat to a soldier who disobeyed his higher officials was: "I'll send you to Sardinia" (Roggeri 2022). In imagining the beautiful beaches of the island, its many fascinating places, the good weather, and the many pleasant people living there, the phrase seems paradoxical, but it was not. It mirrored how the Italians mistakenly saw Sardinia for centuries, a kind of deserted place populated by disreputable people without any interest in cultural exchanges.

Banditry

Not by chance, what Italian people talked about referring to Sardinia was, in the majority of the cases, negative. Without any doubt, banditry played a role in the construction of this view. The island, exactly like Sicily, was prey to criminals called *banditi* (people who had a ban for the crimes they committed and had to go away from their homes), who terrified honest people and lived on robbery, extortion, blackmail, and assassinations.

Sconocchia (2020) explains that bandits were not ordinary criminals. Rather, they very often fought the central State or power, to vent their anger and rebellion against those who had banned them. They also robbed rich people to fund their crimes. For this reason, they were hardly seen by the poor as a peril; conversely, many peasants and shepherds considered them as a kind of Robin Hood, doing what they did not dare to do. This made banditry a cultural problem difficult to solve, as ordinary people tended to protect them from the search of police and armies. From a sociological point of view, thus, banditry is interesting because it has social, cultural, and political meanings.

What is interesting, however, is the different representation that Italian culture constructed around Sicilian and Sardinian banditry. The idealization of the Sicilian bandit went well beyond Sicily. Many national magazines, books, and newspapers represented, for example, Salvatore Giuliano, the most notorious Sicilian bandit, as a fascinating and courageous man, seducing women and helping needy people. This never happened to Sardinian bandits, whose romantic construction did not trespass the Sardinian borders. This is a relevant point to understand how Sardinia was viewed by the rest of Italy: a remote place never romanticized, different from Sicily, that in some sense deserved different treatment.

Matriarchy

Another Sardinian element that affected the way the rest of Italy looked at the island was matriarchy. Sardinia was, in Neolithic times, a matrilineal society, as many archaeological sites and artifacts demonstrate. In many Neolithic houses and towns, in fact, many small statues of female goddesses have been found by archaeologists (Sirigu 2007). They are made up of clay, alabaster, limestone, kaolinite, marble, bones, or quartz sandstone. One of them is half a centimeter long and is currently on display at the Sanna Museum in Sassari (Fiocchetto 2003). Many of these goddesses have their arms open to symbolize cordiality and hospitality. They may be involved in a bigger group of female deities of the same period, found in many places in the Middle East, Mediterranean countries, and North African areas. In Sardinia, they have been found in many *Domus de Janas* (houses of fairies), where the dead were buried. These buildings have female shapes and sometimes resemble the form of a uterus, linking birth and death in the name of the woman.

What is important, however, is that matriarchy continued to exist in Sardinia well after the Neolithic age. During the *nuraghe* civilization, female deities implied priestesses, who mediated between the goddesses and people. The *Tombe dei giganti* (gants' tombs), funerary monuments scattered through the entire island, seem to confirm this theory, as they also were places where ill people used to go to heal and where priestesses supervised the cult (Fiocchetto 2003). Importantly, the *Tombe dei giganti* were dedicated to the *Dea Madre* (mother goddess) or *Grande Madre* (great mother), a mythical female deity who recurs in many prehistoric cultures.

Dea Madre was the deity for excellence of the Sardinian matriarchy. She is represented as a robust woman, often naked and sometimes with three breasts, to underline the abundant prosperity that she embodies (Sirigu 2007). Even during the Phoenician era, goddesses and priestesses were central to Sardinian cults. Tanit was the goddess who protected the dead infants. She sometimes wore a mask to fight evil spirits while at other times she played a tambourine for funeral ceremonies. Other goddesses with lotus flowers in their hands were represented with statues that have been found close to Carbonia, in the southern part of the island (Fiocchetto 2003). The tendency to adore female deities may also be found in Roman times in the cult of Goddess Diana, who has left many signs of her presence in toponymy and nursery rhymes.

Fiocchetto (2003), interestingly, lists female characters in Sardinian legends and cults showing people's devotion to female deities and legendary charac-ters. The *Gioviana* (female of Thursday) is a woman coming to many women's homes on Thursday, the day women spin until the middle of the night, to help them. *Coga* is a vampire imposing justice on humans. The *panas* or *pantamas* are spirits of women who died while giving birth, populating the banks of rivers and streams. The *Saggia Sibilla* (wise sibyl) lives with other *janas* in the caves close to Ozieri and supervises the leavening of bread and the creation of lactic ferments. The *fadas* lives in the *nuraghe* and weave good and bad luck with a golden loom. The *orassionarjas* were experts in herbs, who healed ill people with salt and magic formulas. The accabadòras (from the Phoenician "hacab," which means "putting an end") accompanied people in their journey to death to relieve them (there is a fascinating museum dedicated to them in Luras, very close to Costa Smeralda). Finally, the already mentioned *deinas* knew how to heal people hit by physical or psychological illnesses. All of these women come from old legends but their presence is still evident in Sardinian culture.

Even today, in the most traditional areas of the island, people usually put a small white canvas or wax doll of one of these goddesses in the coffin of a dead relative. These dolls, called *sa piedda* or *sa pizzinedda* in the Sardinian language, demonstrate that till date, female deities play a fundamental role in Sardinian culture and collective imagery (Fiocchetto 2003).

What is more, Sardinia has always been a place of female shamanism. *Deinas* were the women able to foresee the future, talk to the dead, and be in direct contact with gods and goddesses. They have crossed the entire history of Sardinian culture. Witches have also been a continuous presence in Sardinian life. Between 1562 and 1688, there were 767 inquisitorial processes against them (Fiocchetto 2003), most of them women who were well-credited in their towns as healers and experts in medicine.

In the end, Sardinian culture and religion have been, for long, based on the idea of the sacrality of women (Idea Sardegna 2013). The prominent role of women in society may also be seen in the practice of giving children the surname of the mother, rather than that of the father (Pittau 2018). The relevance of the woman in Sardinia is also the recurring element of many works by Grazia Deledda (Izzo 2021), the Sardinian writer who won the Nobel Prize for Literature in 1926, being the first Italian woman to win the Nobel Prize in general.

While what happened in prehistoric times, that is, the established matriarchy, may be called into question (Bonu 2021), the centrality of the woman in Sardinian culture is evident. This element is in this book for two reasons: firstly, because it constitutes a relevant cultural value for the island, and thus may be a piece of valid information to orientate the reader of the next chapters; secondly, because it is interesting to observe the way Italian culture has processed all of this. Matriarchy and the prevalence of the woman in Sardinia have contributed to giving the island a sense of archaism and a savage nature. In another study (Buscemi 2018), I have delved into the way the British media represented Scotland. They do it to pigeonhole Scotland as the archaic room of the bigger house of the United Kingdom. It is not a negative representation, but it refers to difference. Scotland is a part of the UK, the British media seem to say, but is different from the other parts.

I find something similar in the way Sardinian matriarchy and the relevance of the woman, in general, has been represented in Italian media. Sardinia is somehow savage, archaic, and thus different from the rest of Italy. It is a part of it, but it is positioned in a different room. The next chapter will clarify this point, as it focuses on the construction of Costa Smeralda in a land that was very often represented as savage, archaic, and thus different.

Conclusion

This chapter has demonstrated two things: firstly, that Sardinia has a very profound culture that has developed independently from the Italian one and that has given the island a corpus of traditions and habits that till date animate its inhabitants; secondly, that the people governing it or sharing nationality with it (the rest of the Italians) ignored this culture, its people, and even the beauty of those places.

Sardinia was almost a mystery for the majority of people and I hope this does not apply to the readers of this chapter, which has summarized more than two millenniums of history to prepare those who will read the next chapters. What we can see, thus, is that Costa Smeralda was built on a land that, because of its past, was not neutral to people arriving from abroad. Constructed as archaic and savage, Sardinia was perfect for a tourist paradise. However, just because of the fierce past of the Sardinians, it was also perfect for contrasting the tourist enterprise.

CHAPTER 3

The 1960s: The Age of Hope

Introduction

This chapter delves into the very first stage of the construction of Costa Smeralda. At this stage, hotels and villas had not been built yet and this tourist destination was only in the minds of a group of people who, first separately and later together, arrived on the island, remained enchanted by it, and created the plan. Prince Karim was not the first to disembark, having been preceded by other investors and bankers. However, he was the man who would transform the idea of an investment into a concrete commercial project. This chapter describes his profile and his career before Costa Smeralda. As he became a celebrity in a short time, a section here also looks at how the Italian media depicted him and what this meant for the Italian cultural scene of the 1960s.

The other founders are the focus of another section. They had different roles and interests, but together, they formed a powerful group. An interview with Gisele Podbielski, the wife of one of the founders, supports this claim, as do other aspects highlighted in the following pages. The chapter does not forget to discuss the decisive role played by the Sardinians in the process of construction, and it investigates their spirit and mood shown to the new visitors. Finally, the making of the Consortium is explained and a concluding section analyzes, through Baudrillard and Foucault's theories, what this story means at a more profound level.

Karim Aga Khan

Prince Karim Aga Khan IV is the protagonist of the story of the construction of Costa Smeralda. Some accounts give equal importance to Giuseppe Mentasti, an Italian entrepreneur discovering that part of Sardinia at the same time as con

Karim, as well as to Duncan Miller, one of the others exploring northeast Sardinia since the end of the 1950s along with the Aga Khan, collaborating with him and constituting the first Consortium, the decisional board of the tourist enterprise. What favored the birth of a unique group of investors was that both Mentasti and Miller were actually Aga Khan's friends, and thus it was not competition, but collaboration, that was at the basis of their commercial adventures.

Certainly, Karim Aga Khan was the main character of the Sardinian business in the media representations, in the political interactions with the Italian and the Sardinian governments, and in the conception of the project. Knowing this man better would provide a better understanding of the construction of Costa Smeralda, the reasons behind its conception, and the internal nature of this broad project.

Prince Karim Aga Khan was born in Geneva on December 13, 1936, the son of Prince Ali Aga Khan and Princess Tajuddawlah Aga Khan. He is the forty-ninth Imam of the Nizaris, the principal group of the Ismailis, a branch of the wider Shiite Islam. Nizaris are about 15 million globally and principally live in the Middle East, Europe, and North America. The term Aga Khan is a noble title; the prince's real name is Karim al Husayni, and he inherited the role of Imam from his grandfather (*Il Post* 2020).

The Prince has been very popular in the Western media for different reasons: his wealth (which has been helped by donations from his supporters), his entrepreneurial goals to help improve living conditions in poor countries, his private life as a playboy (which he inherited from his father, who also married the actress Rita Hayworth), and his passion for racehorses and skiing, to the point that he participated in the Winter Olympic Games in Innsbruck in 1964 as a member of the team of the Islamic Republic of Iran (Ottone 2023). Karim studied in Switzerland and Harvard and became Aga Khan at age 20, before completing his degree in Islamic History in 1959 (*Il Post* 2020), 3 years before founding Costa Smeralda.

Just after graduating, the Prince stated that he would improve the conditions of Nizaris in the world by boosting the relationships between them and the nations they lived in. His first order of business was to establish in 1961 an independent media group in Kenya to push democracy in that nation and hence guarantee pluralism, which would help Nizaris and other minorities. The Nation Media Group is still the most important media company in central Africa today (*Il Post* 2020). In 1963, the year after he started working on Costa Smeralda, he created Alisarda, an airline company that aimed to take tourists from many parts of Europe to the new tourist destination. Over the years, Prince Aga Khan

activated commercial businesses and social projects in poor countries such as
Uganda, Myanmar, Tanzania, Tajikistan, and others, to build infrastructure and
establish hospitals, schools, universities, and local companies in order to improve
local people's lives.

He also created tourist resorts for very rich people, bought an island in the
Bahamas archipelago, and created large commercial companies, all of which
allowed him to rank eleventh among the richest people in the world, as published
by the magazine *Forbes*. He was married to the British model Sarah Frances
Croker-Poole (from 1969 to 1995) and later to the German heiress Gabriele
Renate Thyssen (from 1998 to 2014), and the media have frequently hinted at
his numerous extramarital relationships, which clashed with his religious role
(*Il Post* 2020).

Aga Khan's popularity in Italy began to build around 1960, when he started
visiting Sardinia frequently. He was romantically depicted as a Prince and was
very often featured in newspapers and magazines without any relevant news,
but just for being Aga Khan. In *Corriere della Sera* (1961a), for example, he
is represented in a photo along with an aircraft pilot, with no article to go with
it, just a caption of two lines that the Aga Khan is in Italy and the photo is in
Rome's Airport before he took a flight to Sardinia. Evidently, here there was no
news worth publishing, as nothing really happened. This mode of representation
of the Prince was really frequent in the Italian press during those years.

Analyzing this photograph through the lens of multimodality may be interesting. The context in which this photo was published was not gossip. On the same
page, in fact, the other articles referred to the problems of the Italian system of
justice, the difficult relationships between France and Algeria, and a fire that
broke out in North Carolina due to the explosion of an oil tanker. All the news
on this page, apart from Aga Khan's arrival and the fire, was in the written mode
exclusively, in the form of long articles; the article about the fire in the U.S. presented two modes: the visual (a photo of the tragic event) and the written word
(a long article). Only the Aga Khan piece did not have an accompanying article
and was the only one exclusively made up of a photo and a very short caption.

Even the mode relating to clothes suggested something: in the photo the Aga
Khan is in a suit and tie and seems older than 25, his age at that time. He is
walking fast along with the pilot, probably toward the gate. He communicates
seriousness and credibility, and appears to have many things to do. The pilot,
wearing the uniform, is shorter than him and seems to be trying to keep up with
the Prince's pace. Most importantly, the photo suggested the opportunity to go

to Sardinia by air. Two years later, Karim would establish Airsarda, the airline company that would take many tourists to Costa Smeralda. The presence of the pilot in uniform reminded the viewer of this link between flying and Sardinia, very useful for the success of Costa Smeralda.

This style of representation was not a one-off event in the depiction of the Aga Khan. Around two months later, *Corriere della Sera* (1961b) published a new photo of the Aga Khan without any related article on its cultural pages. Between articles on paintings, films, and Pope John XXIII turning 80, Prince Karim was shown skiing in Cervinia, with the title: The Aga Khan inaugurates winter. Here the caption was shorter than the previous one, just one and a half lines. Again, there was no news, no event that may have been interesting for the readers. The Aga Khan was simply in Italy, and his presence was a piece of news in itself for the entire country (he is not connected to Sardinia here) and the entire year (he is linked to winter). The written mode suggested his powerful position and role in 'inaugurating winter'.

Thus, the Aga Khan was gradually connected to Italy as both a businessman and a rich Prince enjoying the beauty of the country. Everything was ready for the acknowledgement of the Prince and his adventure in Sardinia.

The Prince and the Italian Media

News of the Costa Smeralda project landed in the media at the beginning of 1962. *Corriere della Sera* (1962) presented it in an article listing all the points of the future tourist destination. The first account was just institutional. The Prince met at the Sardinian airport of Alghero the Italian Minister of Foreign Affairs and presented him the plan. Later he went to Cagliari to meet all the most important institutional figures of the island: the president of the region and two regional council members. He talked to them about issues concerning tourism and the rebirth of the region, respectively. Finally, it was said that he would go to Rome to meet the minister again and other members of the Italian institutions. The written mode here communicated that the Aga Khan was on familiar terms with some of the most important representatives of Italian institutions. He met them in Sardinia and at Rome, at a local and national level. After inaugurating winter, this was a further step from taking on a cultural to an institutional role.

The article said that the Prince had constituted a Consortium along with his brother and French, British, and Italian entrepreneurs, to value the area of northeast

Sardinia between Capriccioli and Olbia. The Consortium was already the owner of the area, which it had bought from Sardinian shepherds for 3 billion lire (the Italian currency before the Euro). The sum corresponds to approximately to 1.5 million euros. The place's name would be Costa Smeralda, said the article. It comprised eleven hotels, five of whom were open to all the tourists, while the other six would be clubs reserved for members; three villages would be for the fishermen; there would be three ports built with all the modern technologies; new roads, schools, barracks, churches, golf clubs, tennis courts, two museums, aqueducts, and power lines would be set up; finally, three thousand new, semi-detached houses would be built and Costa Smeralda would be able to host around twenty to twenty-five people in total (*Corriere della Sera* 1962). After the meeting, the Prince was interviewed by journalists where he told them that some friends had told him about the beauty of the Sardinian coast between Capriccioli and Olbia, inviting him to buy the land, and that he did so.

A photo depicted the Prince and the President of the region smiling at each other and shaking hands (Corriere 1962). Both the article and the image changed the role of the Prince in Italy. While the previously analyzed pictures referred to the Aga Khan as a businessman and a protagonist of high society, here Karim became a man connected to Italian institutions. In the visual mode, the photo of the Aga Khan and the President of the region dressing the same way, smiling at each other, and shaking hands made the two men specular, where both of them do the same things. There is total equivalence between the two men here, the President and the Prince. The connection between the Prince and the Italian State is also underlined by the written mode. It described this link in three steps: firstly, the Aga Khan meets the Minister of the Foreign Affairs at the airport of Alghero in Sardinia; secondly, Prince Karim meets with local institutions such as the President of the region and the regional council members; thirdly, Karim would go to Rome to meet the minister again. There is a narrative structure in all of this. The first meeting with the minister in Sardinia introduced the Prince to Italian politics; the second meeting immersed Karim in the Sardinian system; and finally, the third meeting with the minister would happen in Rome, certifying the complete belonging of Karim to Italy and its highest institutions.

Another relevant element of these messages is the centrality of Sardinia. Certainly, Rome is the capital of the nation and the place where all the major institutions are situated. However, the minister goes to Sardinia to meet the Prince for the first time, and Sardinia is the place of the meeting between the Aga Khan and the local politicians. Only when he has met these relevant people in Sardinia is he allowed to go to Rome. This was unusual for an island that, as we have seen earlier, was an almost unknown place in Italy in those years.

However, the written mode also revealed something, or rather, what had not been written did. The press talked about Costa Smeralda when the Prince had already bought it. The later contested negotiations occurred far away from journalists and cameras. Only in the subsequent years would the negotiations become an issue. This confirms the suspicious complicity of the Italian State in not participating at that stage and in leaving a group of very expert British investors to deal with the price of the land with some ignorant Sardinian shepherds and farmers.

The last point regards what happened after these first Italian media representations of the Prince. Looking at these three images, one might think that the rich businessman very often present in gossip news was replaced by the new image of the Aga Khan, that is, the man close to and somehow consistent with the Italian institutions. Actually, this did not happen. Rather, the two images coexisted and the two sides of the Prince alternated and sometimes merged to give an idea of the complexity of the character.

When he got involved and later got married, for example, the gossip dimension certainly became dominant; when the media focused on the building of Costa Smeralda and the benefits this brought for the entire country, the institutional side of the coin was highlighted more.

In *Corriere d'Informazione* (1961), for example, the Prince was seen through the lens of gossip. It was said that the religious group he was the leader of, the Ismailis, wanted him to marry a Muslim woman and that the promised spouse was Princess Mirza, a beautiful girl living in Lebanon. The Aga Khan was however described as a "young and strong man" with a liking for women belonging to the jet-set, such as Anouska von Mehks, Tracy Pellissier, and Silvia Casablancas. What would these girls do if the prince married the Lebanese princess, the journalist asked.

Sometimes the news relating to the Prince mixed up gossip and institutional characters, as in the case of *Corriere d'Informazione* (1964), where an article said that Karim's yacht crashed on a rock in Sardinia while the Aga Khan, along with his girlfriend Anouska von Mehks, was showing the wonders of Costa Smeralda to Princess Margaret, her husband, and her mother-in-law. Because of the accident, Princess Margaret fell into the sea. The Prince was the only person on board wearing shorts, so he dove in and saved the Princess, taking her to the nearest beach while his yacht almost sank. The group was later rescued by people from the mainland.

This article interestingly contributed to the construction of the character of the Aga Khan, as here the Prince merged two modes, gossip and institutions, *la dolce vita* and politics. The Prince is a rich man enjoying his life and at the same time is a good friend of the Princess of the United Kingdom. He is strong and young, as said in the article previously analyzed, and even saves princesses when they risk drowning. Importantly, Sardinia is the land of this encounter. The formerly savage and archaic island is still risky, but the Prince is transforming it into a safe place.

The impression that the Prince gave to Olbia's inhabitants was different. Many of them still remember this boy going around the town in a red Volkswagen Beetle and very often having dinner at Pizzeria del Romano on Sassari Road (*Coast Magazine* 2021), a place certainly never touched by the international jet-setting crowd. Moreover, the more the image of the Aga Khan circulates through different modes, the more his representation becomes more appealing to a major number of readers. The playboy, the serious and credited businessman, the friend of Italian politicians, the rich man dining in a pizzeria in Sassari... the more the modes, the more the sympathy surrounding the main character.

The list of articles depicting the Aga Khan as a rich man involved in politics and able to change Sardinia, or at least a part of it, could go on. What is important, however, is that the two sides of the main character coexisted perfectly and produced a robust narrative. Over the years, the Aga Khan became a trait d'union between gossip and institutions, lightheartedness and political commitment. In the grey scenario of the Italian politics of those years, he was a sort of colorful, exotic presence aiming to animate the scene and to render Italy's field of politics more pleasant and appealing to the Italians. In about three years, Karim changed from being unknown to being considered a credible entrepreneur able to revolutionize Italian tourism.

This happened to the point that in 1964 the Aga Khan's influence over Sardinia expanded to other areas in Italy. In *Corriere della Sera* (1964b), it was said that some entrepreneurs in northern Italy wanted to sell Valtellina (a mountainous area in the Lombardy Alps) to the Aga Khan. Given the success obtained in Sardinia, they hoped to boost tourism even in that remote region, where people were still attached to the peasant culture and ignored the tourist potentialities of their land. Thus, the Aga Khan was considered as the savior of the many things that did not work in Italy. He actually never bought Valtellina, but few could doubt his abilities to resuscitate at least Sardinia.

The Other Founders

On March 14, 1962, six people gathered in Olbia with the notary Mario Altea by Tempio Pausania, to create the Consortium Costa Smeralda. The Aga Khan was accompanied by John Duncan Miller, Patrick Guinness, André Ardoin, René Podbielski, and Felix Bigio. The six men had already met in 1961 along with Giuseppe Mentasti, an Italian entrepreneur and owner of San Pellegrino, a well-known brand of mineral water. They had established some general criteria that would regulate the entire area. Mentasti later decided to leave the project. The meeting of 1962, thus, marks the official birth of Costa Smeralda. In this section, I briefly explain who these five people collaborating with Prince Karim were.

John Duncan Miller, born in 1903, according to many accounts, was the first of the six people who discovered the Sardinian area where Costa Smeralda would be born. An original document by the World Bank (1955) summarizes his career well. Miller graduated from Cambridge, was an officer of the British Army during WWII, and was the Director of the British Information Services for the Middle West. Later, he joined the Washington staff of *Times of London* in June 1947 and became chief Washington correspondent of *Times* in July 1948 (World Bank 1955; Ottone 2023). Above all, he was one of the richest British magnates at those times. He was also a special representative of the International Bank for Reconstruction and Development, the bank aiming to reconstruct Europe after WWII. Miller was passionate about and financially interested in Italy. Another official document, this time by one of the most important Italian banks, Mediobanca (2024), is of direct relevance in this regard. Miller wrote a letter to Enrico Cuccia, the president of this Italian bank and universally recognized as one of the most powerful people in Italy ever. Miller said to Cuccia that he loved Italy and that he wanted to do some business in this country. Cuccia was certainly the right person to ask, as it was widely acknowledged that he could move money and people around in Italy as he liked.

Miller, in his late 50s, used to sail around Sardinia at the end of the 1950s to verify the extinction of malaria from the island, for his work at the International Bank for Reconstruction and Development. He said that one day he happened to come across Cala di Volpe, one of the most beautiful beaches in the area. He was enchanted by the beauty and purity of the sea and called his friend Ronnie Grierson, another banker, telling him to come to Monti di Mola to see that sea resembling the Caribbean but closer to home, a two-hour flight from London. Going back to the city, Miller told his friends about Gallura and its wonders while meeting them in the exclusive London clubs. He finally persuaded them to invest in what was still a vague tourist enterprise, which would be fine-tuned by Prince Karim, one of his friends who listened to his travel accounts about Sardinia and decided to make a business of it.

Supported by his role in the International Bank for Reconstruction and Development (later the World Bank), Miller started buying land in the area called Monti di Mola, followed by his friends, among whom the Aga Khan was the most active.

Patrick Guinness (1931–1964) was Aga Khan's half-brother. Before Rita Hayworth, in fact, Karim's father was married to Joan Guinness, who had a son from her previous marriage, Patrick. Karim and Patrick, almost the same age, became friends and shared many adventures in the international jet-setting scenes in those years. Patrick married Dolores Maria Agatha Wilhelmine Luise Freiin von Fürstenberg-Herdringen when she was 19. Dolores was the daughter of Gloria Rubio y Alatorrenata, a Mexican fashion model who later was the cofounder of Harper's Bazar, and who previously had married one of the Fürstenberg-Herdringen, becoming a baroness and a member of the jet-set in those years. Dolores's father was Thomas Loel Guinness, so Patrick Guinness was both her husband and her half-brother. She and Patrick became regulars at many social events around the world.

Unfortunately, Patrick died at the age of 34 in 1965, in a car accident in Turtig, at the Simplon Pass in Switzerland, when the sports car he was driving crashed into a tree. The accident happened just a few years after the birth of Costa Smeralda, and thus Guinness could not see the successful development of the tourist enterprise he started along with the other investors.

André Ardoin (1922–2016) was a lawyer and one of the most trustworthy collaborators of the Aga Khan. He started working with Karim's family much before the adventure of Costa Smeralda. In the 1950s, as a young lawyer working at Lloyd's, he was a consultant for the testament of Karim's grandfather Aga Khan III. Karim continued to benefit from his experience and ability to solve the many legal problems that a businessman has to face and the two became friends soon. He also became one of the buyers of the Sardinian land, owning the area close to the Pevero beach and Liscia di Vacca.

Ardoin was also the director of many companies founded by the Aga Khan, like for example, the Berkeley Hotel Company in London. Until he died in 2016, he was the director of the Aga Khan Fund for Economic Development (*La Nuova Sardegna* 2016). Prince Karim also admitted that the idea of the Consortium was Ardoin's, who identified this legal instrument as the perfect one to guarantee Costa Smeralda's independence from other political and economic powers. Ardoin was also famous for his beautiful villa in Porto Cervo Marina, which he sold later to the Italian tycoon and politician Silvio Berlusconi (*Italia Oggi* 1994).

René and Gisele Podbielski (1914–1981): René was a Polish-German writer famous for his book *Kindheit des Herzens* (The Childhood of the Heart), which was a bestseller in Germany before WWII. As a Jew, he escaped Nazism and had an adventurous life in Australia, London, Geneva, and finally Italy. He arrived in Monti di Mola in July 1960, following the accounts by John Duncan Miller in London. He arrived with his wife Gisele (1918–2006) and fell in love with that part of Sardinia. In summer 1961, they came back and remained for many days. In doing so, they were the first foreign tourists who spent their holidays in the future Costa Smeralda. They in fact rented a *stazzo*, a traditional local house, in Liscia di Vacca. They had no electric power, lights, and hot water and were on good terms with many local people, starting to buy land from them.

At the beginning, they lived in a *stazzo*, but later the *stazzo* became a discotheque, the Pedro's, and they bought a very nice villa by the sea close to the villa of Bettina Graziani, a fashion model who was the fiancee of Karim's father. That beach, close to Liscia di Vacca, is today called Liscia Renè, named after Podbielski. The couple also became the first winter tourists, as they enjoyed Monti di Mola over the course of the entire year. For twenty years René was the CEO of the Consortium. After he arrived in Sardinia, Podbielski stopped writing and dedicated his time to his entrepreneurial career, also hosting guests in their villa of primary importance, such as Princess Margaret and Lord Snowdon (Galleria Francesca Antonacci 2006).

His wife Gisele was the ace up his sleeve. A woman of great intelligence and knowledge, a speaker at the United Nations, an internationally renowned economist and essayist, and a tennis champion too, Gisele was as passionate about Costa Smeralda as her husband was (Marestelle 2024). Her book *Two European Lives* (Podbielski 1993) is a wonderful insight into her and Renè's lives together and a eulogy to European citizenship, which they felt was their real identity. Her long and relevant interview about her years in Costa Smeralda is analyzed in the next section.

When he and his wife died, their son René, as requested by them, buried both parents in the cemetery of Santa Teresina, between Porto Cervo and Arzachena (*Consorzio Costa Smeralda* 2019b).

Felix Bigio was for a long time the personal assistant of Karim's father and later became the Prince's assistant. His role in the group was that of the controller and accounting officer. Basically, he had to strictly control all the expenses, allow the good ones and stop the bad ones (Camillo 2023). His severity was in contrast to the rest of the group, that was made up of men who were certainly not austere. There is very little news about Bigio, but the visual mode of a photo on Instagram (*Coast Magazine* 2021) explains his role more than a written page. In it we can see Bigio, an austere man wearing a suit and tie, glasses and a grey 1950s hairdo, just getting out of a car at the airport of Alghero still with an unpaved airstrip. He is welcoming a beautiful girl who probably just arrived on the plane that we can see in the back of the image. To sum up, Bigio represented probably the severe and austere side of the group, which was probably in need of him, given the carefree nature of the rest of its members.

The Spirit of the Founders

In the previous section, we introduced the six men, and the only woman, who created Costa Smeralda along with the Aga Khan. In this section, we delve into the spirit of these eight people through the only woman of the group. Gisele Podbielski was the person who spoke most about the feelings and the emotions experienced by the entire group, especially at the beginning of their adventure. Her account is certainly biased as she was a member of the group. In her words, however, we do not look for absolute truth; rather, they are relevant as they explain the mood and the reasons why the founders chose that destination, along with what prompted them to construct Costa Smeralda. In the next section, I focus on the spirit of the locals; while even their accounts are somehow biased, as in Gisele's case, I am not looking for the truth, if it exists. Here I examine an interview (Barone and Di Francisca 2015) that Gisele released to the Italian public television channel, RAI, telling her story about Costa Smeralda and its founding.

At the beginning, Gisele says that in July 1960 she was an economist at the United Nations. She was invited by a friend who was an ex-colleague at the UN and worked in a bank in London at the time. He invited her on a journey to see

Sardinia along with other friends (Guinness and the publisher Roy Thompson). At that time the Prince was still extraneous to Sardinia. Gisele accepted enthusiastically and she and her husband, the writer René Podbielski, flew from Nice to Alghero. Gisele came to know that his friend was informed about Costa Smeralda by John Duncan Miller, the head of the World Bank in London. He loved the beach of Capriccioli and pointed it out to Gisele's friends.

That is why Gisele, René, and the rest of the group went immediately to Capriccioli, where some fishermen on a boat were waiting for them. They soon became some kind of celebrities of Monti di Mola. The mayor of Arzachena welcomed the group with local wine and foods, and showed the visitors some sights. Gisele and the others were astonished by the wonder of the place, remote but also close to the main European cities. Before this discovery, they used to go to the Caribbean or the Pacific islands to see similar places. They decided to remain there, without knowing for how long.

Gisele goes on to explain that at that point the entrance of the Aga Khan, a common friend of the group, transformed the project from a tourist adventure among friends to an ambitious commercial plan. The Aga Khan convinced the group to constitute the Consortium and René was part of it as a cofounder. Gisele and her husband bought a *stazzo* in Liscia di Vacca with a beautiful view. They started leading a more rustic life there, without electric power, having a shower from a tube, without lights and gas. When they wanted to shop for something to eat, they had to go to Olbia, so they bought a jeep. Life was not easy in those early days, and to revisit the life they'd been used to, they would sometimes book a room at the Jolly Hotel, the only hotel in the area, to have hot water, a shower, and everything they were missing in Liscia di Vacca.

In Arzachena and Liscia di Vacca, they saw poverty and even signs of malaria that persisted then, Gisele tells the interviewer. They became good friends with many people, who were curious to know why they left their city to live in Sardinia, and even worse in a place by the sea, which they did not consider a good place at all.

In Barone and Di Francisca (2015), she talked about the Orecchionis, a wonderful couple who wanted to understand why that corner of Sardinia was so wonderful for the new visitors. To help them understand, Gisele and René gave them binoculars as a present. This was the relaxed spirit of the first period, she says, when they were a small group living there, visiting the houses of many local people and having good relationships with them to the point where they would go very frequently to their weddings. Even the Aga Khan was a part of this lifestyle, at least at the beginning. Later, however, he moved to Cala di Volpe, becoming more distant after starting his commercial enterprise. Local people were displeased by this and the relationships started worsening.

Many people who sold the land were women, Gisele adds, as those who usually inherited the areas by the sea were the daughters, as coastal areas were less valuable than the inner parts, which usually went to the sons. Gisele also remembers that buyers and sellers used to go to the notary, who did not have an assistant who typed the text of the act, but handwrote with a pen the entire agreement really slowly. It took hours, and if someone wanted to change something, the meeting was postponed to the subsequent day (Barone and Di Francisca 2015).

The creation of a place requires many things, Gisele says, as it means inventing a civilized life where there is not; but it was beautiful, as life in 1961 and 1962 for them was divided into two parts: the commercial one, with them going around with a jeep to buy land, and the stressless one, with hours spent on wonderful beaches that were deserted as local people did not catch the beauty of the place they lived in.

Gisele also says that the pioneers discovering that area were exclusively foreigners, as the Italians, especially women, were used to more luxurious places such as Capri or Portofino and did not like the remoteness of Sardinia. After the first stage, the explorers coming from abroad became a crowd and they also included well-known celebrities such as the Prince of Luxembourg, Alain Delon, Romy Schneider, Princess Margaret, Catherine Deneuve, Brigitte Bardot, and even international politicians. The Aga Khan, Gisele says, wanted them to attract visitors to the newly born tourist destination. Bettina, the fiancee of the Prince's father, had a specific role in the plan. She lived in a beautiful villa by the sea and attracted many people from the fashion business. She also invested money in the enterprise and soon became a sort of internationally renowned luxury guide who spread the word of this beautiful new promised land among the international jet-set (Barone and Di Francisca 2015).

It was a daily show, Gisele says, which has disappeared today. Today there is not someone to look at, she regrets. Certainly, it was a commercial adventure, she says, but also a matter of love for this place. Transforming it meant loving it. On the contrary, people investing today in Costa Smeralda do not care about Sardinia and the Sardinians. The ideal reasons that pushed us have disappeared and they only invest in making a business.

The Spirit of the Locals

The same documentary (Barone and Di Francisca 2015) abundantly cited in the previous section also offers an interesting account of the other side of the issue, that is, on how the Sardinians perceived the arrival of the founders of Costa Smeralda. The shepherd Giommaria Pilieri talks about the very hard work he did day and night in those years for 365 days each year. Maddalena Pasiello similarly says that in the 1960s she worked a lot, first doing agriculture and later rearing animals. Paolo Fresi explains the strangeness of not considering going to the beach as a nice activity when he was young. They only knew one beach, Cannigione, and used to go there rarely. Similarly, Giovanni Azara says that they did not get satisfaction from going to the beach and that the foreigners were instead more intelligent, as they took the best places that the locals had ignored.

Some Sardinians perfectly understood that the Aga Khan and his friends were setting up a big business, but did not prevent him from doing so because they believed that it was a business for the locals too. As the Prince started buying the first piece of land, in fact, many people hoped to sell theirs. Even owners from inland towns tried to sell cultivated fields to the Consortium, hoping to make a business like in the coastal areas. This land, however, was useless for the new investors and these owners thus did not succeed.

Lucio Cucciari worked at the local council of Arzachena. He remembers the absolute poverty of many people and the change in their lives brought about by the construction of Costa Smeralda. Francesco Azara was a shepherd who sold his land to the Aga Khan. He became a millionaire, bought a car, and established a factory making bricks. What many shepherds did after selling their land was to buy a house in their town. Giommaria Pilieri says that people were eager to sell their land and that some of them did it for 300 lire per square meter. The Aga Khan, he says, looked for poor people selling their land. Giannandrea was one of them. He lived in Golfo Aranci and had twelve sons and daughters. The Aga Khan gave him 5 million lire, but he did not know what 5 million meant actually. So he dilapidated the entire capital (Barone and Di Francisca 2015).

Simone Azara says that many people considered the Prince as the solution to the problem of poverty. Giovanni Azara (many people have this surname in the area and are not necessarily related) says that his relatives sold their land at 40 lire per square meter. He did not want his family to sell the land, at least at the beginning. Later, he realized that selling was a good idea, even at such a low price. Antonio and Francesco Meloni are two shepherds who wanted to sell the land as they needed money to live better. They succeeded and their lives thus changed when they were almost 90.

Nicola Azara worked at the local council in Arzachena and in the documentary he shows the agreements signed by Patrick Guinness and other people of the group buying land from the locals. He is one of three brothers who sold an entire island, Soffi (a land of 42 hectares), for 16 million lire. The three brothers wanted to get rid of that territory as it did not give them any money. While the other two continued to rear animals, he became a real estate agent. The island of Mortorio was sold to the Italian entrepreneur Mentasti (who has been mentioned earlier) for 3 million. Azara adds that certainly the founders of Costa Smeralda were eager to buy; however, he concludes, local people equally wanted to sell. It was a gold rush, he says, which brought wealth to that area.

Another interviewee (Barone and Di Francisca 2015) says that he sold his land at 400,000 lire each hectare, and that today (the documentary was shot in the 1990s) it was worth 4 or 5 million each hectare. He says that he was cheated. A man says that selling did not change his life. His family was composed of many members and when they divided the money no one became rich. A car seller states that many people, after selling the land, bought a car, either a luxury one or a small van to help them in their jobs, as cars replaced horses in agricultural work. A man and his wife decided to build a hotel. They went through troubled times and made many sacrifices, caused by the fact that they did not have any experience in the field of tourism. However, in the end, they managed to make a good business.

A shepherd suggests that if he were one of these entrepreneurs coming from outside Sardinia he would remain in their places of origin. Without any doubt, he concludes, these foreign entrepreneurs made Monti di Mola more valuable. Many images of the documentary, in addition, show cows led by the shepherds in the early 1960s going around the beaches that would become famous all over the world after the construction of Costa Smeralda.

One person who behaved differently from the majority of the locals was Luca Azara, who sold a mountain for 90 million lire. Later, he did nothing and decided to live in a hotel. He just bought four suits, elegant shirts, and two palaces in Olbia that give him enough to live well.

At the end of the documentary (Barone and Di Francisca 2015), these people explain how all of this has changed their lives in Monti di Mola. Time is the major change, one advances: after the establishment of Costa Smeralda, everyone started running or flying, and people were always in a hurry. Even sound changed, Pilieri adds: Costa Smeralda brought silence to Monti di Mola, which he regretted, as unfortunately it cancelled the sound of the cowbells that he used to hear in the past.

The Consortium

So far in this chapter, I have investigated the personal traits and the spirit that animated the construction of Costa Smeralda on both sides, the investors and the locals. In this section, conversely, I delve into the materiality of the Consortium Costa Smeralda, the legally recognized organism that set the rules and decided what Costa Smeralda would be.

The first legal agreement predated the constitution of the Consortium in 1962. It occurred in September 1961, when the Prince, the Italian entrepreneur Giuseppe Mentasti (producing San Pellegrino mineral water), and other friends of Karim signed a handwritten letter of commitment that fixed some rules relating to the development of the future tourist destination (*La Stampa* 2022).

However, on March 14, 1962, the Consortium was officially created. The members were Karim Aga Khan, Patrick Guinness, John Duncan Miller, André Ardoin, René Podbielski, and Felix Bigio, all the people whose profiles I have outlined above, apart from Gisele Podbielski. She did not enter the group probably because she was René's wife. However, she showed a great awareness of what the group was doing, its pros and cons, and the destiny of the development that they contributed to.

As stated in an official document of the Consortium (*Consorzio Costa Smeralda* 2020), at the beginning, it controlled around 1,800 hectares of land and was nonprofit. It was created to govern and supervise the urban, territorial, and architectural development of Costa Smeralda and prevent it from any attempted building speculation.

For this reason, the Consortium also established an architectural committee, aiming to set the rules of development in relation to the measurements of the buildings, the materials to be adopted, the colors of houses and hotels, and all the other specific visual and aesthetic details. The committee had to control whatever building would be constructed in Costa Smeralda without any exception, the smallest included. Even vegetation was put under the control of the Consortium. In short, even an olive tree or a brick could not be placed without the authorization of the architectural committee.

Since the beginning, it has been clear that the wish of the architects, as suggested by Prince Karim, was to preserve the preexisting natural heritage of the area and to shape an architectonic style combining natural beauty and local architectural traditions. The architectural component of Costa Smeralda is discussed in the next chapter. However, here it is important to anticipate some of its aims and the names of the four architects who were involved: Luigi Vietti, Jacques Couëlle, Michele Busiri Vici, and Antonio Simon Mossa. They were among the most important architects in the world at that time (*Consorzio Costa Smeralda* 2020).

Importantly, since its constitution, the Consortium has been the owner of the brand named Costa Smeralda. What has not been said so far is that Costa Smeralda is not a toponym. This name is not written in the maps (apart from the tourist ones) and in any official document. The original name of the area is Monti di Mola. Costa Smeralda, thus, is a commercial name, the name of a product like Coca-Cola or General Motors.

The initial budget of the Consortium was 14 million lire. It had one hundred employees that, over the summer, became two hundred. Among their duties were also (and still are) security and fire-fighting. All the owners of land, hotels, villas, and apartments were obliged to join the Consortium even in the future. The six founders and their descendants would hold the majority share inside the Consortium.

Since the beginning, the territory of Costa Smeralda has belonged, for the major part, to the council of Arzachena and the rest to the council of Olbia. It comprises 55 kilometers of coasts spanning from Pitrizza in the north to the Gulf of Cugnana in the south. Being a commercial name, no official road sign contains the writing "Costa Smeralda," but just the commercial ones. However, two huge stones made up of local granite, one on the north border and the other on the south one, display this name and inform tourists that they are entering this territory.

Magro (2022) says that the rules set by the Consortium seem to be written today, in the era of sustainability, rather than in 1962, when these principles were still unknown by the majority of tourism professionals. In Italy, preserving traditions and protecting the environment were rare principles, as those were the years of the so-called *boom economico* (economic boom), when buildings were constructed by the sea and the major cities remained suffocated by new huge palaces overwhelming the city centers.

According to Magro (2022), the Consortium found the right balance between new buildings and respect for traditions, highlighting the beauty of the place and the fact that those twenty-two beaches were unique in Italy, with their tropical elements, white sand, pink granite, and Mediterranean vegetation. It was a case of environmental and social sustainability before these concepts were conceived and practiced, especially in Italy. The Consortium also established that the owners could build only in 4 percent of the total territory and that those who removed even one plant were obliged to plant another two. For the first time, at least in Italy, very strict rules were imposed to preserve nature and the beauty of a tourist destination (Magro 2022).

Costa Smeralda Between Hyperrealism and Heterotopia

What has been said so far may be better understood if we look at it through the theories that I have developed in Chapter 1. What this chapter describes is the first stage of a really interesting process of social and media construction. Well before its material establishment, in fact, Costa Smeralda was constructed virtually. Here "virtually" does not refer to the digital meaning that we recognize today, but to a kind of construction that is not material, but impalpable and only to be found in a changing culture, its media representations, and in people's minds.

What for me renders Costa Smeralda an illuminating and original example of social construction is the fact that it perfectly explains how social phenomena are much more shared than they sometimes appear, that what seems imposed in a top-down way very often implies mutual interests. Costa Smeralda was somehow needed by all the agents present in the field. Certainly, it was a commercial enterprise resulting in a very good business for the group of international entrepreneurs investing in it, who speculated and sometimes took advantage of the ignorance of many owners. We have seen that some people selling their land sometimes did not understand what they were doing and did not know the right price to ask for. However, if we look at it in more depth, we can see the inner processes that animated the entire project and made it possible. How can we explain this massive sale? More specifically, would the Sardinians have sold their land to other people than this group?

Addis (2016) has already semiotically analyzed the role of John Duncan Miller and his relationships with Sardinia, underlining how his rationality and cultural profile made him the perfect interlocutor for the Sardinians. However, it is the entire group that brought something new to the island and that, interestingly, received something else from it, the land. Certainly, the group brought to Sardinia progress in the form of hospitals, roads, schools, etc., and an incredible amount of money. However, thanks to the media coverage that I have analyzed in this chapter, and also to the profiles and the forms of representation that the members adopted, they also represented something else.

The Aga Khan, in this sense, is a straightforward case study. He had the perfect profile to suggest something new to the Sardinians. I have explained in Chapter 2 how Sardinia was a world in itself within Italy and unknown to the rest of the world. It was a closed society, not communicating with the outside. On the one hand, other people did not try to communicate with Sardinia; on the other hand, the Sardinians did not try to communicate with the external world. However, society was changing; the Sardinians appeared to be tired of this situation and signs of curiosity toward Sardinia had emerged in Italy.

The situation was ripe for someone to break the deadlock. This happened to be the Aga Khan. No one but him represented what the Sardinians needed at that precise moment, fulfilling their wish to escape the isolation they had felt for centuries. An Arab Prince with an international profile, well-connected in various parts of the world, and showing a passion for a part of Sardinia; he was a rich person seemingly able to solve the many problems of the island and connect it to the rest of the world.

It does not matter if this was reality or not, and if the Aga Khan really had these abilities. What counts is that people from Monti di Mola perceived him in this way. The critical way in which the Sardinians perceived Costa Smeralda is pertinent to subsequent periods and may be explained just by the disillusionment they faced after the first impression they had. Costa Smeralda was different from what they had hoped for. However, this is a more recent issue and will be analyzed later in this book. Instead, the feeling of the Sardinians towards the Aga Khan in the early years of Costa Smeralda was certainly positive and is expressed in their wish to encourage the project, sell their land, and dream of a better future for themselves.

All of this was envisioned on a new map, in Baudrillard's sense of the word, that covered the area of northeast Sardinia. We could say that the map of Costa Smeralda covered the old map of Monti di Mola. Exactly like Baudrillard's Disneyland, Costa Smeralda was an invented place giving people the idea that it had always existed as a real place. However, Baudrillard also writes that there is a matter of context. Only in today's U.S., in fact, can Disneyland exist. This suggests another point: only in 1960s Sardinia and Italy, could Costa Smeralda exist. Why so?

I wrote earlier that I do not consider Costa Smeralda a top-down project, at least in its early stages, because somehow all the agents in the field wanted it.

Costa Smeralda satisfied the commercial wish of the group and the will of the Sardinians to be part of the new world that was forming in those years. Thus, if we go back to Baudrillard's map, we should say that the new map of Costa Smeralda, covering the old one of Monti di Mola, was created by both the group of international entrepreneurs and the inhabitants of the area. Certainly, it was conceived by the six men and the woman, but the Sardinians also participated in its making. In this sense, what Baudrillard says about the U.S. context for Disneyland is also true for the Sardinian context in the case of Costa Smeralda.

Another interesting point to study is the relationship between the Sardinians and the international group from the point of view of the entrepreneurs. If it is important to see how the Sardinians perceived the Aga Khan, it is even more important for me to see the reverse, that is, what Monti di Mola meant for the group and what the members of the group took from the island on an island.

We can see that, along with the commercial reasons, the group of entrepreneurs found in the project forms of Foucault's utopia or heterotopia. More precisely, for the people of the group, apart from the Podbielskis, Costa Smeralda was first a kind of utopia, and later, as we will see, a heterotopia. In the beginning, it was a utopia, because while in the rest of their careers, these men set up their businesses within their habitual environment (the bank, the family, their companies), Costa Smeralda allowed them to enter a fantastic space. Later, it became a heterotopia, when business became dominant. It separated them from their everyday business lives in London and projected them into a world governed by different space and time rules. As happens with heterotopias, Costa Smeralda represented for them short periods of suspension that alternated with habitual business life.

And what about the Podbielskis? For them, on the contrary, Costa Smeralda, or better Monti di Mola, continued to be a form of utopia to be realized. They discovered that part of Sardinia and immediately decided to remain there for the rest of their lives. After adventurous lives that led them to many parts of the world and to play various professional roles, they had found their place, their utopian space wherein to live. But utopias do not exist, someone may object, and instead the Podbielskis found a real space. We have already seen that Costa Smeralda was a nonexistent place and they lived in it just as in a nonexistent utopian place. They lived their personal Costa Smeralda, which was different from what the other members of the group or the Sardinians could perceive. They were aware that they were seeing another version of the place, a different Baudrillard's map that they had sketched together.

For this reason they gave Orecchionis binoculars: to help them see what they, René, and Gisele, could see. When things changed, and one of them, René, passed away, the utopia came to an end, and Gisele said that in the new Costa Smeralda after the 1980s there was nothing to see, no one to look at. The perception of that dream, of that utopia, had gone away forever.

Conclusion

This chapter has shed light on the beginning of the construction of Costa Smeralda. It has emerged that the profile of the Aga Khan, or at least the way it was represented by the media, was the perfect one to impress the Sardinians of the 1960s.

However, if Costa Smeralda could be invented in just a few years and become so powerful, this was also due to the way the Sardinians, at least at the beginning, perceived it. The Prince and his project were considered as the solution for every problem, and this also happened more generally to the whole of Italy. As often happens in such cases, this would turn out to not be true, and in the next chapters we will investigate this. But at this first stage, there was a mutual interest and a win-win exchange in the realization of the project. The investors would make their business and the locals would solve their problems, poverty first of all.

As often happens when social constructions are more profound than they appear, the exchange was even deeper: on the one hand, the Sardinians found in the Aga Khan, his international profile, and his happy life, a perfect means to fulfill their wish to overcome the isolation they had lived in since centuries, as demonstrated in Chapter 2; on the other hand, the group of investors could make their business also satisfying their desire to escape from their habitual business lives. They found in Costa Smeralda a form of Foucault's utopia and later heterotopia, a different time and space dimension that projected them out of their usual setting. Just two people in the group, René and Gisele Podbielski, interpreted Costa Smeralda as a utopia even later and for their whole lives, remaining there until their death, not escaping however, in the case of Gisele, the final discovery that the utopia, if it ever could exist, had disappeared.

CHAPTER 4

The Age of Enthusiasm: The Material Construction of Costa Smeralda

Introduction

This chapter is about materiality. In its first part, it centers on the negotiations and deeds that allowed the founders to buy the land and, in the second one, on the actual making of hotels, villas, houses, other buildings, and infrastructure, with an aim to attract tourists from all over the world.

The construction of Costa Smeralda certainly had a very important immaterial side. Media representations, symbolic elements, and cultural values have already been explained in this book and will also be explored in the next chapters. However, materiality also played a relevant role in the birth of this tourist destination. I am here referring to the walls, roads, hotels, and other concrete buildings that constituted the actual aspect of the business.

However, materiality and immateriality intertwined more than I expected. In fact, the materiality that is the center of this chapter allowed the Aga Khan's invention to acquire even more immateriality, as these constructions, as we will see, contain straightforward connections to culture, symbols, social structures, and other impalpable meanings. Costa Smeralda became thus a fascinating system of signs waiting to be interpreted to fully understand its position in our universe of signification, well beyond its being a simple space destined for holidays.

Materiality meant first of all architects, who are the topic of the central part of the chapter. They were some of the best professionals in Europe, and in Sardinia they defined the so-called "Costa Smeralda style," a way of visualizing things aesthetically charming and intrinsically obeying the directives expressed by the Prince and the Consortium. The final result was a fruitful combination of the two components: elegance and philosophical stance, merged to become objects. In the end, the island on an island also resulted from the creativity of the people projecting its concreteness.

What is more, Costa Smeralda was the product of a complex legal and economic plan guided by the nude rules of the market. The founders bought the land and reached relevant agreements with the Sardinian political institutions, benefiting from great independence in the management of the area. Interestingly, even these negotiations and the deeds stipulated in those years acquire semiotic relevance. In the final part of the chapter, we will delve into the semiotic analysis of what the founders bought in the form of land pertaining to Monti di Mola and what later they had in the form of Costa Smeralda.

As we will see, the Italian media did not miss the opportunity to celebrate this physical construction and to represent it as an opportunity for economic growth and tourist expansion, giving back immateriality to what was mainly material. Images of roadworks, construction sites, new buildings, and transformation flooded the Italian magazines and newspapers to pay homage to a business that in the articles was welcomed as a great opportunity: to change Sardinia forever.

The Absurd Negotiation and the Great Absentee

We have mentioned in the previous chapter a documentary (Barone and Di Francisca 2015) showing some shepherds talking about the details of the sales of their land to the Aga Khan and the other founders. However, it may be useful here to focus on other purchases that can add more information to the whole picture. Giuseppe Mentasti, the owner of San Pellegrino, a company known for producing mineral water, bought in 1954 the island of Mortorio (42 hectares) for 3 million lire. The owner was Luigino Demuro, who ran a tobacco shop in Arzachena (*La Nuova Sardegna* 2012a), thus not a rich landowner living on his properties.

Mentasti went on and five years later, on June 14, 1959, in Antonia Orecchioni's *stazzo* in Liscia di Vacca, signed the first deed of sale regarding the future Costa Smeralda: 145 hectares of land, where today is Porto Cervo, passed from the local family of the Orecchionis to Mentasti. The Italian entrepreneur, at the beginning, seemed interested in being part of the group of founders, but he left sometime later and in 1959, sold what he had bought to Prince Karim. As we have already seen, Mentasti owned San Pellegrino, a brand of mineral water, and since the early 1950s, he used to sail around that area, enchanted by the beauty of the place and intrigued by the commercial opportunity that it offered. The land he bought in 1959 was previously entirely devoted to grazing animals and no building was ever built on it (*Inside Sardinia* 2020).

At that time, the Aga Khan was still unaware of Monti di Mola. He arrived later and started buying land too, but hid his name, signing every document in the name of a company based in Lichtenstein (Piga 2014). The first act that he signed as a person and not in the name of his company was in April 1961. With it, the Prince bought the *stazzo* called *fucareddu* ("small fire" in Sardinian), close to San Pantaleo. *Fucareddu* was a hidden jewel: it was oriented to the southeast to be sunnier and protected from the wind. The *stazzo* was composed of two rooms: a dining room and kitchen with a fireplace; and a bedroom, which also had a corner used as a cellar. The roof was supported by juniper wood. However, as the *stazzo* was on a hilly area, its incommensurable surplus was the view, comprising on the left a large part of the coast including Capriccioli, Cala di Volpe, and Razza di Junco; in the center the islands of Mortorio and Soffi; and on the right, Capo Figari (Piga 2014).

After these inital purchases, the gold rush began. The two acts we have described above demonstrate that owning land in that Sardinian area was not a great business. Probably, the group could sense that and bought the land at the lowest price they were able to obtain. The business had to be easy. The scenario pitted expert businessmen coming from London against Sardinian shepherds who were incapable of making business from the land they owned. The entrepreneurs won easily. All of this was far from the romantic representation of the media, which hid that the Prince accurately planned the financial investment along with the other British entrepreneurs. In the end, a group of businessmen made their business, not a novelty at all, but with one point to examine: the price.

Whether the prices were low or fair has been the focus of a long debate that has never stopped. However, the businessmen bought the land at the price that was established by the market, which was low, as owning land was not a business in those times for the Sardinians. The owners used it to graze animals and used to leave it to their daughters and not to their sons, as it had poor value. In the end, the businessmen paid the sum that the owners asked.

This explains why many Sardinians strove to sell their lands to the new investors. They considered that amount of money huge for the value they estimated for that land. For the new investors, that money was very little, as they perfectly knew that Monti di Mola had enormous potential in terms of the tourist industry. So, the locals were, in short, expropriated from their properties and, as reported by Barone and Di Francisca (2015), did not know how to spend what they had earned.

So, basically, the two groups sold and bought two different goods. The locals sold useless land only good for grazing animals; the businessmen bought the land to establish a mega tourist business. The price, however, was that of the useless land. Money had arrived in a region of peasants and shepherds, who immediately decided to sell it to have the money that land could not give. The Aga Khan and the others were gentle, polite, and sincerely enthusiastic about the innovations they foresaw. Piga (2012b) estimates that the investors paid around 2 billion lire in total to acquire Monti di Mola. Some of that land belonged to the major families, such as the Orecchionis and the Azaras; the remaining one was owned by single shepherds and farmers. They immediately agreed to sell it. In the end, Piga (2012b) sustains, whoever would not do it.

However, in this unbalanced and, in some aspects, absurd negotiation, there is a great absentee—the Italian State. Today, the State always intervenes when a company from abroad attempts to buy an Italian firm speculating or profiting from a moment of weakness of a national brand. So it seems strange that in 1962 this did not happen. The Italian State is today the same as in 1962, the Constitution that regulates the basic organization of the State is the same, and its aims and duties are the same. How thus this discrepancy in its behavior in front of a speculation coming from abroad?

Certainly in 1962 this happened for the first time, so the State was unprepared for it. In addition, it is easy to see that many Italian politicians saw the arrival of the Aga Khan as an unhoped-for help for a region that was in strong need of a financial restoration, a lot of work that the State could not do. A private company could do the job that the State was unable to do.

In any case, the State did not intervene to balance that unequal negotiation. Indeed, many politicians encouraged this intervention, pretending not to see the low prices that the foreign investors were paying. Thus, apart from not intervening in the negotiation, they did more, as is explained in the next section.

The Regulations Between the Investors and the Italian State

The Italian State, apart from refusing to intervene in the negotiation with the local owners, accepted the birth of what the journalist Guido Piga defines as "an autonomous principality within the Italian Republic" (2012b). In those times, Piga (2012b) explains, there were no urban plans, no regional laws limiting the number or the measures of the buildings or their proximity to the sea. The State decided not to intervene and not to limit the Aga Khan and his friends. They could have done whatever in Monti di Mola, build skyscrapers wherever they wished, the buildings they wanted in the quantity they desired. They did not do it, luckily, probably for ethical and moral reasons but certainly because this would have not helped their tourist business. They were in fact targeting a high-level class of tourists, who appreciated beauty, elegance, discretion, and pure nature. Moreover, Piga (2012 a and 2012b) adds, they had an international reputation that would have been irremediably damaged in this case, especially in the case of the Prince. Incidentally, the presence of the Aga Khan in Italy was not limited to Costa Smeralda. He was also treating with the major Italian automotive brand, FIAT, in order to set up some plants in Pakistan (Corriere della Sera 1965b) and was well known in the European political scenario, to the point of being mentioned among the very important people to send a telegram to the French President De Gaulle after a surgery (Bocchi 1964).

Thus, for their interests but also the good of Sardinia, the entrepreneurs decided to save the beauty of the place and enact the first sustainable tourist project in Italy, well before the birth of the concept of sustainability.

On the national level, we have already seen the meetings between the Prince and the Italian ministers (*Corriere della Sera* 1962). In 1964, the Italian media (*Corriere della Sera* 1964a) reported a three-day meeting in Sardinia between the Aga Khan and a powerful representative of the Italian State: the minister for Southern Italy Pastore, the vice-Ministry Mannironi, the President of Cassa del Mezzogiorno, the public office devoted to finance investments in southern Italy, the Senator Monni, the MP Isgrò, the Prefects of Nuoro and Sassari, and "numerous authorities on the Regional and Provincial levels" (*Corriere della Sera* 1964a, 17). The minister Pastore also took advantage of the meeting to announce new works to improve Sardinian infrastructure, clearly paid for by the Prince.

No one can thus say that the Italian State ignored what the Aga Khan was doing in Monti di Mola. Rather, they ignored the price of the land sold by the Sardinian owners but benefited from the public works included in the project.

On the local level of the Italian institution, the Regional Councilor Giovanni Filigheddu (who later would become mayor of Arzachena) played a pivotal role. He persuaded his colleagues to reject a project to set up an oil refinery in Gallura and conversely suggested investing in tourism, more precisely in the plan of the Aga Khan and his friends (Piga 2012b). Again, Costa Smeralda seems a business that avoided worse initiatives: the industrialization of Sardinia is widely recognized as a failure in Italian industrial history, with many plants closed or not giving the expected results.

The Aga Khan was thus accepted in the Italian political system. He started meeting ministers and regional politicians who accepted his plan. Unconventionally, the

and Jacques Prevert, who nicknamed him for his anarchism "the an-architect" (Archilli 2023), he produced works that are very often defined as sculptures. He founded in 1930, the *Centre de recherches des structures naturelles* (Research center of natural structures), striving to merge architecture, sculpture, and the natural forms of plants and human bodies (Archilli 2023). In 1958, he projected Castellaras-le-Neuf, a group of houses overlooking Cannes's bay, which seemed a part of the rocky complex naturally present around it. Before constructing it, Couelle tested the future inhabitants of the houses through the so-called Test de Tristan. He drew the perimeters of the rooms on the sand and left the people to move in the potential future house, seeing whether they were at ease in it or not, and adjusting what seemed to be wrong, to design the perfect house for its inhabitants.

The Aga Khan gave him the task of building the Hotel Cala di Volpe, which is analyzed in a later section, and other buildings and villas, which he projected and realized with a bigger aim, to involve human intervention in the preexisting natural shapes. His most innovative work in Costa Smeralda, however, was the villa that he built for himself and his wife, Villa La Grotta, in Monte Mannu. It is a sculpture in the form of a house. He built it without any preexisting map or precise project. The architect only made a small model in wire and terracotta and brought it to the construction site, modifying it continually. The house has a concentric map in which the dining room with a fireplace is the central part. The windows project colored light into the rooms, and walls and ceilings are curved and sinuous, as if they were modeled by the Sardinian wind or recalling the natural caves of the area. The facade is covered with worked coppery and colored tiles that perfectly insert the house into the natural scenario, as may be seen in some photos (Archilli 2023).

Jacques Couelle's son, Savin, was not a member of the architectural committee in Costa Smeralda. He joined the work later but, in the end, settled in Sardinia for many years. He had been an architect focusing on film sets and celebrities' houses. He had designed the scenography of *King of Kings*, *55 Days at Peking*, and *The Fall of the Roman Empire* and projected or refurbished the houses of many personalities, from Serge Reggiani to Jacques Prevert. His father involved him in the project of the hotel Cala di Volpe when the worksite was already in progress. Jacques did not have time to follow the day-to-day development and passed this task to his son. Jacques and Savin agreed on adopting local materials to give birth to new forms of buildings recalling the traditional ones. Savin also built some of the most elegant villas in Costa Smeralda (Domus 2024).

Michele Busiri Vici

Michele Busiri Vici was an architect whose father and brothers were architects too. He was involved in the construction of EUR in Rome, focusing on gardens and parks, as he did in Ostia Antica, close to Rome. In 1939, he projected the Italian pavilion at the Expo in New York, also receiving the honorary citizenship of the city. In 1955, he created the master plan of Sabaudia, a coastal city created by the Fascist regime close to Rome, also projecting many churches and villas in the same areas, very often in white or green and recalling the Mediterranean landscape.

In 1960, Busiri Vici was involved in the project of Costa Smeralda to build Bettina Graziani's villa. Graziani, who has been mentioned in the previous chapter, was a French fashion model (her real name was Simone Bodin), the partner of the Aga Khan's father and one of the trendsetters that attracted the jet-set to northeast Sardinia. Her house was the first villa built in Costa Smeralda, really close to the one which would be built later for the Podbielskis.

In projecting Graziani's villa, Busiri Vici set the rules of the so-called Costa Smeralda style. The house was white and resembled the *stazzo*, the traditional rural house of Gallura. It was made up of natural materials and was well-camouflaged by the Mediterranean vegetation and the rest of the natural context (Scarpellini 2019). This is the base of the Costa Smeralda style. Strictly Mediterranean, the architecture of Costa Smeralda presents low buildings with simple shapes and curved and sinuous forms, as if the wind has created them, with arches, bright colors, and local materials such as juniper and granite (Real Estate Costa Smeralda 2024).

Close to the bigger building, Busiri Vici also built another house, smaller and closer to the beach, which was considered as a *dependance* of the major villa. This smaller building is on the cover of the 1965 album Costa Smeralda by the Italian singer (and actor) Renato Rascel (Scarpellini 2019).

After the first villa, Busiri Vici projected many other buildings in Costa Smeralda: The hotels Romazzino and Luci di la Muntagna, the Stella Maris church, the condominium of Sa Conca, and many other private villas (Scarpellini 2019). Almost all of his buildings have soft shapes and white or other bright colors, and recall the Mediterranean natural materials and colors.

In an interview (Costa Smeralda 2019), Busiri Vici's son, a young architect who collaborated with his father in Monti di Mola, recalled the adventure in Costa Smeralda. He underlines that the Aga Khan, at first, wanted to create a new tourist destination in Corsica but that Duncan Miller persuaded him to invest in Monti di Mola. He also remembers the good relationships between the architects of the committee who found together the so-called Costa Smeralda style but managed to maintain a personal style within those collective rules.

Antonio Simon Mossa

Antonio Simon Mossa was the only architect of the committee with Sardinian roots. He was born in Veneto, but arrived in Sardinia at the age of 27 and never left it until his death at the age of 54. Mossa was a curious intellectual and radical politician. He wrote scripts for many Italian films and poems, worked as a film assistant director, and animated a Sardinian radio station. He organized cultural events and literary awards, and became a supporter of the Sardinian independence from Italy, being part of the Partito Sardo d'Azione (Action Sardinian party).

As an architect, he projected the airport in Fertilia, refurbished Santa Maria Cathedral in Alghero, and planned the Hotel Cala Reale in Stintino, the Hotel L'Abi D'oru in Olbia, and Villa Rafael in Porto Rafael, which will be explored later in this chapter.

He was involved in the project of Costa Smeralda as an expert in stazzi, nuraghi, and other traditional Sardinian buildings. Moreover, he participated in the making of the town planning in Porto Cervo.

Jean-Paul De Marchi

The French architect Jean Paul De Marchi joined the project of Costa Smeralda in 1964, two years after the birth of the Consortium and the architectural committee. He soon became passionate about Sardinia and lived there until he died in 2012, at the age of 76. He helped protect La Celvia, a beach close to the Hotel Cala di Volpe. In that area, he also projected a villa called La Celvia, with a swimming pool that was famous for its waterfall. Savin Couelle remembered him after his death, saying that he was fundamental to defining the Costa Smeralda style (La Nuova Sardegna 2012b).

Raymond Martin

Raymond Martin was a French architect specializing in urban planning. Similarly to Mossa, he did not project specific buildings in Costa Smeralda. Rather, inside the committee, he was responsible for creating (and making the other architects respect) the rules that they all together had decided to stick to.

What the Architects Built

Porto Cervo

Porto Cervo is a city built from scratch. It did not exist before the arrival of the people who wanted that bay to become a coastal town. In this sense, it is a straightforward example of Baudrillard's map covering the original territory and hiding reality. Even physically, the image of Porto Cervo covering the previous territory perfectly renders Baudrillard's concept. The new town, in a few years, changed forever the features of the territory, adding a town where shortly before there was only countryside.

Again, the person who discovered the place and bought the land is a man we have already mentioned various times, an Italian entrepreneur who was not a part of the founders, Giuseppe Mentasti, the owner of the San Pellegrino mineral water brand. In 1954, he had bought the Island of Mortorio. In 1959, as he remembered in an interview (Consorzio Costa Smeralda 2019a), he was going around in a Jeep along with one of his friends and found a place he had never seen from his yacht. It was a wonderful bay that, from the sea, appeared to be a piece of the coast without any interest. As by car it was inaccessible, he decided to visit it arriving from the sea. He fell in love with that place and, once he knew that the owners of that entire land were the Orecchioni family, he started negotiating its price. In the end, Mentasti persuaded the owners and bought the entire area (Consorzio Costa Smeralda 2019a).

In the deed, dated June 14, 1959, the name Porto Cervo is never mentioned. The whole area was roughly indicated by an ancient name. People from Gallura named the bay "Poltu Mannu," which means "the big port." That day, for the first time in Sardinia, such a big portion of territory was sold from a Sardinian owner to a non-Sardinian buyer. Four years later, in 1963, Mentasti sold everything to Prince Karim (Consorzio Costa Smeralda 2019a), who had already built a small port in the bay.

Mentasti is also key to the choice of the name "Costa Smeralda." In 1961, he was in Monti di Mola, just while the Aga Khan was buying great quantities of land from the local owners. The Prince told Mentasti about his project and Mentasti suggested Vietti as the perfect architect for what Prince Karim had in mind. Mentasti and Vietti also talked about the name to give to the entire new area, something different from Cot d'Azur or Costa del Sol. Mentasti suggested

"Esmeralda," the name of his daughter (Piga 2012b), and Vietti decided to cut the "E" and leave "Smeralda," which also suggested the color of the emerald, in Italian "smeraldo." Prince Karim loved that name and this is how the name Costa Smeralda was born.

After about one year of work, Porto Cervo was officially inaugurated on August 15, 1964 (Consorzio Costa Smeralda 2021). As the Prince and Vietti wanted, the village was built following the forms of the Mediterranean style. The square is the very center of Porto Cervo, as in any Mediterranean coastal village. Vietti had done something similar in Portofino, in Liguria (Ducci 2021). The village is on a superior level to the port, which resembles the form of a deer (in Italian "Cervo").

Hotel Cala di Volpe

The hotel Cala di Volpe was another key architectural moment in the construction of Costa Smeralda. It was projected by Jacques Couelle and was the first hotel built in Costa Smeralda. As theoretically stated before the construction, Couelle aimed to merge human intervention and nature. The hotel, inaugurated in 1963, is like a little town by the sea. The walls have rustic resemblances, the roofs look like those of the huts, and in many cases the wood is not fully refined. All of these elements and many others recall the rural architecture present, rather than specifically in Sardinia, in the whole of Italy and the Mediterranean more broadly. The entrance has been positioned through a wooden bridge, which leads to the restaurant. The many objects fixed on the walls are made up of juniper and recall Sardinian craftsmanship (Balducci 2024). Each room was designed to be different from the others and some suites had private swimming pools (*La Stampa* 2022).

The hotel was considered one of the most beautiful in the world and welcomed celebrities from all over the world. Some photos show Peter Sellers wearing a swimming suit, Marisa Berenson leaning on the white curved walls, Ringo Starr in flared jeans, and Grace Kelly with her daughters (Colosimo 2023). Today, the hotel is different from how Couelle projected it, but the processes of refurbishment have striven to maintain the original style. It is still one of the most refined and famous hotels in Costa Smeralda and is available on the internet to be booked (Booking 2024).

Related to this, the entire area became much easier to reach. Roads, harbors, a heliport, churches, and security agencies started flourishing along the coast.

A new airport was built in Olbia on the old one, called Venafiorita, to allow the flights of the new airline, Alisarda, opened by the Prince (*La Stampa* 2022).

Olbia International Airport and Alisarda

What made the utopia of Costa Smeralda reachable was the new airport that the Aga Khan wanted in Olbia, the bigger town just out of the new destination. Before Costa Smeralda, Olbia had a really small airport, called Olbia-Venafiorita. It was inaugurated on May 21, 1927 and also had a seaplane base. However, its small size and dirt airstrip did not allow international flights to land on it. In 1954, Alitalia, the Italian national airline, had to close the route Rome-Olbia as no passengers were traveling to Sardinia.

However, this was the airport that the Aga Khan and the other founders used to arrive at and leave from. The Prince financed the construction of a longer runway but as the tourist destination started to be targeted by people from all over the world, it was clear that the airport had to be renovated radically. Some memories from those days can help us understand better what the airport Villafiorita was: airplanes landed in the dust caused by the sheep running away because of the airplane getting closer, as Prince Karim said. Moreover, there was only a low drywall between the airstrip and the street, and many times the airplanes touched it while landing; a small hut was devoted to the check-in, while sometimes it was made under a tree, to protect the passengers from the sun—a momentary and improvised office with a wooden table and four chairs. A motorist said that there was no water around and that they used to go to a stream nearby to fetch water (*Sardegna Abbandonata* 2015).

On April 1, 1964, Prince Karim inaugurated Alisarda, an airline which was a relevant part of the project "Costa Smeralda" and one of the satellite companies revolving around the tourist destination, along with Cerasarda (making Sardinian pottery) and others. Alisarda started operating with two twin-piston-engined Beechcraft C-45, each of them allowing eight passengers (*Coast Magazine* 2021). In 1964, Alisarda had 186 passengers. In 1966, the number rose to 5,640. At the beginning, the only air route was Rome Fiumicino—Olbia and return. In 1968, the airport was also connected to Milano Linate and Nice. New aircrafts were bought, such as McDonnell Douglas DC9/14 and others. It is still possible to see a photograph portraying one of The Beatles, Ringo Starr, who just arrived and walked on the clay strip of the airport carrying his luggage.

The new airport was an evident need for Costa Smeralda. The old one certainly nurtured that romantic feeling of adventure that had accompanied the first pioneers, but was insufficient for the new tourists. Thus, the Aga Khan decided to dismiss Villafiorita and to build a new airport in another area surrounding Olbia.

The new airport, inaugurated in 1974, led to new businesses. In 1978, the Italian Government gave Alisarda a connection between Cagliari (in the south of Sardinia) and Milan. The airline expanded in a few years and in 1985, the number of passengers became 791,439, connecting Sardinia to Catania, Venice, Paris, Dusseldorf, Frankfurt, Zurich, and other European cities.

Porto Rafael, an Alternative to Costa Smeralda

In a documentary that I have already mentioned (Barone and Di Francisca 2015), Gisele Podbielski talks about a strange episode involving her and her husband while they still lived their wild life without electric power and hot water. They used to go to the only hotel in the area to experience some material comforts. During one of these excursions out of the future Costa Smeralda, they happened to see a small house and hear some voices coming from it. They also saw some smoke coming out of the house and approached it. Immediately, a lady with a strong British accent came out, asking if they would like some Bloody Mary. They entered and met a Spanish noble, a Count, who made paella for them. The Count was Rafael Neville, Count of Berlanga, and he was there not by chance. He was establishing a really small community with about ten or twelve houses, which he called Porto Rafael.

In the interview, Gisele Podbielski describes Porto Rafael as much more personal than Costa Smeralda and mainly targeting British people. Built close to Palau, thirty minutes by car from Liscia di Vacca, Porto Rafael was another material utopia constructed in northwest Sardinia in those years. Rafael Neville was the son of Edgar Neville, an intellectual and writer who produced some of Charlie Chaplin's films and was a good friend of Pablo Picasso (Andovino 2021) and of Angeles y Rubio Arguelles y Alessandri, writer and patron of the arts. Born in Malaga, Rafael had already experienced the tourist industry. He had managed a property in Torremolinos, making this small town a tourist destination for Spanish celebrities. He arrived in Palau at the beginning of the 1960s, when Costa Smeralda was in progress; however, Rafael wanted to do something different, a really small community in which the elite easily could know each other, live informally, and have relaxation away from the crowd.

The Sardinian entrepreneur Domenico Manna and the Italian lawyer Paolo Riccardi understood the relevance of Rafael's project and supported it. Riccardi would become, some years later, a precious collaborator of the Aga Khan and the secretary of the Consortium Costa Smeralda (Camillo 2000). Neville created with them, a small town with a square in the center, as in the Mediterranean tradition, and a few white houses and villas around. Neville and Manna bought the land and constructed the new center. Rafael wanted that town to be his realm and his residence was called Il Municipio (the city hall). Every year, on his birthday (in August), he opened his house to the other inhabitants and guests, like a head of State (Andovino 2021).

The idea of tourism implied by Porto Rafael was even more elitist than in Costa Smeralda. Many celebrities spent their holidays in Rafael's realm, but in a place that was more detached from the rest of the world than Costa Smeralda.

Rafael Neville, Count of Berlanga, died in December 1996, alone, ill, and poor, after a car accident in Marbella and after dilapidating his huge patrimony. In April 1996, he had to sell his Sardinian villa to pay his health expenses (Andovino 2021).

Roland Barthes in Costa Smeralda

In this section, I examine what has been said so far, mainly the negotiations to buy the land and Costa Smeralda's architecture, through the lenses of Roland Barthes's (2013) mythologies and semiotics.

As has been explained in Chapter 1, mythologies for Barthes (2013) are elements represented as natural and already existing, but actually socially constructed. Every form of representation in the consumer society implies forms of mythology. Our society, in brief, produces mythologies as means of signification and representation. To convert them into mythologies, the represented elements are deprived of their content to become something else.

Thus, here I try to analyze what happened between 1959 and 1964, in greater depth, focusing on what Costa Smeralda was before the arrival of the Prince and what it became after it. The fact that Costa Smeralda is a form of mythology is quite evident. This results from the many media representations we have seen so far and will see in the next chapters, which fully match Barthes's definition. In fact, we can see a territory that is presented as natural but that has certainly been socially (and materially) constructed. It was deprived of its actual elements (the land to graze animals, the peasant's civilization) to become something else.

To better understand all of this, we must answer three questions: What kind of mythology is it? What relationships between nature and culture does it imply? And finally, how did the territory change from Monti di Mola to Costa Smeralda? Incidentally, we will also see in the next chapter that Costa Smeralda's mythology has changed over the years. In this section, we look at the form of mythology pertaining to the years before (1959–1960) and immediately after the destination's construction (until 1964), which is the chronological range of this chapter.

Certainly, the relationship between nature and culture is of paramount relevance in the Costa Smeralda architecture, going by the founders' and architects' statements. The Aga Khan and all the architects involved in the project continually said that they wanted to hide human intervention in the beauty of nature, which had to remain pure and untouched. Aesthetically speaking, it was certainly a good idea, as even today many buildings cannot be seen and are totally immersed in the beauty of nature, not disturbing the perception of the tourists. In comparison to what happened in the Spanish Costa del Sol or many other Italian tourist areas, Costa Smeralda saved the natural scenario and till date is preferable to other destinations just for this.

What strikes the analyst is the cutting-edge philosophical view behind the construction of this destination. What Costa Smeralda's construction says in terms of the nature/culture relationship is that nature may only be saved through culture, and that culture may turn nature into something that helps and does not oppress humans. In fact, Costa Smeralda was built respecting the pre-existing nature, which was saved and became the main scenario of the new tourist destination. We can call it pure nature, that is, a form of nature without an evident human intervention. The land was totally wild, without buildings or other forms of human intervention, and only used to graze animals; it was something that remained untouched by humans. However, this kind of nature did not secure for its inhabitants a comfortable life.

Pure nature was the dominant paradigm in Sardinia for centuries and we have seen that it did not overcome poverty or exclusion. Since the 1960s, however, two other paradigms came up. The first, and opposite to pure nature, was the paradigm entirely based on culture, summarized by the fast process of industrialization that happened in other areas of Sardinia and aiming to cut unemployment and poverty. In this case, culture was meant to expropriate nature. Thus, again, nature and culture were seen as separate and in conflict, as in pure nature. We can call this paradigm the entirely culture-based one.

Costa Smeralda was the third way; we can call it the balanced paradigm. In it, exactly as theorized by Sebeok and explained in the theoretical framework of this book, culture is seen as a part of nature. The two elements coexist and support each other. The shift from pure nature to the balanced paradigm implies a more equilibrate relationship between the two elements, as it emerges from a more accurate analysis of two elements: firstly, the negotiations for the land and the consequent deeds; secondly, the product Costa Smeralda that the Prince sold to the entire world as a tourist destination. If semiotically, we look at the denotative level, we can see the commercial interests in both elements: some land is bought, reworked, and finally sold in the form of a new status, a tourist destination, with an impressive money surplus. But what did the Aga Khan actually buy and what did he actually sell, more in depth?

The connotative level here unveils that the Aga Khan bought the traditional perceptions of nature and culture considered as separate and in contrast. He, in fact, bought hectares of land without any building or forms of human presence. Put simply, he bought pure nature. What he sold, instead, in the form of a tourist destination, was a new and more balanced conception of nature and culture, with the two entities merging and completing each other. Prince Karim had also another option, the remaining paradigm, the entirely culture-based one. This would have meant creating a tourist destination that looked like the Costa del Sol in Spain or other locations in Italy. Costa Smeralda was instead born under the balanced paradigm.

This may be found in the general architectural rules regarding the hotels, villas, and houses we have analyzed above. In all of them, natural elements have been spontaneously or artificially reintroduced in human (and thus cultural) artifacts. Three examples may clarify what I mean: firstly, the frequent use of local materials, which come from nature but become cultural objects; secondly, the representations of local natural elements, for example the sea in the Hotel Coda di Volpe, which bridges the gap between the real sea and the hotel, merging nature and culture again; thirdly, the curved shapes of the walls, in the same hotels and in other buildings, recalling the wind hitting Sardinia very frequently, which represent a natural element in an object that is exclusively human (a wall) to give natural shape to culture. In all of these cases, it is evident that nature and culture are never in contrast; rather, culture recreates nature and the two elements support each other. On the one hand, culture saves the existence of nature in the new human artifacts, while on the other hand, nature contributes to cultural materiality.

However, what is historically relevant here is that while Sebeok theorized his revolutionary view of this philosophical field in the second part of the 1960s and the 1970s, Costa Smeralda's founders and architects did it between the end of the 1950s and the first part of the 1960s.

In conclusion, in the language of business, thanks to the revolutionary ideas of the Prince and his architects, the project of Costa Smeralda rendered the mythology of the wilderness palatable for high-class tourists who would have had trouble adjusting to the absolute nature existing before the emergence of Costa Smeralda or to a destination designed under the totally culture-based paradigm. They conversely enjoyed the place's mythologized version. In the language of nature/culture relationship, instead, we may say that culture helped to mediate the natural essence of that land and to transform it into a commodity targeting a very high class of tourists.

All of this served the purpose of creating mythologies relying on two paradigms out of three: the first, pure nature; the second, the balanced model; and the third, which was luckily discarded, the entirely culture-based one.

Finally, looking at Peirce and his concepts of icon, index, and symbol, it is evident that the Prince bought an icon, lived an index, and sold a symbol. In the case of the purely natural land that he bought, signified and signifying almost coincide. The images of that territory corresponded to the territory almost completely. Later, when the Prince and his friends lived in Monti di Mola without electric power and hot water, that land acquired an indexical component; the images of that land for them meant wildlife, runaway from civilization, and adventure. The wild landscape was there, but it was added to with a more general signification. Finally, when Monti di Mola fully became Costa Smeralda, it became the symbol of a status, the perfect idea of a holiday for a very rich class of tourist. In this case, signified and signifying were linked through a convention. The juniper or the curved walls do not mean exclusivity and wealth in themselves. They acquire this signification through the process of construction and promotion of the final product branded as "Costa Smeralda."

The material building of Costa Smeralda was thus also an adventure of meaningful construction. A territory was bought and ingeniously reworked in order to make it acquire new signification. The shift from Monti di Mola to Costa Smeralda is a straightforward case in which even a deed to buy land or the shape of a wall reveals a semiotic itinerary that helps us understand the fascinating system of the signs revolving around us.

Conclusion

In this chapter, I have explored the actual construction of hotels, villas, houses, the airport, and other buildings that, all together, formed what was called Costa Smeralda. This construction had connections to Italian politics, social issues, aesthetics, creativity, economic laws, and symbolic meaning; all of them have been investigated, as they constitute the fascinating material and immaterial interconnections that make Costa Smeralda so relevant and meaningful.

As regards Italian politics, the chapter has reported its absence when it came to protecting the Sardinian owners from the speculation and its obsessive presence in boosting the Prince and his adventurous business. This allowed the State to solve some problems regarding Sardinia without spending money.

As I said in the introduction to this book, it is really difficult for me to take any one of the two opposite sides that usually people assume when talking about Costa Smeralda. For some of them, it was an endless romantic adventure; for others, it was a pitiless financial speculation. For me, it was both, as contrasting things are not necessarily separate. The financial speculation, however, was caused more by the absence of the State than by a group of businessmen buying hectares of land at the price asked by the sellers (usually businessmen do worse things, actually).

I have moreover pointed out the creative efforts of the architects, chosen and supported by Prince Karim: not only did they conceive a tourist destination from scratch, but they also set aesthetic and environmental rules that guaranteed a development based on sustainability before the term "sustainability" even existed in the public debate.

Finally, this chapter has demonstrated that, as semiotics says, everything means something. Those buildings, hotels, walls, and infrastructure all together formed a powerful system of signs well beyond their being part of a tourist destination. The relationship between nature and culture, Peirce's icon, index, and symbol, and Barthes's mythologies and speculations about the level of connotation were the semiotic keys that I adopted to understand more in depth what Costa Smeralda's construction signified and why the things it tells us are so important even today.

However, history never stops. New periods add new representations, maps, and meanings, and so it happened with Costa Smeralda. This will be the focus of the next chapter.

CHAPTER 5

The Age of Inaccessibility and Its Crisis

Introduction

Now we can see the map, geographically but also in Baudrillard's sense. The old configuration of Monti di Mola was canceled and a new place appeared in that territory, Costa Smeralda—a new city, new hotels, and even a new spirit surrounding those beaches, abandoned for years and now rethought for a new class of people.

In the 1960s, the island on an island was built; adventurous entrepreneurs had shaped it ideally, while architects did the same materially, giving shape to what those entrepreneurs had envisioned. Costa Smeralda started working, entering its *age of inaccessibility*. The new area was represented as the exclusive place where people from all over the world belonging to the jet-set and the show business spent their free time.

The 1970s, however, changed this picture. Abruptly, Sardinia was discovered by the Italians, thanks to the football club Cagliari winning Serie A championship in 1970; bandits took advantage of all those rich people coming to Sardinia, enacting the criminal business of kidnapping. After years of success, both as a tourist destination and a media message, Costa Smeralda had to cope with its first period of crisis. Many international tourists, worried by the many kidnappings, sold their villas or did not renew their rental contracts.

Together with this, the Aga Khan surprisingly unveiled Phase 2, the development of Costa Smeralda as a mass tourist destination. The project is exaggerated; it aimed to enlarge the built area in Costa Smeralda from less than 2 to more than 5 million cubic meters. I try to demonstrate that in this plan there was certainly something threatening the natural beauty of the area, but there was also something wrong from a communicative point of view. Phase 2 was the Aga Khan's decisive misstep in the history of Costa Smeralda. After that, the place would not be the same and would lose its identity. Crime, Phase 2, and other accidents thus took Costa Smeralda into a long night of crisis.

Inaccessible Holidays Until 1967

In a memoir (Camillo 2023), an executive of the estate agency of Consorzio Costa Smeralda explains that tourists in Costa Smeralda, in the years analyzed in this chapter, preferred not to be visible to the media. As a result, they used to go very little to public places such as restaurants and bars, so as not to be seen by photographers and journalists. Rather, they preferred to go around barefoot and wearing shorts and enjoy the very new architecture of the place.

It is not by chance, thus, that I have had much more difficulty in finding articles and media items relating to those years. While until 1964 the media were full of pieces of information about the construction of the site, and from the 1980s to 2000 no event in that area remained uncovered, from 1965 to 1979 there is a gap that is impossible not to note. There were fewer pieces of news about Costa Smeralda, and those that were published did not regard its visitors and their dolce vita.

In 1965, for example, the new tourist destination was considered a big success but also a field of political battle. Madeo (1965a) sustains that in 1964, the number of yachts anchored in the Porto Cervo harbor was four hundred and that in 1965, it was supposed to be seven hundred, also supering Cannes and thus giving Costa Smeralda the European leadership. Holidaymakers were of the highest profile: Beatrix of the Netherlands and Princess Margaret; Sean Connery, Rockefeller, and Ford; the most popular Italian actors, from Virna Lisi to Ugo Tognazzi. The Consortium already invested 40 billion lire, and another 50 would be spent on the new development plan.

However, the Italian Communist Party (PCI) did not see all of this as a positive contribution to Italian development. They found that the Sardinians were not benefiting from the business, while the prices in the area were going up. Moreover, Costa Smeralda was becoming a center of power, able to influence politics, and this could have led to political decisions damaging Sardinia, its natural beauty, and its people and only supporting business. This could have also transformed Costa Smeralda into a small State within another State, it is said.

Finally, the article (Madeo 1965a) advances the suspicion that prices of restaurants or businesses in general are different according to the buyer. If the buyer is a celebrity able to promote the tourist destination or a company listed on the stock exchange, the price to buy that restaurant will be lower. The wind was changing, and the tone of voice describing the island on an island became either brief and mainly written, or more critical. The first category is analyzed here, while the critical representations are investigated in the next section.

As regards the principally written mode, the subsequent year, in 1966, an anonymous comment (usually these articles that have no author name are written by the director) appeared on one of the first pages of *Corriere della Sera* (1966a), the most important Italian newspaper. It was an endorsement of both Costa Smeralda and the Prince. The fact that Princess Margaret used to spend her holidays in the ex-Monti di Mola meant that the Aga Khan is capable of attracting the highest class of tourists, and this would benefit Sardinia and the entire Italy, the article says. Only in its last part, the article has an ironic hint, by asking what holidays these people take, holidays from what, as they actually never work. However, Costa Smeralda is treated positively, and there is also praise for the Aga Khan and his ability as a businessman, even when he bought the land from the peasants.

In 1965, a photo without an article (*Corriere della Sera* 1965a) shows Princess Margaret in Costa Smeralda close to another woman wearing Sardinian traditional clothes. Princess Margaret has a kerchief on her head, as does the other woman; moreover, both women are wearing bright clothes, so they seem to dress similarly. A brief caption says that Princess Margaret is on holiday in Costa Smeralda along with her husband Lord Snowden. Similarly, one year later, another photo without an article (*Corriere d'Informazione* 1967) depicts Princess Margaret and her husband taking their holiday in Costa Smeralda. A blurb (*Corriere della Sera* 1966b) says that even Brigitte Bardot and Gunther Sachs were in Costa Smeralda that summer, after Grace Kelly and Ranieri of Monaco. They thus preferred Sardinia to Saint Tropez, the article advances.

These were small pieces of news which were based more on the written mode than on the visual one, contrary to the past. Costa Smeralda was becoming something to mention rather than to show. Photographers were not allowed in the restaurants or hotels and the written mode was the unique way of informing people, who in any case were not the target of the tourist destination, trying as it was to attract a rich class of tourist. As a result, Costa Smeralda was not promoted in the newspapers, just briefly represented to remind the Italians of its successful existence.

This invisibility of parties, dinners, and an exclusive class of tourists on the beaches, sunbathing in places inaccessible to photographers, became a powerful medium of myth-construction in Roland Barthes's sense. Paradoxically, the inaccessibility for its expensiveness that Costa Smeralda showed off, increased

its popularity among the middle class. The media continued to negotiate a place
that was the setting of a fairy tale, forbidden to "normal" people, and coveted
by those who were not allowed to go there.

The Critical Account About Costa Smeralda Since 1967

In the following years, however, these short and written pieces of news became
even rarer, but Costa Smeralda did not disappear from magazines and newspapers.
What was represented was a critical side of Costa Smeralda. For the rest, the people
going there from all over the world to enjoy themselves, the place remained hidden.

What was shown by the media was the surrounding environment of inaccessibility. If Costa Smeralda's rules did not allow photographers in, the solution was
to insist on the rest, on what was around those inaccessible places. So the press
contributed to shaping a sort of dark side of the island on an island.

Banditry

First of all, let us examine banditry. In August 1967, a group of bandits tried to
set up a roadblock to rob some tourists passing by the street between Olbia and
Arzachena, near the exit to Porto Cervo. However, they were intercepted by the
police. They engaged in a firefight and in the end they ran away. Luckily, the
article says, the tourists who were there at that moment were not involved or
injured (*Corriere della Sera* 1967a). Another article (Ghislanzoni 1967) adds
more details. The already reported one was not the only firefight in Sardinia that
day. Close to Orgosolo, the police heard the sound of a shooting and of a hand
grenade going off. It seemed to them the settling of scores among peasants.
They thus went to the place but did not find any signs of what had happened.

The principal crime committed by bandits was kidnapping. Another article
(*Corriere della Sera* 1967b) informs the reader that some bandits tried to kidnap
a German industrialist trying to get into the villa he inhabited, built a few years
before the episode. The man managed to barricade the entrance, so the criminals,
after a couple of attempts to force the door of the villa, went away.

Drugs

Drugs are another recurring theme of this period in the news regarding
Costa Smeralda. On the night between August 19 and 20, 1969, police

officers entered the most popular discotheque in Costa Smeralda, Pedro's, and discovered people selling and buying individual quantities of hashish, marijuana, and cocaine—in total one kilo of various substances (F.P. 1969a). Nine people were arrested in total, the list including American managers, English holidaymakers, African dealers, and Italian businessmen. The article described how the drug was introduced in the discotheque: it was hidden in a silk slipper made in Morocco and then offered to the people present at Pedro's that night.

Relating to the previous episode, again in 1969, an article (*Corriere della Sera* 1969) reported that three people were arrested: two brothers and an "avvenente" (charming) English girl, who was the girlfriend of one of the two brothers. The two brothers worked at Pedro's, the same discotheque as in the previous piece of news. The villa where the three were arrested was Baby Pignatari's home at Porto Rafael, out of Costa Smeralda (while the subtitle of the article refers to "Costa Smeralda"). Pignatari, a famous playboy, had given his villa to a friend, a film director. It is not explained how the three people arrested ended up there. However, the police found "traces" of parties based on hashish and a machine to make cigarettes.

The news about Pedro's and its drug issue goes on. F.P. (1969b) explains how the drug was hidden in the oriental slipper and that it was introduced to the discotheque for the delight of the tourists. It is underlined that the discotheque was close to Porto Cervo and in front of the villa of the model Bettina. From some time earlier, voices about drugs in Costa Smeralda had come up in Sardinia, so some police officers disguised themselves as "hippies or capelloni" (hippy or boys with long hair). Among them, there was also a policewoman. The technique adopted to sell the drug was simple. The employees of the discotheque, says the article, kept the small envelopes inside their oriental slippers, and when a client requested the drug, they bent over pretending to adjust their shoe but took the envelope and passed it to the client. Another article (*Corriere d'Informazione* 1969) reveals that many of the people arrested were wearing a swimsuit and that they were taken to the police office that way.

The last part of the article is relevant too. It reports a statement by the Consortium Costa Smeralda, which is worth reproducing entirely:

> Mentre ci congratuliamo con le forze dell'ordine per aver così brillantemente compiuto la difficile operazione di polizia che ha liberato la Costa Smeralda da un gruppo di persone che vi svolgevano attività illecita, desideriamo chiarire

quanto segue: il night club Pedro's, come del resto altri locali pubblici esistenti in
questa zona, opera indipendentemente dall'organizzazione della Costa Smeralda
ed opera a iniziativa privata fuori dal nostro controllo.

   Da tempo avevamo segnalato alle autorità competenti le voci che circolavano
su questi locali e sull'attività che vi si svolgeva. Desideriamo che questi dubbi
vengano chiariti e che la Costa Smeralda venga liberata da persone che risultas-
sero implicate in loschi traffici.

(F.P. 1969b)

The article ends with the statement of the Consortium, with no comment added
by the journalist.

I reported the entire statement in Italian because I will analyze it even gram-
matically, as it gives important accounts of the whole situation. Here I translate
it into English.

   While we compliment the police on their brilliant, difficult action that has freed
   Costa Smeralda from a group of people illegally operating, we want to clarify
   what follows: the nightclub Pedro's, like other private places existing in this
   area, works independently from the organization of Costa Smeralda and works
   as a private initiative out of our control.

      For a long time, we had pointed out to the competent authorities the voices
   revolving around these places and the activity existing in them. We want these
   doubts to be cleared and Costa Smeralda to be freed from people who are involved in trouble traffic.

Some weeks later, Pedro's affair was updated (F.P. 1969c), as it seems that a
noblewoman from Milan was involved in the investigation. The article also
explains that the only drug that was found was hashish.

Accidents

Before analyzing all of this, we examine the other news coming out from the
archive of the *Corriere della Sera* (and its evening version *Corriere d'Informazione*). In 1971, Costa Smeralda was again on the front page of the newspapers. An
entrepreneur from Pavia, his fashion model fiance, and another friend, disappeared
while they were on their rubber dinghy. They were unprepared for the rough sea
that since many days had ruined the holidays of many people in Costa Smeralda.

They did not have lifesavers or other objects able to help them. The three people, the article continues, had been in Costa Smeralda for a few days and many other holidaymakers had recognized the model, who was famous at that time. A big photo (bigger than the article) shows the model smiling in a swimming suit.

Another accident leads Costa Smeralda to the news. F.P. (1968) reports that six people died in a flight accident that occurred close to the Olbia airport. A Belgian aircraft crashed and all the people onboard, a family with two daughters aged 4 and 8, passed away. The private airplane had taken off a few minutes before the accident to go to Alghero. The Belgian family was spending some days in Costa Smeralda on holiday and wanted to visit Alghero.

A much less relevant accident is reported in Madeo (1965b). The actress Virna Lisi was in a nightclub and was dining with her husband. Both of them appeared to be bored, certainly silent. The place was The Night of Costa Smeralda, it did not have a name. It was one of the most refined places in the world, the article says. You could find there Princess Margaret or other high-level friends of Prince Karim. But unfortunately, the article continues, Margaret was not there, like Karim and his rich friends. Lisi was there with her husband, and on the other side of the room, a noisy group of important Roman families were dining.

When they started dancing, a young man of the family said to his girlfriend: the next I invite to dance is that woman, Virna Lisi. Lisi's husband went up and started fighting with the man. There also should have been paparazzi, the article complains, but there were not there, as holidaymakers in Costa Smeralda did not let them in.

1971: The Turning Point

The turning point in the way Costa Smeralda was perceived by the media, and thus by the Italians, occurred in 1971. It was a criminal case that is not among the most represented by magazines, newspapers, or television, but that perfectly links many elements we have revolved around so far in this book. At the beginning of April, Giovanni Maria Ghilardi was kidnapped along with his son Agostino, who was 9, close to Arzachena. Giovanni Maria is the son of Salvatore Ghilardi, who was a Sardinian farmer who had become a billionaire after selling his land to the Aga Khan and the Consortium. By selling 200 hectares of terrain from Abbiadori to Liscia Ruja for almost 1.5 billion lire, Ghilardi, a few years earlier, had become one of the richest people in Sardinia.

Salvatore Ghilardi also became famous for an interview on Italian television where he said: "Who wants to buy my land has to pay millions, not billions," demonstrating that he did not know that billions are more than millions. This mistake became the perfect example to explain that the Aga Khan was buying land from people who did not have any idea of what they were doing. He was 80 at the time of the kidnapping and immediately tried to contact the kidnappers to pay a ransom for their liberation. The police also slowed down its research to encourage a happy ending of the story (*Corriere d'Informazione* 1971b).

The event had two elements that impressed the Sardinian people. The first one was that the hostages were Sardinians. Bandits, until that time, seemed to target only foreign or northern Italian entrepreneurs and industrialists. The fact that they kidnapped a Sardinian farmer changed the perspective on the criminals. The second element was that they also kidnapped a child, Agostino, showing that they would not stop at anything to get money. This last element also produced anger in many Sardinian bandits who were not involved in this kidnapping, as according to them it broke a code of honor among the local criminals.

The two went on to be freed after 36 days and after the payment of a ransom of 100 million lire from Salvatore Ghilardi to the kidnappers (Lullia 2012). The sum was only the first part of the entire payment of 250 million, which however never happened, as after the payment the police identified and arrested the kidnappers. The criminals were sentenced, all except four of them. After being called "Mister Miliardo" (Mister Billion) in the news, Agostino had a "normal" life, out of rumors and the news, marrying a woman from Sardinia, and managing a stationery shop in Baja Sardinia, where he died in 2012 when he was 52 from a heart attack (Lullia 2012). It is easy to see the kidnapping of Giovanni Maria and Agostino as a form of short circuit.

A Change in Perspective

The articles that have been analyzed above clarify a neat change in the perspective from which the media represented Costa Smeralda from 1967. Even the Aga Khan had to face a new approach of the media to his personality and aims. F.P. (1971) reports that the Aga Khan would not step down from the Consortium of Costa Smeralda, as looked likely to happen. There was an article titled "Karim rimane in Sardegna" (Karim remains in Sardinia). The Aga Khan, as said in the article, seemed to step down because the Regional Government of Sardinia blocked Phase 2 of Costa Smeralda, the plan of developments presented by the Consortium that would menace the natural beauty of the area, according to the Italian politicians.

The atmosphere changed for the Aga Khan, not only in the field of Italian politics. Even the media were modifying their points of view. The man was not portrayed anymore as the generous Prince discovering a beautiful place and saving it from uncontrolled tourist development but as an entrepreneur wanting to enlarge his business at any cost. Costa Smeralda was defined as "l'approdo dei miliardari" (billionaire's harbor), while the Aga Khan was said to have acquired "graniti d'oro" (golden granite), as what he bought from the shepherds was turned into a billionaire business. Now his plan, it was said in the article, may destroy Sardinia's natural beauty. Now the fight was around the "programma di fabbricazione" (fabrication program). It consisted of about three hundred thousand new rooms for three hundred fifty thousand visitors.

The Italian institutions, at both the regional and the national level, defined it as paradoxical and did not pass the plan. At that point, the Consortium answered that the ban would have caused the closure of some companies of the Consortium, Alisarda (the flight company), Cerasarda (pottery), Biancasarda (the company managing the washing of bedsheets and towels of the hotels), and of some hotels. This meant that many people, the majority of them Sardinians, would lose their jobs. Voices concerning the exit from the Consortium of the Aga Khan started flourishing. The article is quite short and on just one column, but the title is wide, four columns on the page and written in a very big font.

Costa Smeralda from Utopia to Heterotopia

We have seen that until 1967 the media representation of Costa Smeralda centered on a few princesses and other representatives of an ultra-high class of tourists, mostly celebrities, seen from a distance. Very often, they were photographed at the airport on their arrival, while what they actually did in Costa Smeralda was rarely reported. This confirms that these people were inaccessible at those times. Semiotically speaking, following Peirce (1960), we may say that Costa Smeralda is an index in these cases. The presence of Princess Margaret or Brigitte Bardot signals the existence of Costa Smeralda as a destination for high-class people, but the place, however, is seldom directly shown, like the fire in the case of the representation of smoke, as said in Chapter 1.

Thus, if Princess Margaret and the other celebrities are the smoke for the Costa Smeralda fire, what type of society is argued to be the new tourist destination? Until 1967, it was a nonexistent place, as we rarely see it, only populated by princesses and other celebrities, where everything was perfect. Could "normal" people go there? Certainly not, as it did not exist for them.

As regards the modes, it is very interesting that many of the items regarding those celebrities are photos without articles, and thus relying on the visual mode and not on the written one. This means that there is nothing to say about that piece of news. It is something to show, a visual index that cannot be deepened because there are no concrete things to add to the image.

To go directly to the point, we may say that Costa Smeralda, until 1967, was represented by the media for the public as a utopia. It does not exist, it is a wonderful place populated by princesses and actors, its visual display is pleasant, and words cannot add anything to its visual value. Among those analyzed, the only journalistic genre using words adopted to talk about Costa Smeralda is the blurb, the shortest written article at all (probably, there were no images of Brigitte Bardot and Gunther Sachs, and thus publishing the usual photo without an article was not possible).

Finally, the utopian nature of Costa Smeralda for the public is underlined by the article without signature published in the *Corriere della Sera* (1966a). It highlights the immaterial character of the people making holidays in Costa Smeralda by reminding the reader that they are detached from the material need for work.

Such great immateriality contrasts with the sometimes tragic materiality of the news concerning Costa Smeralda after 1967. Criminals shooting in the streets, drug dealers and consumers, deadly accidents with both aircrafts and boats, kidnapping, banditry, and other ultra-concrete problems seem to hit Costa Smeralda all of a sudden. We know that they had already existed, some of them like banditry for centuries, and drugs probably even when newspapers did not talk about it. However, these pieces of news had been banned from the news. From 1967, they become the dominant ingredients of the representation of Costa Smeralda.

Sardinian Popularity After 1970

In the second chapter, we have seen that Sardinian culture contributed to pigeonholing the island as an ancestral place having little to do with the rest of Italy and made it an inaccessible place for the majority of the Italians. However, this did not last forever. Since 1970, in fact, Italian culture has started considering Sardinia differently. This is truly relevant for this book, as Costa Smeralda started in 1962 and thus in a period when Sardinia was still surrounded by this atmosphere of diversity. A few years later, however, the new perception of the island accompanied the success of the new tourist enterprise of Costa Smeralda. What brought about this change was Italian popular culture, specifically football and music. But banditry did not stop affecting the idea that the Italians had of the island.

Cagliari Football Club

The last Sardinian element that culturally signified something in Italian culture was football. However, while the previously mentioned cultural elements contributed to detaching Sardinia from the rest of the country, football unified or, more accurately, clarified its position. In 1970, the Sardinian football club of Cagliari won the Italian *Scudetto*, the national championship of the Serie A (the Italian premier league). In a competition usually dominated by the teams of the big cities (Milan and Inter from Milan, Juventus from Turin, Rome, etc.), for the first time the *Scudetto* was won by a team from a city south of Rome, and it was considered a big surprise for the Italians. The surprise of seeing a club that was not credited until 1968 (in 1969 Cagliari was second and started being taken into account) became even bigger as that club belonged to a land that many people did not know—Sardinia.

The most important Italian sports journalist has certainly been Gianni Brera, who was also a novelist and historian. In his many books and articles, he used to connect football to Italian cultural history. As regards the victory of Cagliari in the Serie A in 1970, he wrote:

> Cagliari's victory represented the real entrance of Sardinia in Italy. It was the event that permitted the insertion of Sardinia in the history of Italian culture. Until the 1960s, this region represented another galaxy. To go there, it was necessary to get a flight and many Italians have an atavistic worry of it. Sardinia needed a victory and it got it from football, defeating the big teams of Milan and Turin, which traditionally were the capitals of Italian football. Scudetto allowed Sardinia to be free from old inferiority complexes, and all of it was a positive enterprise, a joyful event. (*Guerin Sportivo* 2011)

Brera's account well clarifies the place of Sardinia before the Cagliari football team's victory, and the subsequent change after it. The mood of Sardinia before and after the victory is also exemplified by the website of the Cagliari football team:

> The *scudetto* in 1970 unified Sardinia to Italy, according to Brera. Before it, we were shepherds, bandits. No one came to spend their holidays here, Costa Smeralda did not exist. The films about Sardinia, if viewed with today's eyes, would be considered racist. The higher officials threatened their subordinates saying "I'll send you to Sardinia." Everything changed and the island became a paradise for tourists. (Montesi, n.d.)

The discovery of Sardinia among people passionate about football and the Italians in general had an extraordinary guide: Gigi Riva. Riva, who passed away in 2024, was the striker of the team and with his many goals, was decisive in Cagliari's victory in Serie A. Importantly, he was not Sardinian but from Leggiuno, in Lombardy, the richest Italian region, alsocomprising Milan. Some years earlier, Riva had accepted an offer to go to Cagliari from Lombardy and he later confessed that he knew nothing of the island and the city. He was in a difficult period of his life; his parents had died some years earlier and he felt at war with the entire world. His sister persuaded him to change his life and go to Cagliari.

Shortly after Riva arrived in Sardinia, he was enchanted by everything: the city, its people, the beaches… He was happy with the affection he received from the Sardinians and understood that Sardinia was his place in the world. In fact, he remained there for his entire career, rejecting offers from Juventus and other big teams (Oriolo 2023), and also after his retirement, until his death.

Riva very often delved into his relationship with Sardinia in the many interviews he released:

> People used to call us shepherds and bandits, and I got angry. Bandits were bandits for hunger, as at those times people were hungry, like today, unfortunately. The Cagliari football team was everything for everyone and I understood that I could not cancel the unique dream of the shepherds. (Cerruti 2013)

Graziano Mesina, a bandit who was wanted by the police and lived in hiding, started writing to Riva (at his private address) every time he would go to the stadium in disguise, so as not to be recognized by the police. Riva never answered but never told the police and also said that sometimes he had the impression that he was a man with a long beard in the first raws among the public (Cerruti 2013).

Riva started his family in Cagliari and, as said above died, on the January 22, 2024 at the age of 79. He was a friend of Fabrizio De Andrè, an anarchic singer and songwriter, who in his songs represented people who were rejected by society and in danger. He is the topic of the next subsection.

Fabrizio De André

Fabrizio De Andrè was the most important of the Italian *cantautori*, singers who wrote their politically engaged songs between the 1960s and the 2000s. De Andrè was from Genoa, but in the middle of his career, in 1975, when he was 35, he decided to move to Sardinia, where he established a farm in Tempio Pausania, really close to Costa Smeralda. From that moment on, he split his career into two parts, continuing to write and sing songs and managing his farm.

The decision was a polemic reaction against industrialized life and the result of his wish to immerse himself in nature. De André repeated many times that Sardinia was the right place to live, a paradise and an opportunity to start a new life without worries and apprehensions (*Cagliari Magazine* 2020).

Unfortunately, he was wrong. In 1979, a group of bandits kidnapped him and his partner, the singer Dori Ghezzi, and kept them prisoners for four months close to the town of Pattada. In the end, De André's father, an ex-executive of a big sugar company, paid the ransom and De André and Ghezzi were freed. The kidnappers were arrested shortly after the release of the two singers, who at the trial brought suit as a civil party against the instigators of the kidnapping but pardoned the wardens, who had treated them well (*Cagliari Magazine* 2020).

Surprisingly, nothing changed in the two singers' lives after this event. They remained in Sardinia to manage their farm and sometimes in their interviews, De André hinted at the fact that he often saw their kidnappers in the central square in Tempio Pausania after they were released. SISDE, the Italian intelligence service, suspected for years that De André's farm was actually a refuge for the Italian terrorists of Brigate Rosse (red brigades) and spied on it for a long time, without finding any suspicious person or event (*Cagliari Magazine* 2020). De André and Ghezzi got married in 1989 and remained in Sardinia for almost the entire span of De André's life. They came back to the continent to cure the cancer that he suffered from, dying in 1999.

De André and Ghezzi's sequence of events had a large echo in the Italian media. In the first part of their stay in Sardinia, the media underlined the untouched life that the singers lived there; later, magazines and TV highlighted the archaic and savage spirit of the island, considering inexplicable the pardon and the decision of the couple to remain in the same place where they were kidnapped.

The Crisis After Popularity

Meaningfully, the crisis of Costa Smeralda coincided with its popularization in newspapers and magazines, in Cagliari winning the Serie A trophy, and in its becoming famous among the Italians and all over the world. It might seem a paradox, but it is, instead, in line with what we have found so far.

The key to comprehending this apparent contradiction is in Porru (1970), an analysis of the tourists spending their holidays in Costa Smeralda written in 1970, a year when popularity was hitting this destination but the crisis was still far, or underground. The article states that the actual clients of Costa Smeralda were those we do not see, living in their villas without showing off in the press, and arriving in the winter. The article underlines that the destination worked this way, as it was based on the invisibility of those rich clients. However, Porru (1970) says, something new was happening: Costa Smeralda had appeared on the leaflets of the big travel agencies, and many people were arriving, but they stayed only a few days and left. This wasn't good business for Costa Smeralda. However, the management of the Consortium seemed not to understand it, and in the same article it is written that the architect Couelle presented a new project for the Hotel Cala di Volpe, transforming it from a 70-bed hotel to a 210-bed one.

Phase 2 was in the air, and this was probably the beginning of the transformation. To sum up, Costa Smeralda was promising to remain exclusive but was conveying it to millions of people. It would be impossible to keep up, as it was too large a contradiction.

Popularity also made new problems emerge: till 1980, there was no medical center in Porto Cervo. It was inaugurated on May 31 of that year by the mayor of Arzachena Filigheddu and the Aga Khan. Relevantly, the center was a gift of the Consortium to improve the health of both the tourists and the Sardinians (*Corriere della Sera* 1980b). Another problem was that of scamming: in 1981 (Zasso 1981), Costa Smeralda had the problem of the many tourist initiatives bearing the name Costa Smeralda but actually extraneous to it.

Zasso (1981) also points out the danger of Phase 2—in ten years, the number of buildings increased from 1870 to 9350. Costa Smeralda was becoming an industry, the article says. Many celebrities who used to spend time in the island of an island in the 1960s were abandoning it and were looking for other places, some "new Costa Smeraldas."

Finally, we come to the problem of criminality. Zasso (1980) looks at the tourist numbers: 1979, he says, was a triumphant year for Sardinia, with 4 million tourists; despite it, Costa Smeralda lost visitors in comparison to the previous years: Arzachena -4.4 percent and Olbia -16.8 percent. While the rest of Sardinia increased its tourism business, criminality damaged Costa Smeralda. Many villas were on sale and many northern Europeans did not want to go back to Costa Smeralda and Porto Raphael because of the frequent criminal events.

The tourists' concerns were understandable. So far, we have talked about prominent kidnappings, involving either important people (De André and Ghezzi) or local entrepreneurs, and thus relevant to the fears of tourists. However, kidnappings in Sardinia (and in another poor Italian region, Calabria) were so frequent that it is difficult today to paint a clear picture. Just to hint at some of them, here is a brief list with some details.

In 1977 the ex-journalist, aviator (under Fascism), and industry executive Leone Concato was kidnapped in Cala di Volpe. He was of Sardinian origin but had lived in Rome for long. Concato worked for a private company and was building a garden in his villa in Costa Smeralda. He used to go to north-east Sardinia regularly, by plane, renting a car at the airport and going to his villa. These regular movements probably made his kidnapping easier for the bandits. The kidnappers asked for 5 billion lire and the family answered that they could never pay such an amount of money. A negotiation started between the bandits and the Concatos who, like many other families in the same situation, appointed a spokesperson to negotiate (*Corriere della Sera* 1977b, 1977a). The family adopted the same strategy that many others resorted to in these cases. They used to release interviews to the press saying that they were ready to pay, thereby inviting the kidnappers to make contact with them (*Corriere della Sera* 1977b). They would then explain to the journalists that they were not so rich as to be able pay the requested amount of 5 billion lire, thus sending an encoded message to the kidnappers to start the negotiation. The bandits lowered their request. In the end, the family collected 600 million lire and paid the ransom. Concato, however, never came back home, killed by the bandits (*Corriere della Sera* 1977c).

His corpse was never found. In 2012, four people were found guilty of his kidnapping. Every now and then, when skeletons are found in Sardinia, DNA tests are carried out to verify if the bones are Concato's or those of the other kidnapped people who have never been seen thereafter.

In 1979, an entire family was kidnapped in Porto Rafael: the father, Rolf Schild, 55, his wife Daphne, 51, and their daughter Annabel, 15, who was deaf-mute. The article also reminds the reader that there were eight people kidnapped in north Sardinia around the same time. The journalist did not know that three days later there would be the kidnapping of the singers De André and Ghezzi, resulting in a total of ten kidnapped people in August 1979.

G.Z. (1979) adds worrying details to the crime scene. The family was spending a night at an English friend's house, 300 meters from their home. They were kidnapped in the center of Porto Rafael, a small village by the sea, which has been discussed earlier in this book. So, even the most serene villages suddenly became unsafe, in Costa Smeralda or near it. Rolf Schild was freed two weeks after the kidnapping, to collect the money to pay for the liberation of the two women. The wife was released after five months and the daughter four days after the mother (G.Z. 1980).

In 1980 a Swedish man, Fritz Aberg, was kidnapped in Orosei and freed after six months (*Corriere della Sera* 1980b). He was not rich at all, and his wife adopted the same strategy to negotiate with the kidnappers but with a small change—she used to talk to the Swedish Embassy to communicate with the kidnappers. When the man was released, he told the journalists that no ransom had been paid and that he almost became friends with one of the kidnappers, who treated him well.

The list could go on, but what is important here is to make clear the degree to which all of this threatened tourism in Costa Smeralda. It is really difficult to find exact data on this. However, the more optimistic accounts say that from 1960 to 1990 there were 177 kidnappings and that 25 people never came back home (Melo 2021; Ledda 2019). This clearly discouraged tourism and brutally changed the perspective that the Italians and people all over the world had of this tourist destination.

This negative view also affected the entire representation of Costa Smeralda. Even accidents were highlighted in the newspapers much more than in the past. *Corriere d'Informazione* (1971a), for example, in an article on the first page of the newspaper, reported that three people going out in the sea on a boat totally unfit for the bad weather lost their lives. Reports and articles about this accident went on for weeks.

The Long Night of Costa Smeralda

What has been said so far marked the beginning of the long night of Costa Smeralda. The night was totally different from the shining ones enjoyed in the 1960s by the Aga Khan, his friends, and the exclusive tourists who spent in northeast Sardinia their amazing holidays. This night was instead dark and difficult for those who managed this tourist destination.

Certainly, they tried to react. Costa Smeralda in some newspapers remained the tourist destination of the past years, but it is evident that it had lost its allure. In 1972, Jacqueline Kennedy and Aristotle Onassis were reported to have spent some days in Costa Smeralda to find an agreement in their stormy relationship (*Corriere d'informazione* 1972). The happiness and lightheartedness of the past years seemed to be lost, even when the main characters were the same as in the past.

What strikes the researcher is the change in the representation of people in Costa Smeralda even visually. Jovane (1977) is key to introducing the reader to this new atmosphere. The article reports that many of the wives of the Italian footballers were in Costa Smeralda, and that "Lady Zoff," the wife of the goalkeeper Dino Zoff, had been elected the most beautiful. The quality of the images, the other photos on the pages, the article, the social level of the represented people, and everything else had abruptly taken Costa Smeralda to the same level as many other tourist destinations in Italy and abroad.

Brigitte Bardot, Princess Margaret, and Mick Jagger had been canceled forever. People spending time in Costa Smeralda were changing, that page says; the old ones were now looking at other places, worried by what was happening in that place in terms of crime and kidnapping.

However, this change was evaluated and wanted by the Aga Khan and his collaborators. At the beginning of the 1970s, the Prince and his architects tried to expand the tourist attraction that they had conceived as an elitist place, proposing to the Italian institutions the second step in the development of Costa Smeralda, called Phase 2. Costa Smeralda, according to them, had to be remade, and rethought in its deeper elements. Just to give an idea, Phase 2 aimed to take the built areas in Costa Smeralda to 5 million cubic meters (in 2016 they were less than 2 million cubic meters) (Piga 2016). Phase 2 comprehended many new (and big) hotels in Monti Zoppu, Cala di Volpe, Liscia Ruja, Razza di Juncu, and other places (Piga 2016).

It is evident that almost tripling the built areas of Costa Smeralda would have changed not only the visual scenario of the place but also the tourist aims of the enterprise and the level of the visitors. The idea of a remote place only accessible for a narrow class of international tourists was lost forever. What the Aga Khan wanted to do was to transform Costa Smeralda into a mass tourism place like many others. The photos of the footballers' wives and the relatively changed representation in the press were thus only a part of a larger plan. The idea of turning a serene nest for a few rich tourists into a mass tourist destination was probably aimed at a bigger and easier business. However, things did not go in that direction. The Aga Khan and his collaborators had not considered some changes in the Sardinian political equilibria.

When, in 1971, Phase 2 was examined by the Sardinian Regional Government, it was considered too damaging for the natural scenario. One of the strictest enemies of Phase 2 was Alessandro Ghinami, the Councilor for Public Works. The Regional Government, conversely, approved the plan for tourism development for other Sardinian areas, such as Pula and Villasimius, both in the south of the island. What had been a success in the north could have been replicated in the south, the Regional politicians thought.

This made the north protest. Arzachena, the closest city to Costa Smeralda whose municipality was responsible for Costa Smeralda, became, for one day, the epicenter of a riot. On January 21, 1971, six thousand people moved through the town to oppose the Regional Government's decision. Piga (2019) points out that they were principally people working in the tourist industry of Costa Smeralda, their relatives and all the local people in some way benefited by the tourism business in the area.

However, the manifestation seemed to be well-organized and strategically directed. The focus of the protest was the uneven treatment of the south and the north. People from Arzachena shouted slogans implying that the south was helped by the Regional Government that was based in Cagliari, the regional capital, which was in the south; and that the north remained penalized. "The Region is of Sardinian people, not of Cagliari people" (Piga 2019), they said in chorus.

Moreover, the mayor of Arzachena, Giovan Michele Digosciu, was much less seduced by Costa Smeralda and the Aga Khan than his predecessors belonging to the Filigheddu family, one of the fairest Sardinian allies of the Prince. Digosciu participated in the protest but without the full endorsement that the Filigheddus would have had.

Six days after the manifestation, the Regional Government stepped down and the new one had a new Councilor for Public Works. It took one year for the Aga Khan to see Phase 2 accepted: on January 4, 1972, the restyling and rebuilding of Costa Smeralda was approved by the Regional Government. Twenty days later, the Government stepped down because of the controversies relating to Phase 2. The Aga Khan and his collaborators had won at least that battle. The war, however, was in the end, lost, because the new Regional Government and the

Municipality of Arzachena changed their political components and continually postponed and changed the plan.

The 5 million cubic metres built area was never realized and this led to the detachment of the Aga Khan from the Sardinian project in general and to the continuation of the long night of Costa Smeralda.

Narratology and Costa Smeralda

All of a sudden, Costa Smeralda was thus in a state of crisis. What had perfectly worked in the 1960s, went wrong in the 1970s. Various elements contributed to it; however, the most important change was the attempt to change the nature and the aim of the enterprise, from elite to mass tourism.

Assuming that Costa Smeralda is a medium, as we have done since the beginning of this book, and that it tells stories, like any other medium, we can explain the problem with narratology. Narratology is the literary and media theory analyzing the communication system that is inside a story, and looking at the structure and the most relevant element inside a narrative text (Fludernik 2009).

We can see that Phase 1 and Phase 2 of Costa Smeralda tell two different stories. Phase 1 tells an elitist story, the story of a rich Prince discovering a sort of paradise on Earth, taking his friends there and constituting a sort of untouched realm where "untouched" people such as princesses, actors, very rich people from all over the world could find their nest out of their everyday life. It was a Foucault's utopia, especially in the first years, for the group of investors; and a utopia for the public, who perceived this place as nonexistent and unreachable.

The story worked, attracted many people, and fascinated many others who could not afford holidays in Costa Smeralda but consumed it through the media, watching the photos of the rich people at the airport, of the yachts close to the beaches with all of those special people on board, etc. There was full coherence between who told the story (the Aga Khan), the content of the story, and the readers, who wanted to read exactly that utopian story to dream of it.

Phase 2's story was totally different in its content. The place that was a paradise on Earth promised access to a mass of people. In many representations, it lost its magic, and this was right, as it had to attract many more people, so it would have been wrong to represent it as untouched. However, the problem was that the storyteller was the same, the Aga Khan. People had seen the paradise he had built, while in the second story, he banalized that land to sell it to much more people. The narrator had transformed a utopia into a more common and concrete heterotopia, for both the group of investors and the public, killing a dream. This did not work.

While losing its magic, the story also lost its credibility. Even when in the 1970s Costa Smeralda increased the number of its visitors, the real business had gone away, as those people would go to other, similar, tourist destinations in subsequent years. In short, Costa Smeralda became similar to many other places, while in the first story it was unique, and the lucky people spending time there would not go to other places, for the simple reason that there were no similar tourist destinations.

What is more, the political change also prevented the Aga Khan from enlarging Costa Smeralda, given that the basis of any mass tourist place is its size. In a couple of years, Costa Smeralda became massive without the massive structures to accommodate the mass—a contradiction too big to overcome in order to win the race in the competitive market of tourism that exactly in those years prepared for deep changes.

Conclusion

This chapter has been particularly articulated. It started happily with the big success of Costa Smeralda as a tourist enterprise and a mass medium conveying utopian messages to people scattered all over the world. What we had seen in the previous chapter, the material and architectural construction of Costa Smeralda, bore fruit. The place became soon one of the most exclusive tourist sites in the world and was represented in the media as such.

Then the chapter suddenly became worrisome. What started to change things in Costa Smeralda was popularity, the accessibility that was excluded from the 1960s, and the age of inaccessibility, as we have termed it. Being almost invisible had been the secret of its success, but it lasted for a short time. Being visible and accessible meant its ruin.

Sardinia gained popularity in Italy and in the world for many, sometimes contrasting, reasons: football, crime, accidents, the beauty of its places. Costa Smeralda was frequently represented in the media and its popularity also worsened its situation, as the presence of many rich people also attracted criminals.

Kidnappings also involved popular people and these criminal events were impossible to hide. Rich people went rapidly away from Costa Smeralda and, at the same time, the Aga Khan put forward his Phase 2. We do not know if the crisis and Phase 2 were linked to each other; if the Prince proposed Phase 2 to transform Costa Smeralda into a more affordable place, attract the middle class, and bring down or eliminate kidnappings in that area.

By looking at the dates, Phase 2 was imagined at the end of the 1960s, in years when crime was not yet a problem in Sardinia. However, this matters to a certain extent, because the two factors were hand in hand at the beginning of the 1970s and took Costa Smeralda to what we have called its long night.

As narratology has suggested, when the storyteller remains the same it is difficult to change the story, especially when the new is the opposite of the old. There was a need for another change, either of the storyteller or the story. It happened in the second half of the 1990s. Both elements changed and, as difficult as it is to imagine, when Costa Smeralda woke up after its long night, the new day was even worse than the dark.

CHAPTER 6

The Age of Showing off

Introduction

This chapter tells the story of an earthquake. We have seen in the previous chapter that the old exclusive model conceived by the Aga Khan failed because of criminality, changing times, and also because the Aga Khan changed his mind in terms of what Costa Smeralda should have become. He became the person least able to change the island on an island, as he initially perfectly embodied the spirit of the first Costa Smeralda, and was not credible when announced his wish to betray that spirit. The problem, as has been underlined in the conclusion of the last chapter, was that the message was changing but the storyteller remained the same.

In this chapter we will deal with the entrance of a new storyteller, who would change Costa Smeralda profoundly, overturning everything. Keep in mind every aspect we have discussed so far, because in this chapter you will see its opposite.

Actually, after the crisis of the previous model, there were two changes. The first was the change of the property ownership of Costa Smeralda. The Aga Khan was disappointed with the rejection of his dream of Phase 2 and sold, or more accurately, lost, as we will see, the control of the tourist destination. The second change was the entrance of Silvio Berlusconi into what Bourdieu would call the field of cultural production of Costa Smeralda.

It is difficult to understand what happened first, if one of the two changes caused the other. What is certain, instead, is that the coincidence of the two events constituted an earthquake that changed the tourist destination profoundly.

Berlusconi found in Costa Smeralda the perfect stage for his character, based on a blended mixture of entertainment and politics. On the one hand, he transformed Costa Smeralda into a sort of medium feeding the programs of his TV channels; on the other hand, he turned Villa Certosa, his hyperluxurious Sardinian residence, into the place of very relevant international meetings. Moreover, the two elements very often also cooexisted.

Media scholars can read all of this as the demonstration of the mediatization of people's lives, while sociologists may find in Costa Smeralda's destiny the actualization of the metaphor of Baudrillard's map. Whatever it was, Costa Smeralda in those years was a really interesting research field in which it was possible to see postmodernism taking over modernism and how powerful economic and political change can be when they happen together.

The Failure of Phase 2

In the complex language of Italian politics, the approval of Phase 2 voted by the Sardinian Regional Council meant that the plan was rejected. The project was continually postponed and changed by the Italian institutions between the second half of the 1970s and the early 1980s. In 1984 (Zasso 1984), the Aga Khan did not hide his annoyance and hinted to the Italians that he could abandon Costa Smeralda.

In those years, the press reported the news about this issue in two different ways: articles reporting the backstory sounded the alarm, saying that Prince Karim wanted to leave Italy to concentrate on other areas where politicians would encourage tourism enterprises; and official statements of the Aga Khan and his team said that the Prince would never abandon Costa Smeralda.

When in 1985 Prince Karim bought CIGA, many thought that the die had been cast. CIGA was a company controlling some of the most luxurious and famous Italian hotels, from the Hotels Excelsior in Venice, Rome, and Naples, to the Grand Hotel in Rome and Stresa, to the Principe di Savoia in Milan. The company also owned many hotels in the U.S. and other countries.

However, the purchase of CIGA did not change the media reports about Costa Smeralda: on the one hand, there were frequent rumors about the fact that Prince Karim bought CIGA to leave Costa Smeralda to its fate; on the other hand, interviews with the Prince and his staff served the purpose of reassuring the Italians and the market that the Aga Khan would never give up managing Costa Smeralda (Pinna 1985).

A conference about the future of Costa Smeralda was held in Sassari in 1985. During that event, the management of the Consortium unofficially leaked information about the relationships between CIGA and the Sardinian business of the Prince. The two companies would be kept separate, but some synergies would facilitate the organization of the tourist destinations (Pinna 1985).

At the conference, a group of academics from Bocconi University underlined the importance of Costa Smeralda for the entire economic system of north Sardinia. However, they highlighted that since 1983 the number of tourists spending their holidays in Costa Smeralda had decreased, and found that the tourist enterprise had entered a new stage. Moreover, even the number of people with a second home in Costa Smeralda were diminishing. Finally, the number of people permanently employed in Costa Smeralda was decreasing while the seasonal contracts were higher.

This data may also be read as the signal of a change of the target audience—Costa Smeralda was becoming a tourist destination like many others, to be consumed in summer, while it was losing the old target of rich people having on the island on an island a second home, and spending holidays in north Sardinia scattered over the entire year. However, revenues were up and while the crisis was looming, it was hardly damaging the business. To sum up, Costa Smeralda was still the economic engine of the area, but it was slowing down (Pinna 1985).

The change was already visible at the beginning of the 1980s. Pinna (1981) pointed out that VIPs, well-known people, had disappeared from Costa Smeralda. This had divided the opinion of local people and investors into two groups: the nostalgic ones believing that the area had lost its allure; and the others, especially entrepreneurs of the tourism industry, supporting the new trend, which was, according to them, more commercially fruitful.

The new tourists turned out to be mainly from the U.S., with a different mood, less attachment to traditions and the past and more concrete when it came to spending money. Princesses and actors had had a precise function, an executive says—making Costa Smeralda famous in the world. Once this had happened, we did not need them anymore (Pinna 1981).

Pinna (1981) reports that many people think that among the collaborators of Prince Karim there was a split into hawks and doves, those who wanted to save traditions and an exclusive target, and those who preferred to sell tourism more widely and massively as other goods, and that the latter finally won.

The split that occurred in Costa Smeralda in those years also led to a radicalization of the two views which also affected the island symbolically. In August 1993, the stone naturally sculpted and representing a turtle in Cala Girgolu, close to San Teodoro, was seriously damaged, and in 1997, was destroyed forever. The natural sculpture was the symbol of the nature and beauty of the Sardinian coast. The attack was carried out by two Italian entrepreneurs, who arrived on their yacht and hammered the sculpture. People on the beach immediately intervened, surrounded the yacht and called the police, who arrested them.

It happened a few days after the TV program *Moby Dick*, when environmentalists and advocates of Phase 2 had clashed in a violent way. Many believed that the destruction of the sculpture was a reaction of some radical supporter of Phase 2 as an affront to the environmentalists (Zasso 1997), but whatever the case was, the crime remained unpunished.

The Aga Khan Leaves

In 1994, Prince Karim lost Costa Smeralda. "Lost" is the exact term, instead of "sold." After buying CIGA Hotels, Prince Karim merged this company with his most important activities in Costa Smeralda. CIGA Hotels, however, was not in good health, and nine years after Prince Karim's purchase, it was placed in receivership. Thus, in losing control of CIGA, the Aga Khan also lost control of almost all of his activities in Costa Smeralda, the hotels principally. To sum up, what the Prince still owned was the Yacht Club, Villa Cerbiatta, and a few other businesses (*La Stampa* 2022).

Certainly the Prince was tired of the opposition of the Italian politicians to Phase 2. What people working on Costa Smeralda say about those years is that the Prince was simply not there. He was always abroad to manage his other businesses and Costa Smeralda was not at the forefront of his commercial activities. Thus, his absence cost him his assets in Costa Smeralda and he also lost interest in its old creation. Many think that he probably would have sold Costa Smeralda in a short time even without this accident relating to CIGA; however, this is what happened and thus is what has to be told (*La Stampa* 2022; Masneri 2022).

The financial refurbishment of CIGA finished in 1995, when the group, and Costa Smeralda with it, was bought by the global hotel chain Sheraton. From Sheraton, in a short time, CIGA (and Costa Smeralda) passed to another U.S. hotel company, Starwood.

When Starwood in 2003 announced that they wanted to sell Costa Smeralda, the most important Italian companies showed interest in it: Leonardo Del Vecchio, Pirelli, Diego Della Valle, and even the Sardinian entrepreneur Renato Soru.

Moreover, some Sardinian and Venetian business people formed a group to buy it: they were the families Tabacchi, De Rigo, Loi, and Corbeddu (Pinna 2003).

Surprisingly, none of them would be successful. Starwood, which had taken ownership of Costa Smeralda from Sheraton, sold everything in 2003 to the U.S. entrepreneur Tom Barrack, who paid 300 million euros for it.

Barrack would go on to have a troubled future. He became one of the most important advisors to Donald Trump, directed some branches of his electoral campaign and ended up being arrested for his questionable activities in the Arab Emirates, which also implied lying to the FBI.

When Barrack bought Costa Smeralda via his company Colony Capital, however, he said that the tourist destination would have saved the original shape desired by the Prince and that there would not be new areas built (Pinna 2003). The old idea of Prince Karim was already gone at those times, but indeed, Barrack did not cement new areas, disagreeing with the Aga Khan, who had projected Phase 2 and 5 million cubic meters of new buildings.

What is more surprising is that Prince Karim opposed the new buyer. After losing Costa Smeralda, the passage from Sheraton to Starwood to, finally, Barrack, was probably seen by the Prince as a progressive loss of quality.

The control of the Consortium Costa Smeralda, the assembly of the owners, was the battlefield between the two businessmen. Barrack had a large majority and won the elections to the leadership roles, appointing his collaborators and controlling the Consortium. The collaborators of the Aga Khan contested this election saying that many votes supporting Barrack actually came from owners of the buildings that were never built. The opposition went on and many hoped that the Prince could come back.

The Aga Khan, however, never spoke about this issue. His collaborators tried to invalidate the elections but failed. The Prince was always abroad and never intervened or showed interest in what was happening. Some questions remained unanswered. Among them, till today, it is not certain if the Prince was a candidate for the election to the presidency of the Consortium, or if he knew that Barrack would win easily and thus gave in. What emerged through his collaborators was that the Prince was pleased that the new Costa Smeralda did not satisfy many people who were nostalgic about the old one, to the point that many hoped that he would come back (Pinna 2007).

This may also be true, but what is important to remember is that the Prince started to change the nature and identity of Costa Smeralda and that any other change descended from his masterplan, or Phase 2; his plan would have destroyed

Costa Smeralda more than what the subsequent owners did and that, in the end, Tim Barrack won.

A New Storyteller

So far we have focused on issues linked to the ownership of Costa Smeralda (and the chain of its owners is not finished yet, as we will see below). However, apart from these economic disputes around controlling the business of this tourist destination, what also changed in those years was the storyteller. The economic change was in fact only a part of a bigger restyling of Costa Smeralda in terms of culture and taste.

The departure of the Prince and the abandonment of princesses and film stars meant that other people replaced them. In the previous chapter, we have briefly looked at the footballers' wives in some photos as a signal that something was changing. The 1990s were the decade of another, deep change in the nature and aims of this place. Costa Smeralda became the holiday site of a new class of rich people, profoundly different from the previous, based in Italy and destined to also affect the political life of the country.

The differences between the old main characters and the new ones are evident; the old ones in order to be satisfied by their stay in Costa Smeralda relied on its inaccessibility. The new ones made Costa Smeralda a media place and, I would say, a medium in itself. The great protagonist of this stage of the history of Costa Smeralda was Silvio Berlusconi, the television entrepreneur who also became Prime Minister in 1994.

Silvio Berlusconi based his summer life in Costa Smeralda, specifically in the town of Porto Rotondo. He lived in Villa Certosa, a huge complex system of buildings (described in detail in the next section). Villa Certosa soon became for Berlusconi something more than a place just to spend holidays. It served in fact for the Italian Prime Minister to create a system of power. Villa Certosa was the place where in Sardinia Berlusconi was able to combine the two main aspects of his life, entertainment and politics. Not by chance, Villa Certosa ended up being spied on by many photographers for the sexual scandals that he was involved in, and at the same time was a branch office of Palazzo Chigi, the official Italian Prime Minister residence in Rome (Muresu 2023). In Villa Certosa, Berlusconi organized very important meetings—with the British Prime Minister Tony Blair in 2004, the Russian President Vladimir Putin in 2003 and 2008, and the US

President George W. Bush in 2005. These visits were of huge relevance, not just in the political scene, but in how the Italian entrepreneur and politician used them to construct his image. We will analyze all of this in more depth. Before doing that, however, it is relevant to take a closer look at the summer headquarters of the Italian Government, Villa Certosa.

Villa Certosa

Villa Certosa is one of the biggest villas in Costa Smeralda. It is situated close to Porto Rotondo, is about 4,500 square meters large, and has 126 rooms and 174 parking spaces. The garden surrounding the villa is around 120 hectares in area. Berlusconi's refurbishment added other pieces to the original shape of the estate. Around the building, there are four bungalows, two houses, a Greek-Roman amphitheater, a tower, a greenhouse, a gym, five swimming pools, thalassotherapy, a medicinal garden of 297 square meters, and a fake, electric volcano able to erupt (and in fact the first time that Berlusconi turned it on, the firefighters soon arrived at the gate of the villa) (Jattoni Dall'Asen 2024). In 2022, an estimate established that the approximative value of the building is 259 million euros.

The villa had been owned by the Sardinian entrepreneur Gianni Onorato and later by the fixer Flavio Carboni (Jattoni Dall'Asen 2024). Carboni was sentenced to eight years and six months in jail for the bankruptcy of Banco Ambrosiano. Pushed by creditors, Carboni had to sell the villa. He found two buyers who disappeared at the last minute. Being in jail, Carboni had to accept Berlusconi's offer, which Carboni said was much inferior to the real value of the villa (Jattoni Dall'Asen 2024). The original name was Villa Monastero but Berlusconi renamed it Villa Certosa. Around one hundred people worked permanently at it when Berlusconi owned it.

In May 2004, probably because of Berlusconi's wish to organize in the villa international meetings with political leaders from all over the world, Villa Certosa was officially considered an alternative place of maximum safety for the Italian Prime Minister. This implied that the totality of the activities inside the villa became top secret.

On the one hand, this fed a series of legends concerning Berlusconi's refurbishments. Rumors became widespread about the "pier 007," an underground harbor able to host even submarines in case of emergency; archaeological remains scattered over the garden, including Phoenician tombs; a perfect copy of Solomon's Temple; a bunker; a Nuraghic village in Las Vegas-style; a magic forest; Caribbean turtles, and many other incredible elements. Villa Certosa sparked the imagination of the Italians and became a kind of fantasy setting, certainly for the enjoyment of its owner. However, no one, apart from those who have visited it, can say how many of these rumors are real and how many have simply been invented by journalists.

On the other hand, the top-secret stamp also made it difficult to verify the legality of the many refurbishments carried out by the owner of Villa Certosa. The environmentalists accused him of carrying out work that did not adhere to the standards requested by the regulations of Costa Smeralda. The Italian tycoon always maintained his innocence, even though there was a lack of documentation relating to the top-secret issue (Jattoni Dall'Asen 2024). As a result, there was a legal trail from which Berlusconi left acquitted.

In 2007, the photographer Antonello Zappadu published in the Magazine *Oggi* some of the seven hundred photos that he managed to take in Villa Certosa's garden. He found a place from where he could covertly capture images of what happened in the secret area. The first published photos depicted Berlusconi with five girls, some from TV programs, hand in hand with the prime minister or sitting on his knees. Zappadu would publish other photos that provoked fewer reactions, such as those of the Czech Prime Minister Mirek Topolànek naked with a couple of girls around, in one of the swimming pools of the villa (Jattoni Dall'Asen 2024).

The sexual scandals that would involve Silvio Berlusconi with serious consequences for his political trajectory would come from 2009 to 2011. In 2007, the year when Zappadu's photos were published by *Oggi*, the great majority of the Italians ignored Berlusconi's private life, or at least did not have concrete proof to be sure of it. Thus, the photos taken of Villa Certosa, in which incidentally the depicted people did nothing illegal, produced a sense of scandal that today seems strange. Today, we can relate them to the general atmosphere that Berlusconi and his collaborators took to Costa Smeralda, an atmosphere comprising the ultimate degree of spectacularization of politics, which will be discussed at the end of this chapter.

One of the main elements of this spectacularization was certainly the meetings that Berlusconi organized with some of the most influential and powerful political leaders of the time.

Tony Blair and Berlusconi in Costa Smeralda

In 2002, *Sunday Times* revealed a rumor that was causing agitation in the political offices in the Western world: the British Prime Minister Tony Blair, leader of the Labour Party, would spend some days of his holidays as a guest of Silvio Berlusconi in Villa Certosa. The staff of both leaders immediately denied the news, but the British journal seemed to be certain of what it had written (*Corriere della Sera* 2002). An official meeting between the two leaders could have been possible, but in Rome or London. No one could understand why a Labour leader would go to Berlusconi's villa to spend his holidays.

Silvio Berlusconi was already known in Europe for his informal way of representing himself and his disputable views on justice, civil rights, and women, so it appeared strange that Blair would have accepted the invitation, even though the relationship between the two was good.

In 2002, Blair did not go to Costa Smeralda and the *Sunday Times* revelation was forgotten. In 2004, the prediction came true and the two leaders met in Villa Certosa. What many political observers had considered senseless happened, and in terms and styles they could not foresee. The recurring theme preceding the event was that the meeting would be informal and that the visit was to be considered a reunion between friends (Fuccaro 2004a). However, as in the case of Putin, informality and friendship would not prevent the leaders from talking about international issues, particularly, terrorism and migration.

Two weeks before the visit, in Britain, many observers and even Labour politicians considered the visit a political mistake and a tacky choice (Altichieri 2004). Politically, many members of the Labour Party did not understand why Blair chose to go to Berlusconi's villa and thus support a political opponent. However, the majority of the critiques were around the the showiness of Berlusconi and his villa, considered an example of a James Bond-style presentation. Berlusconi was also defined as "slippery" by the *Daily Mail* (Altichieri 2004), and the press in general reminded the readers of the risks implied in the visit. However, it was also highlighted that Berlusconi would certainly take advantage of this visit in terms of credibility, but that Blair also needed visibility and thus the visit to Costa Smeralda could also be of help to him.

The day after the meeting, the reports informed that Blair and his wife arrived in Olbia and from there went to Villa Certosa in a helicopter. In the afternoon, they started a tour on a speedboat along the most beautiful bays of Costa Smeralda and finally, surprisingly, they went to Porto Cervo, which was crowded with tourists. The article again repeats the keywords even in the titles; Fuccaro (2004b) cites Berlusconi saying that it had to be seen as the visit of a friend to a friend (this was also the phrase used at the beginning of the article), and that it was an informal summit.

The article also highlighted the contradiction between the informal aspect that the two leaders wanted to give the visit and the document that they wanted to sign, about the Iraqi crisis (and this presented the opportunity for the journalist to repeat that Berlusconi defined the visit as a meeting of friends). In a side box, the report explains the dinner menuof linguine and crayfish, marinated tuna, and St. Peter's fish. The dinner was reported to occur in Villa Certosa and to be accompanied by songs by Mariano Apicella, guitarist, singer, and one of Berlusconi's best friends. In the end, fireworks illuminated the bay and finished by forming the lettering W. Tony (Stella 2004).

However, what acquires centrality within the page is the article below this one (Di Caro 2004), on the huge crowd surrounding Berlusconi, Blair, and his wife while they were walking in Porto Cervo. They were all in white and Berlusconi also wore a bandana on his head. Blair had asked to maintain a low profile during the entire visit, but the tour in Porto Cervo was crowded, especially when the three talked to the tourists, did some shopping, and even briefly participated in a book presentation by a P.R. professional.

All the security measures, the secret service people, and the police officers scattered over that area were in one moment rendered useless. The two leaders and Cherie Blair walked into the crowd exposing themselves to potential risks that they usually avoided.

Being visible in public was probably the real reason for this meeting, and the low profile requested by Blair would not make sense. Can we imagine a better example to explain populism, even today, than this visit? However, Tony Blair was just one of Berlusconi's guests. Another would come two times, before and after the British PM's visit.

Vladimir Putin and Berlusconi in Costa Smeralda

Vladimir Putin met Silvio Berlusconi at Villa Certosa, in Costa Smeralda, two times, in 2003 and 2008. Along with the visit by Tony Blair in 2004, these two events may be considered today as a watershed of the way politicians meet, set the style of their encounters, and represent themselves to the public.

The first visit was in the summer of 2003. One thousand security people were in Olbia (around the airport), Porto Rotondo (the closest town to Berlusconi's villa), around Villa Certosa, and inside Berlusconi's residence. One entire area of Porto Rotondo was off-limits and closed to everyone. Putin also adopted his own security measures—the Russian ambassador in Rome had come to Costa Smeralda to check every aspect of the visit; a Russian firefighting aircraft flew over Costa Smeralda for the entire duration of the visit; two military ships of the Russian navy were anchored to the military base of Santo Stefano, the destroyer Smitlivy and the cruiser Moskova (still utilized by the Russian in the Ukraine war in the Snake Island in 2022). The presence of two Russian military ships in the Mediterranean had alarmed the U.S. and French Presidents George Bush and Jacques Chirac, but in the end they accepted it (Pinna 2022).

From the airport, Berlusconi and Putin went on a helicopter to Porto Rotondo, held a press conference at the Hotel Abi d'Oru and spent the evening and night in Villa Certosa, listening to the songs of Berlusconi's favorite guitar player, Mariano Apicella (some of the songs had lyrics written by Berlusconi). The day after saw another press conference at La Maddalena, a tour of the archipelago on a yacht, and a final feast in Villa Certosa, with Andrea Bocelli's concert (Pinna 2022).

The second time, on April 17, 2008, the reports on the meeting (Galluzzo 2008a) say that Berlusconi and Putin substantially did two things: talked about international politics and attended a show of *Il Bagaglino*, a theater company holding TV shows on Berlusconi's channels and famous for its ironic look at politics, always seen from a conservative point of view.

Berlusconi is photographed while on the strip of Olbia's airport, where he is waiting for the landing of Putin's plane. He is with a group of hostesses, visibly excited, and with some representatives of the police. In another photo, taken after the landing, Berlusconi and Putin are together with the interpreter in the middle, and again one Carabiniere is in the background.

The visit, Galluzzo (2008a) says, was to repay Berlusconi's visit to Russia six months earlier, when the Russian President welcomed the Italian Prime Minister at Valdai Lake and together they attended a show of a group of lap dancers. At Olbia's airport, before Putin's arrival, Berlusconi told the journalists that they would talk about the complex and difficult relationships between the EU and the Russian Federation. The aim was to improve the relationships between Italy and

Russia, Berlusconi added, as 30 percent of the oil and gas that Italy imported came from Russia.

Berlusconi and Putin were reported to have had lunch together, to have walked through the very big garden of the villa while talking to each other, to have had dinner, and finally to have attended the show. A photograph of the Bagaglino dancers completes the page-long report dedicated to covering the meeting.

The day after, a press conference with both Berlusconi and Putin was organized in Villa Certosa (Galluzzo 2008b). The two politicians arrived on a golf cart crossing the big garden of the villa and answered the questions asked by the journalists. They kept the conference informal and complimented each other on their political successes.

A Russian journalist asked Putin about his supposed lover and his separation from his wife. The Russian President said that they were fake news, that he liked women but that his marriage was good and destined to continue. Galluzzo (2008b) underlines that all the questions were already checked and agreed on by the press offices of the two political leaders, so probably Putin wanted to answer that question just to put an end to the rumors.

As the Russian journalist continued to ask questions to Putin, preventing the other journalists from intervening, Berlusconi pretended to have a machine gun in his hands and imitated the gesture of shooting at her. Some of those present were upset by the gesture, while others took it as a joke, and the press conference went on.

There are two points about Putin's visits to Costa Smeralda that are to be underlined. The first one is the inextricable intertwining of politics and entertainment. If since the 2000s politics have become entertainment, these two visits are an illuminating example of how the two elements feed each other to finally give the public a different representation of politics. Dancers and international politics, Andrea Bocelli and navy destroyers, hazardous gestures and global energy issues merge to construct the meeting of two international leaders.

All of this leads to the second point: if the same meetings had happened in Rome, they would not have been the same. Undoubtedly, Costa Smeralda played a pivotal role in this sense, as it helped the two politicians keep the meeting informal.

The gesture of the machine gun against a journalist, at a press conference in Rome, without the golf car, the dancers, and the garden, would have been condemned globally. In Costa Smeralda it was meant as a tacky joke, either to condemn or to gloss over. Costa Smeralda was also the opportunity for Putin to overtly answer a question about his supposed lover. The Russian President took advantage of the informal atmosphere to also touch upon this delicate issue. Thus, the informality of Costa Smeralda helped the two informal politicians better represent themselves to their audiences.

The informal style was one of Berlusconi's main political strategies. It served the purpose of playing down some of his weak points and divert the attention of the public from sensitive issues to insignificant ones. In this sense, we can see that Costa Smeralda was for him not only a place to find relaxation, go to parties, enjoy his holidays, and sometimes meet other politicians. Rather, it was a part of a bigger strategy to orchestrate his politics and seduce his voters.

George W. Bush and Berlusconi in Costa Smeralda?

The most important meeting between Berlusconi and an international leader in Costa Smeralda never happened. In 2005, Berlusconi tried to organize a meeting with the U.S. President George W. Bush. He had worked two years on it, and on June 6 of that year eventually obtained a promise from Bush (Pinna 2005). Berlusconi's dream seemed to become reality. He wanted to have a cold tea with Bush and his wife in the garden of Villa Certosa, take a helicopter and fly with them over the wonderful bays of Costa Smeralda, and sing with the President in the evning in the Greek-Roman theater of the villa.

Berlusconi and Bush also agreed on the days, July 9 and 10 of the same year, after the G8 in Gleneagles, Scotland. Both the offices of the two leaders in Washington and Rome admitted the existence of the plan but never put out a precise date, saying that the invitation was always open and that there not was any certainty of its acceptance (Pinna 2005).

What Berlusconi's office did say was that the visit would be private, without any official protocol, but only a meeting between two friends. Security measures were proportionate to the importance of the event: a police cordon would surround Villa Certosa on land and at sea; military ships of the Italian navy would protect the President from attacks from the sea; nuclear-powered submarines, already present in Sardinia at the U.S. military base of La Maddalena, would complete the protection system.

The town of Porto Rotondo was planned to be closed. An entire battalion of Carabinieri and people of the U.S. and Italian secret service were to protect Villa Certosa on land. Closure of airspace over north Sardinia, and U.S. and Italian fighter planes always in the air were to protect from air attacks. Finally, Olbia's airport was considered to be at an appropriate level to let Air Force One land (Pinna 2005).

The scale of the efforts to organize this visit is evident. If it occurred in Rome, it would have been much easier to organize and it probably would even have occurred. It was decided instead to organize it in Costa Smeralda. Similar to the previous cases, being perceived as informal get-together with the most powerful politician in the world (this was at those times the unofficial qualification of any U.S. president) would have allowed Berlusconi to overcome the simple image of the ordinary politician, and to project him to a higher dimension, leaving his Italian competitors aside and making many people forget the many problems regarding Italy, its government, and Berlusconi, specifically.

The Berlusconization of Costa Smeralda

Apart from the political meetings, Berlusconi, or rather, "Berlusconism," branded Costa Smeralda to a degree that cannot be compared to previous cases. I mean that Berlusconi and his television channels, made Costa Smeralda the setting of gossip, news, reports, and communication items stemming very often from TV shows broadcast by the Mediaset channels, and sometimes by RAI, the public service TV that was controlled by Berlusconi.

Apart from Berlusconi, the leaders of this new trend were two of his best friends: Lele Mora, the agent of the TV stars, later sentenced to six years in prison for bankruptcy; and Emilio Fede, the journalist who supported Berlusconi's political campaigns as the Director of TG4, the news bulletin of one of Berlusconi's channels, later sentenced to four years for soliciting prostitution and going bankrupt.

As regards Lele Mora, a photograph that has been published by many magazines around the world explains the atmosphere of those years better than any other account. In it (Fantozzi 2023), Lele Mora is entirely in white, lying on a very big sofa and talking on the phone. Two well-built reality show contestants and models, Fabrizio Arca and Cristiano Angelucci, only wearing a swimsuits and sunglasses, massage his feet. A bulldog, in the foreground, looks at the camera.

In a later interview, after getting out of jail, Mora defined that photo as "stolen" (Tgcom24 2013), and more importantly, for this book, he said that in those cases, he was working, promoting TV stars and TV programs in which his artists participated. "I packaged TV characters" (Tgcom24 2013), Mora says to explain his role in Costa Smeralda in those years. In the interview, Mora also remembers that in Costa Smeralda he earned 10,000 euros for each show he organized with one of his TV show contestants, the amount of money that is enough to feed ten families for one month, he concludes, a bit sheepishly (Tgcom24 2013).

For many years, the two young models were associated with that photo and accused of having done it just to participate in more TV shows somehow controlled by Mora. In Fantozzi (2023), Arca invites the public to consider the entire career of an actor without exclusively dwelling on one episode.

Lele Mora, in the same years of Berlusconi's political leadership, became a central element of Italian popular culture. The TV critic Aldo Grasso (2011) created the term *lelemorismo*, which refers to Lele Mora's aesthetic and economic views. Grasso (2011) says that *lelemorismo* was the symbol of the overpowering power of agents when it came to deciding the content and the aesthetics of TV programs; *lelemorismo*, Grasso (2011) says, led to the worsening of the Italian language level on TV and in Italians' everyday lives. Above all, *lelemorismo* meant simplifying things that are complex and cannot be simplified, and the triumph of carelessness, the arrogance of nothing that wins along with total indifference. Never, Grasso (2011) concludes, have we seen so many incompetent people working on TV, and so many bad programs based on gossip, arguments, and parasitism (Grasso 2011).

Certainly the decadence of Italian TV was not exclusively because of Lele Mora. However, I have reported Grasso's words as they give an idea of how much Mora counted in those years. What is important to underline here is his centrality to both Italian television and to Costa Smeralda, again to suggest that the two were, in the end, elements of the same (Berlusconian) system.

The journalist Emilio Fede had a different role in the representation of the Berlusconization of Costa Smeralda. Fede was the editor, head, and presenter of TG4, the news bulletin of Rete4, one of Berlusconi's TV channels. He held this role from 1992 to 2012, thus following Berlusconi's entire political trajectory. As such, very frequently, Fede went well beyond the limits that a journalist should have, especially when talking about politics. He celebrated every political event having Berlusconi as the protagonist, hid pieces of news that risked damaging the political leader and showed a kind of sentimental link to him. Moreover, he attacked many politicians who contested Berlusconi, regardless of whether they were part of the left or the right wing. To ridicule Berlusconi's competitors, Fede used to distort their names, making them resemble words somehow offensive.

Fede kept a low profile in Costa Smeralda. He was less of a protagonist than Mora was on the pages of magazines and newspapers; however, he never missed an appointment. Since 1999, he was one of the characters in the background of the parties—rarely photographed, but always present. Paracchini (1999) reports his presence at the party in Porto Cervo that the top British model Naomi Campbell also attended. The party was organized by the entrepreneur Flavio Briatore, who at those times had a liaison with Campbell.

According to Pinna (Pinna 2008), Fede was also the co-protagonist of an episode that explains well how the new dominant class of Costa Smeralda was welcomed by a part of the habitual tourists of north Sardinia. In the summer of 2008, the entrepreneur Flavio Briatore, a member of the Berlusconian group, started managing a kiosk on the wonderful beach of Capriccioli. He renamed the kiosk "Billionaire Rubacuori" (heartbreaker), and imagined it as the daytime correspondent of his restaurant "The Billionaire." Briatore used to take clients to the kiosk coming to the beach along with other people from the sea, on motorized tenders, while tourists were still bathing or lying on the beach.

At the beginning of August of that year, Emilio Fede was among Briatore's friends and clients arriving on the tenders at the beach. That day, however, the tourists swimming or sunbathing in Capriccioli did not welcome them. Upset by the frequent tenders disturbing those who were swimming and by the noise of the motors, they started insulting the group and tried to prevent them from arriving at the beach. Fede and the others succeeded in reaching the kiosk, but in the subsequent years, Briatore did not manage the kiosk anymore.

Fede was also present in many parties testifying to the links between Berlusconi and some Arab millionaires. Pinna (2006) explains how the two groups mingled in a series of parties that were also attended by "young and beautiful entertainers" and around one hundred carefully selected invitees. Berlusconi is said to have been the main protagonist of the party, which was organized by the Sheik Al Rashid, whose 36-room-yacht is reported to be 105 meters long, 100 million euros worth, and one of the 10 biggest in the world. The yacht stopped in Villa Certosa, probably to let Berlusconi in, the article says. At the party, all the people danced on the tables until early morning, and among them, there was the ex-coach of the Italian football team, Marcello Lippi (Pinna 2006).

Berlusconi's Arab passion was also evident in the case of Veronica Lario's (Berlusconi's wife) 50th birthday. On that day the couple was in Morocco and Berlusconi surprised his wife by wearing bedouins' clothes (Pinna 2006).

Apart from Berlusconi, always in search of a balance between entertainment and politics, many other Italian politicians were also attracted by Costa Smeralda. The leader of Lega Nord, Umberto Bossi, for example, was photographed during his holidays in Porto Rafael in 2005 (*Corriere della Sera* 2005). It is interesting to note the modality of the representation of this piece of news, which was politically relevant because during his stay Bossi fmet Berlusconi to discuss political issues.

However, the photograph that was first published by the popular magazine *Oggi*, and later by many newspapers and other magazines, displayed Bossi in a swimsuit sitting at a table in the house he had rented. The picture seems to be stolen, as it was certainly taken from a great distance, going by the quality of the image. No news about the political meeting was released, the focus of the news being the fact that Bossi went to Costa Smeralda.

Bossi was in fact a populist leader proud of coming from the working class and always basing his speeches on the popular and peasant origins of his voters. Lega Nord was at those times a territory-based party whose voters predominantly lived in Lombardy and Veneto's countryside. This represen-tation (Lega Nord was also the party of many northern entrepreneurs tired of traditional politics) also permitted Lega to gain many votes that in the past when to the left wing.

Bossi in Costa Smeralda, more specifically in the closer Porto Rafael, thus had a precise meaning. Even the part of Italian politics more distant from the rich and famous surrendered to the appeal of the Berlusconized holidays.

What is more, other people involved in Berlusconi's life found in Costa Smeralda a sort of salvation island after their former failures. Pinna (2007) delves into the character of Giampiero Fiorani, a formerly very powerful Italian banker, who for many years contributed to deciding the economic destiny of Italy. Fiorani was later arrested for various financial scandals and once out of jail, and left by his wife, was the protagonist of many parties in Costa Smeralda, very often along with Mora and other friends of Berlusconi. Magazines and TV channels reported his flirtations with actresses, singers, and showgirls and photographed him during shows and karaoke performances.

Fiorani chose Villa Alberta as his Sardinian home, but Pinna (2007) notices that the villa was very often empty, as the ex-banker preferred to stay in Lele Mora's celebrated estate in Cala Granu. The article also reports on a really significant episode. Fiorani, Mora, and the others also spent an evening together in front of the TV watching an interview given to the photographer Fabrizio Corona talking about the sexual scandals involving many of them. At the end of the program, they congratulated the interviewee on his accounts of the scandal. This episode makes clear the degree of impunity pervading the new class dominating Costa Smeralda in those years.

The obsession for showing off in Costa Smeralda, however, did not spread to the entire team of Berlusconi's collaborators. The politician Gianni Letta, the TV executive Fedele Confalonieri, the football executive Adriano Galliani, and even the entrepreneur Flavio Briatore (who till date runs the Billionaire, one of the most trendy restaurants in the area), participated in Berlusconi's dolce vita in Costa Smeralda without appearing everywhere and kept themselves far from the most dangerous events, such as those concerning sexual scandals and the presence of people with a debatable past. The "crazy" life of Costa Smeralda, in the end, was left to TV stars and other people who were enthusiastic about showing off. Berlusconi bridged the gap between the two groups, the politicians and the entertainers, perfectly.

What has been said so far, and the many other examples that I have not mentioned here, as they would need another book focusing exclusively on them, transformed the life in Costa Smeralda radically. The place became a sort of dreamland obsessively represented by the media as being a place where rich and beautiful people spent their time in a sort of temporal suspension. The tourists going to it principally aimed to see those celebrities. In those years, the term "bird watching," meaning going to places to see birds in their natural environment, in Costa Smeralda became "VIP watching," and referred to the many tourists going around those 55 kilometers in search of actors, TV stars, reality contestants, etc. in their "natural" environment, that is, in Costa Smeralda.

This links to Barthes's conception of denotation and connotation. In the 1990s and 2000s' Costa Smeralda, there was a denotative level comprising parties and scandals, photographs of the tycoon with many girls in the garden of Villa Certosa, and even the Prime Minister of Czech Republic naked among a group of girls. This was connected to the fact that Berlusconi set up his life for about four months a year there. With him there also were many of his collaborators, the actors and actresses working on his TV channels, friends, etc., who moved there to stay with him for the same period.

All these people together implied precise lifestyles, points of view, conceptions, and mindsets. All of this composed the connotative level of Costa Smeralda, a philosophical stance that ended up Berlusconizing Costa Smeralda. Costa Smeralda became something else because it assumed the characteristic, spirit, and nature of what formed Berlusconi's mentality. The tourist destination was briefly transformed into Berlusconi's summertime world, exactly as his TV channels were a kind of representation of his imaginary. Not only did the Italian Prime Minister live according to his way, but he also had the ability to give form to what was around him, and this happened to an entire television aesthetic and a whole tourist destination for about fifteen years. This further Berlusconist influence on Costa Smeralda may be considered the connotative level of the phenomenon that was represented in the media almost every day, which was the denotative one.

From Modernism to Postmodernism

The columnist Pierluigi Battista (2008) defined the shift from the old to the new Costa Smeralda's lifestyle as "the postmodernist scare to good taste." Following from this, we may say that in those years, in Costa Smeralda modernism gave space to postmodernism. Costa Smeralda's hyperreal map, to go back to Baudrillard, became the perfect representation of the ideology of illusion. The system activated a media chain that is worth investigating. Firstly, on TV, ordinary people were allowed to access the jet-set thanks to reality and talent shows, becoming somehow "famous;" secondly, in Costa Smeralda, these people became a model for the new class of wannabe rich people produced by the new postmodern society. This class of wannabe rich people became the new class of tourists in Costa Smeralda.

Costa Smeralda thus became an extension of TV entertainment, with formerly ordinary people turned into VIPs by TV, and tourists assaulting the beaches once frequented by the old inaccessible class. More relevantly, Costa Smeralda also became a place full of discotheques, which marked a big change in comparison to the past, when discotheques were just a few and less invasive. This was however the new style of the tourist destination, perfectly mirroring the new dominating class.

This new map exactly represented what Baudrillard said, as it was entirely formed by people and lifestyles pertaining to the media. Without the media, this version of Costa Smeralda would not exist. This perfectly explains why the Sardinians also at this stage continued to say that Costa Smeralda was not a Sardinian place.

Socially, the new class was totally accessible, different from the previous lot. The success of the new industry was in fact based on the promise that everyone might become popular thanks to TV, and Costa Smeralda became a part of the media system and of this promise. This also explains the obsession to appear there and show off. Appearing and showing off were the hidden engine of the system. The more people in Costa Smeralda appeared in magazines and on TV channels, the more the ideology of illusion could work and seduce the growing crowd of wannabe aspirants.

When Berlusconi became Prime Minister, the sale of that ideology widened and also covered politics. Interestingly, Costa Smeralda also became the place where the new links between politics and entertainment were evident. The image of Silvio Berlusconi, sun-tanned and wearing a bandana, welcoming the Blairs in 2004, is the perfect image if one wants to understand Costa Smeralda in those years.

Politics and trash, high and low culture, the king and the court jester will never be so close to each other, so intrinsically bound, and sometimes so played by the same actor. The lifestyle in Berlusconized Costa Smeralda crowned a new dominant class, which remained in charge and went on partying and having fun deciding the new rules of the Sardinian tourist destination. Whatever idea one may have of the Aga Khan and his idea of that place, it becomes apparent that Berlusconi's was its opposite.

Conclusion

The most important finding in this chapter is that when it comes to talking about Costa Smeralda, we cannot be sure about anything. We had seen Prince Karim realizing his romantic dream of a tourist destination where buildings never dis-turbed nature and where the beauty of the place would be safeguarded. Phase 2, presented by the Prince to the Italian and Sardinian politicians to be approved, actually subverted all of this, prefiguring pouring concrete into one of the most beautiful places in the world. What the matter was with the Aga Khan we do not know. Certainly business, but I must also remind the reader that the approval of Phase 2 would have killed Costa Smeralda as a special place and also menaced, consequently, its business as a unique, exclusive place destined for a very high class of tourists.

The arrival of Tom Barrack, the "imperialist" American entrepreneur, owner of global chains of hotels certainly not famous for safeguarding nature and, even worse, Donald Trump's supporter and friend, would mean, in simple terms, the final destruction of the place. Instead, Barrack's management of Costa Smeralda, in its first stage, never touched the Aga Khan's primordial model, leaving the place as respecting nature and not playing with it. Later, Barrack also tried a sort of Phase 2 and was thankfully stopped again by the Italian politicians.

After a period of uncertainty, Berlusconi's earthquake changed everything. This could happen because what changed was the narrator, the storyteller of Costa Smeralda. The Aga Khan left as owner and narrator of his romantic dream and Silvio Berlusconi replaced him, telling a totally different story.

The first watchword was "showing off." What I have called the ideology of illusion needed people to appear in the media while they had fun in Costa Smeralda. If the Aga Khan's model was based on the idea of disappearing from the media, Berlusconi's was centered on obsessively being there. Not (only) Berlusconi in person, obviously: the visibility concerned those working (and again appearing) on his TV channels, his political collaborators, and people revolving around his activities. Television was in charge of the first step, allowing unknown people to become famous thanks to reality and talent shows; however, Costa Smeralda was fundamental in the second stage of the process, welcoming those new celebrities and transforming them into models to be followed by the many wannabe rich and famous people who read or watched the many media images of the dolce vita in Costa Smeralda in the entire country and abroad.

So, while the Aga Khan's model was centripetal, aiming to save the inner space from the external one, Berlusconi's model of Costa Smeralda was centrifugal, wanting to spread the message to a massive public to sell, not rooms in the Sardinian hotels (too expensive), but ideology and visibility, the most precious material for a politician. The new tourists in fact, as some studies found, stayed in hotels outside Costa Smeralda and used to come in just to see the VIPs.

In this sense, I have said that Berlusconi branded Costa Smeralda. He conferred on the entire territory of the tourist destination his influence, his way of living, and his perspective well beyond politics and his persona. For about fifteen years, Costa Smeralda became the place where Berlusconism took root and triumphed. The combination of entertainment and politics, the centrality of the leader, and the destruction of any formal rule were elements of Berlusconi's politics that became concrete matters in Villa Certosa and nearby.

In this period Costa Smeralda was thus, again, a laboratory. Its history, however, has not finished yet. Not by chance, the next chapter (spoiler) has a new twist regarding its property, even though at present no storyteller is saying to us what will be its destiny.

CHAPTER 7

Costa Smeralda Today and Tomorrow

Introduction

I like it when a history book talks about the past of "X" (an event, people, places, etc.) and in the last chapter it focuses on the present and the future of that "X." At that point, the readers should know enough about the past of the given topic and I find it fascinating that the author offers them a fast overflight over what is happening now and finally a pleasant interpretive dive into the future, hazarding a guess about what might happen tomorrow. Some topics do not offer this opportunity (Punic Wars does not have a present or a future), but books on cultural history very often do. Costa Smeralda meaningfully allows the author to do it. So this last chapter delves into Costa Smeralda's present (which is quite empty and in search of novelties) and future (which actually appears in the form of a big question mark).

However, the first section of the chapter seems to be in line with the previous parts of the book. Again, I dwell on the changes relative to Costa Smeralda's ownership. Tom Barrack's possession of the Sardinian tourist destination only lasted a few years, and sincerely without any big change, for good or for bad. A new owner appears and he reminds many people of the first one, the creator of the universe of Costa Smeralda, the Aga Khan. The Emir of Qatar, who bought Costa Smeralda in a short time, is in fact, like Prince Karim, one of the richest people in the world and hails from the Arab world. The two elements are not so remarkable, actually, but in needy times they were enough to make some people hope that another golden age was ready for northeast Sardinia. So far, however, hope has remained hope.

As a result, Costa Smeralda today is in a state of suspension. Thankfully, the media sometimes manage to explain something better than mere language can.

This chapter thus analyzes Enrico Lucci's documentary, which exactly shows this state of suspension in this territory, between a concluded era, the Berlusconian one, and an unknown future.

The second part of the chapter is a bet. I have selected the main future trends in tourism and have tried to see which of them may fit into Costa Smeralda. Surprisingly, many of my questions have got positive responses: Costa Smeralda seems to be perfect to play a relevant role even in the future of tourism. Some adjustments are needed, however. Thus, I see in practice which strategies could be adopted and how, and advise the hypothetical tour operators reading this book on what might be done. I hope that this will not be considered presumptuous. I believe that research should contain suggestions for people working practically in the field, and the last part of this chapter exactly does this.

The Last Twist so Far: Qatar

In 2012, Tom Barrack's Colony Capital sold for 360 million euros, the entire possession of Costa Smeralda to some financial companies that, through Italy, Luxembourg, and The Netherlands, led to Qatar Holding, a company controlled by the Emir of Qatar, Hamad bin Kalifa Al Thani (Pinna 2013). Several infrastructures constituting the core of Costa Smeralda, that is, all the properties that Barrack had bought from the Aga Khan, including 2,400 hectares of land, various hotels, the entire Porto Cervo Marina with 700 moorings, villas, houses, the Pevero Golf Club, and many other properties, passed to a new owner.

For Costa Smeralda, it was another change. Perhaps it is worth briefly summing up the history of its possessors: Costa Smeralda was founded by the Aga Khan; in 1994 it was sold to Sheraton Hotels; in 2003, it was acquired by Tom Barrack via Starwood; and finally the territory was bought by the Emir of Qatar in 2012 (Ferraino 2012).

What persuaded Barrack to sell Costa Smeralda was the same reason that pushed Prince Karim to leave. As reported by Ferraino (2012), Barrack said that he loved Sardinia, but that the Sardinian and Italian politicians were preventing him from investing more money, so the best decision would be to transfer his business elsewhere.

Al Thani is a huge investor in European and Western businesses. He owns great parts of companies such as Barclays, Sainsbury's, Harrods, the London Stock Exchange, Volkswagen, Walt Disney, Heathrow Airport, Siemens, Royal

Dutch Shell, and the Shard London Bridge building (the highest in Europe). His financial fund, valued at 600 billion dollars, also owns the French football team Paris Saint-Germain, and supports the Italian one A.S. Roma; also the development plan of Porta Nuova and the prestigious Hotel Gallia in Milan are among the most important assets of the fund (Ferraino 2012).

The Emir of Qatar was considered by some as a kind of reincarnation of the Aga Khan, the new savior of an enterprise that had lost its identity in a changing world. Pinna (2012) focuses on the never-interrupted link between Costa Smeralda and the Arab world. In the beginning was the Aga Khan, who invented Costa Smeralda among London's investors and the skepticism of the Sardinians, and left because of the obstacles lifted by the Sardinian and Italian politicians against Phase 2. Later, at the end of the 1960s, Sheik Zaki Yamani, a very powerful Minister of Oil in Saudi Arabia, bought a luxury villa in Romazzino, which he transformed into a sort of bunker: there were cameras every 10 meters, sensors and alarms scattered over the entire park, an operative room like in a James Bond's film, and other measures that became legendary among the locals.

From the villa, Yamani managed contacts and businesses between Europe and the Middle East; sometimes, he met the billionaire Rafiq Hariri, another Arab recurring habitué of Costa Smeralda, whose yachts, Nara and Marana, were frequently anchored in Cala di Volpe as a symbol of his presence (Pinna 2012). Hariri became Lebanon's Prime Minister from 1992 to 1998 and from 2000 to 2004, and was killed by a car bomb in 2005.

Muammar Gaddafi, who ruled in Libya from 1969 to 2011, was never directly linked to Costa Smeralda, but his sons enjoyed their holidays in the Sardinian tourist destination, with some problems: Saadi Gaddafi was kicked out of Briatore's restaurant The Billionaire because he and his numerous friends tried to jump the queue to enter the restaurant; another of Gaddafi's sons, Moutassan, became famous for the money he spent in Costa Smeralda, around 20,000 euros a day only for wines, and for some problems that his security staff caused to journalists and photographers (Pinna 2011). Finally, even the last Costa Smeralda owner before the Qatar twist, Tom Barrack, may be considered a part of this Arab link, being of Lebanese origins, as his grandparents were Lebanese Christians who emigrated to the US.

Qatar's possession of Costa Smeralda has thus been considered the last stage of a long series of Arab interests in the area, and certainly the Emir Al Thani has been associated with the Aga Khan essentially for his wealth. However, we have to say that both Al Thani and Qatar Holding have done nothing to support the association with the Aga Khan. No plans have been developed or promoted, no statement has been made to explain what the future of Costa Smeralda might be, apart from some formal declaration, and no new rule has been established.

The Aga Khan, in the meantime, completed his detachment from Costa Smeralda. When Al Thani was already in charge of the Consortium, Prince Karim made the last journey back to finish dealing with any remaining interests in Costa Smeralda and be rid of them forever. Just the Olbia airport, in fact, remained in the hands of the founder, Prince Karim. He kept it as a symbol of his past life, his last link to Sardinia. In 2020, the Aga Khan sold it to the fund F2i, already in charge of the airports of Alghero in Sardinia and of Milan, Naples, Turin, Trieste, Bologna, and Bergamo in Italy.

Paradoxically, the reports on the sale of the airport had in Italy much more resonance than the sale of the entire Costa Smeralda eight years before. Newspapers, magazines, and TV news focused on the fact that the Aga Khan was abandoning Costa Smeralda forever. This occurred eight years earlier, but the fact that Prince Karim had kept the airport was frequently seen by his supporters as a signal of his wish to remain somehow attached to northeast Sardinia and of hope for his possible return. Any hope died when the news that Prince Karim sold his part of the company Geasar (80%) to F2i, a company worth 5 billion euros (Sechi 2020a, 2020b), was released.

This piece of news was seen as the end of an adventure lasting sixty years. Sechi (2020a, 2020b) acknowledges that Costa Smeralda has lost the person who for long tome owned it and controlled its development and advances that selling the airport to a company extraneous to Qatar does not discharge the Emir Al Thani from liability. For the airport, the referent will be F2i. However, Costa Smeralda has more important problems and the Emir Al Thani is the person who has to be brought into play to solve them. Thus, the Qatar Investments Authority, and specifically its Italian branch Smeralda Holding, must be considered the referents for the answers that people working or living in Costa Smeralda are waiting for (Sechi 2020a, 2020b).

Sechi (2020a, 2020b) explains the sentiment of the Sardinians working in Costa Smeralda and feeling unsure about the future. The fear of this conclusive sale, the article says, was linked to the centrality of Prince Karim. The Aga Khan was not only the inventor of Costa Smeralda, but also the person who had invented the dream of that place, a dream together romantic, tourist-led, and commercial; the narrator of the island of an island, as I have defined him in this book. After many disappointing events, the fact that he had decided to leave to capitalize on his investments was felt by some as worrying.

Meaningfully, Sechi (2020a, 2020b) says that that in Costa Smeralda other people, other people optimistically think that this is not true, that Prince Karim would remain anchored to Costa Smeralda in some way in any case. He has done good business by selling the airport, they say, but he has sold it to a solid company that has great expertise in managing this business and this can be good for the Sardinian future (Sechi 2020a, 2020b). Dreams never end, we could say. Prince Karim, after more than sixty years, is still seen by many people as an irreplaceable element of Costa Smeralda, even though he left in 1994. The creator has left an indelible mark alongside those 55 kilometers of beautiful beaches. Each new Baudrillard's map that has been added to the territory still contains his imprint, every time less visible but however present and recognized by many people.

For the optimists, the demonstration of the Aga Khan's presence in Costa Smeralda, after having sold every asset he owned in the area, was his yacht Alamshar, still anchored in the bay of Porto Cervo in the summer of 2020. He inaugurated the tourist season as in the good old days, and the fact that he did it even in the middle of the COVID-19 emergence was interpreted as a sign of resistance and proximity to Sardinia. In fact, as the COVID-19 regulations allowed travelling, tourists gradually came back to Costa Smeralda (Sechi 2020a, 2020b). However, we must say that the real situation in today's Costa Smeralda is different, as a documentary shows.

Today's Costa Smeralda and Enrico Lucci

While I was preparing this chapter, trying to understand today's Costa Smeralda, I noticed that I was paying much attention to events and issues relating to the ownership of the island on an island and that this was taking some more pages than I had expected. The fact is that the changes in ownership have had strong repercussions on the cultural and social aspects related to this tourist destination. It is difficult to understand what the effect and what the cause was, whether the ownership or the tourism culture came first, but undoubtedly Prince Karim's Costa Smeralda was complementary to the architectural style and the tourists of those years; and that ownership and culture went hand in hand even in Tom Barrack's Costa Smeralda, a place perfectly expressed by Berlusconism, its standpoints, and lifestyle. Closely related to this, we see that today, Costa Smeralda has changed again. Or, at least, has abandoned the past but has not found its future yet. It has an owner, but not a style or a precise identity.

No one has caught this suspended status better than the journalist and satyrical author Enrico Lucci, who in 2018 dedicated the first three episodes of his program *Realiti Sciò: Siamo tutti protagonisti*, (reality show, we are all protagonists) (Monoscoppio TV 2018a, 2018b, 2018c) to Costa Smeralda after Berlusconi. In presenting the episodes, Lucci clearly said that they show "the definitive end of the Berlusconian age" (Grasso 2018).

Lucci's account is so neat, meaningful, and direct that it is worth recounting its entire contents. The first two parts of the documentary are devoted to the interviews of Emilio Fede and Lele Mora after the end of the Berlusconian age in Costa Smeralda and in Italian politics in general. The two interviews have to be contextualized in relation to Berlusconi's political trajectory. To sum up the steps of the end of Berlusconism, we can say that Berlusconi's last government stepped down in 2011. In 2013, the ex-Prime Minister was sentenced to four years in jail for fiscal fraud. Three years were canceled by the pardon and the remaining year was turned into ten months of social service to be carried out at the social cooperative *Sacra Famiglia* (holy family) in Cesano Boscone, near Milan, until March 2014 (Ansa 2015). The condemnation also led to Berlusconi's expulsion from the Parliament (Rai News 2018).

In this scenario, Fede and Mora, due in part to the many judicial investigations into both of them and many others of the group, lost contact with Berlusconi and with each other, while some personal contrasts emerged. Thus, Lucci's interviews try to clarify the status of the relationships among them and, first of all, to satirically underline the sense of the good old days lost forever.

Fede is interviewed at his home (Monoscoppio TV 2018a), where he lives alone aged 87, among medicines and sanitary equipment just in case he needs it. It is the same house where Fede paid his bills with justice for four years, for promoting prostitution. Due to his age and his health condition, he in fact did not go to jail but was condemned to house arrest.

Fede is shown to hold a grudge against all those people who benefited from him when he was powerful and who later abandoned him. In his twenty-four years of work with Berlusconi, he says, he only had a couple of days of holidays, but he was happy with it, because he loved that job. He was always with Berlusconi: during the day at his TV channels, as the director of the news; in the evenings, having dinner and parties with Berlusconi. Now, he says, all of this has ceased forever.

In March 2013, Fede was fired by Berlusconi's TV channels in thirty seconds, as he says, and he has never known why. The episode is meaningfully titled "The

Friend of the King," and Fede explains his almost religious faith in Berlusconi. In the documentary, he is frequently represented walking unsteadily at home, or in pitiless foregrounds that show his face marked by age. In the final part of the episode, where Fede is sadly the guest of a local TV channel, the old days appear to be lost forever.

In the second episode (Monoscoppio TV 2018b), titled "The Other Friend of the King," Lucci interviews Lele Mora, who is about to go back to Olbia to restart Costa Smeralda and reestablish the good old days; at least, this is what he says. Mora settled his bills related to justice: he was sentenced to four years and three months imprisonment for fraudulent bankruptcy and was also convicted of promoting prostitution; that is why he served in prison and at the social services, in total for seven years, as he says in the interview.

Mora immediately complains about the old friends who abandoned him. Berlusconi is the first on the list, as he disappeared when Mora was involved in the Ruby scandal. Ruby was a 17-year-old girl suspected to be part of the famous "bunga bunga" parties organized by trouble managers to please Berlusconi with prostitutes. Mora says that he has been absent from Costa Smeralda for ten years; now it is time to go back, as many people will be interested in his coming back, he concludes.

Lucci and Mora go together to Costa Smeralda. For many years, Mora used to travel in his private jet and, in the interview, he confesses that he has never queued up to get a flight. Fruitfully for this book, during the interview, Mora explains how Costa Smeralda worked in those days. People went to Costa Smeralda to see the celebrities that he took to the island; in other words, to participate in the big, long-lasting show that Mora created in that tourist destination. Mora repeats many times that he "made" Costa Smeralda.

They go to one of the villas owned by Mora in those years. As with the jet and the other houses, it was confiscated and sold again at auction. Mora is moved when he sees the garden from the street. In the end, they meet the new landlady, who says that the villa is really beautiful, and this makes Mora even sadder. He also tells Lucci that in the "golden days," the tourist tours used to stop in front of the house and that the guide explained to tourists that they were in front of Lele Mora's house. They frequently rang the bell and if Mora was in, they were let in to visit the villa.

In Porto Cervo, Lucci and Mora meet a couple: they say that they are there to see celebrities, but that there are no VIPs in Costa Smeralda anymore. Mora is encouraged to restart "his" Costa Smeralda again. Other people miss Lele Mora

in Porto Cervo and say that only he can relaunch that place. Lucci and Mora
go around Costa Smeralda where other people, especially hotel and restaurant
managers and entrepreneurs, complain that there are only a few tourists, while
the celebrities have disappeared.

In the third and final episode (Monoscoppio TV 2018c), named "The Historic
Reconciliation," Lucci makes Fede and Mora meet again after many years. He
brings Mora from the hotel where he stays to a beach, where Fede has been
brought by another journalist. The two are masked: Fede wears the mask of a
horse, as he was "the race horse of Italian journalism;" and Mora has the mask
of a lion on, as he was "the lion of Costa Smeralda." When they pull their masks
off, they see and hug each other. Lucci wears Berlusconi's mask and hugs the
two, saying that Costa Smeralda is alive again. Fede says that Berlusconi's Villa
Certosa is not far from there, and finds this meaningful, so the three sing together
a song dedicated to Berlusconi. Mora also says that he has decided to cancel an
old story that generated enmity between him and Fede, because of an amount of
money given by Berlusconi to Mora and partially subtracted by Fede.

The two ex-friends of Berlusconi remember the good old days and all the good
work they did together. Fede frequently says that Mora made him earn a lot of
money legally. Lucci asks the two if all the legal investigations, the trials, and
the convictions were invented by the judges, and they answer, a bit embarrassed,
that the judges exaggerated the outcomes of those investigations.

Fede mentions mythological accounts about Villa Certosa: he remembers an
island in the middle of the artificial lake, where Berlusconi's favorite guitarist,
Mariano Apicella, played his guitar and sang during parties, with famous guests
participating in them. In the end, they say that Villa Certosa cannot be described
if one has never seen it. Thus, Lucci takes both to Villa Certosa.

Fede and Mora are moved while following the same road they have traveled
on many times in the past, when they were full of joy and emotions. They arrive
at the gate and Fede refuses to get out of the car, as he does not want to come
back to the place where he spent so many good moments and is frightened by
the arrival of the police. Lucci and Mora go to the gate, ring the bell, and a man's
voice says that Berlusconi is not in and that they cannot enter the villa. This is
the final scene of the series.

The three episodes rely on the contrast between Lucci's irony and Fede
and Mora's sincere nostalgia for the Berlusconian era. Lucci humanizes the
two protagonists by representing them as two losers who once were winners.
The documentary splits the verbal and the visual modes. The verbal mode is

the ironic one, thanks to what Lucci says and to the involuntary ironic effects that Mora and Fede's words carry with them. Lucci's account risks becoming too sad and some verbal aspects convey humor, as when Fede is continually accused by the other two of having resorted to Botox to make his face younger. The visual mode, conversely, is deeply sad. It shows Fede and Mora walking unsteadily, tired after walking, and wearing ridiculous clothes when they go to bed. While the verbal mode shows Mora and Lucci accusing Fede of being full of botox, the visual one shows Fede's face irremediably, and comprehensively, marked by age. The two ex-friends of Berlusconi are visually constructed as two old people full of memories and illusions, who try to reconstitute the past nostalgically and sadly fail.

This sad atmosphere also involves Costa Smeralda, which cannot have a verbal mode and only relies on the visual one. The island on an island is seen as almost empty, with only a few tourists who do not find what they are looking for. The beauty of the places remains hidden; Lucci's episodes never show it. The sad visual mode also shows the place where the two old men remember their past. In the documentary, Costa Smeralda is thus shown to be as sad a place as its old ex-protagonists. It is not able to satisfy the tourists as it did in the past under both the Aga Khan and Berlusconism. Many scenes are filmed in silent places, where nobody, or just one person, passes. The beaches where Lucci takes the two protagonists are empty. Visually, the documentary shows a universe where the past greatness is now lost.

Today's Costa Smeralda and the Social Media

What is important about this series is that, thanks to its narrative strategy, it has perfectly caught the suspended status of Costa Smeralda today. At present, in fact, Costa Smeralda has lost its appeal. All the previous stages, among which were unawareness, hope, enthusiasm, inaccessibility, and showing off, had given the island on an island a precise identity, but they disappeared from the entire area after their successful seasons. Costa Smeralda seems a wonderful leftover of the previous ages, stubbornly immutable. The old classes that ruled in it do not exist anymore and the economic crisis has reduced its incomes. Its detachment from the real world is today inconceivable. At present, no public bus takes people to Costa Smeralda from the nearby cities and towns. Sardinians continue to refer to it as a non-Sardinian place.

The last dominant group, the Berlusconians, have gone away quite abruptly, just like the first one, the Aga Khan. However, when the first group disappeared, the Berlusconians took over in a short time. Now that the Berlusconian era is over, it is not clear what Costa Smeralda will be shortly and no new group appears to be about to conquer the field. At the moment, as Lucci demonstrates, everything is in a suspended status, between what Costa Smeralda was and its uncertain future.

What is sure is that Lele Mora's dream to restart "his" Costa Smeralda, as it emerged in the TV series, is just a dream. It is only nostalgia, understandably experienced by one of the protagonists of that era and coveted by those who enjoyed those years. As for the Aga Khan, the storyteller of the last stage has gone, and the same story cannot be told by another voice.

Tourism is culture and culture is always in a state of flux; it continually changes to adhere to new trends and values, to merge with new influences, and to mix tradition and novelty. Why should it be different in Costa Smeralda? Exactly like the first Costa Smeralda was replaced by the second one, the second will be replaced by the third, and so on. The problem is that nobody, at the moment, sees this third one.

An interesting way of having a finger on the pulse of the situation is to look at social media and the internet in general. It is in those virtual places that one may see the most widespread approaches to a given theme. Costa Smeralda is not an exception, as it is a hot topic in the virtual realm and very often splits opinions into two.

What emerges at first sight is that blogs, forums, and social media accounts talking about Costa Smeralda principally can be divided into two groups: the first one contains posts and comments where people nostalgically remember the good old days in Costa Smeralda, where the atmosphere was refined and exclusive and everything went well among well-educated and charming tourists; the second group of posts and comments revolves around the idea that Costa Smeralda is not a part of Sardinia, but is a kind of foreign object that someone (usually first the Aga Khan, later Berlusconi) has inserted in it.

About the first group, on Facebook, more than four thousand people participate in the group *I professionisti della Costa Smeralda di ieri e di oggi* (Costa Smeralda's professionals yesterday and today), (Facebook 2024a), where yesterday seems more relevant than today. The image of the group is a photo of the Aga Khan, and many posts regard the glorious past of the place. In various announcements, the administrator gives the news of the death of the people who worked in Costa Smeralda's hotels and restaurants many years ago, and the comments frequently concern the past, even when the post is related to the present.

On this page, a photograph of Porto Cervo taken in 1968 unchains memories and nostalgic accounts. Someone remembers when he was 14 and used to dive from the bridge to get money from the tourists; someone else recalls his first kiss, and others their work in the kitchens of a closed restaurant or hotel. Interestingly, the Berlusconian period is ignored by those participating in this social media trend. All the people in the group remember episodes well before the 1990s, meaningfully. Similarly, on both Instagram and Facebook, the page *Sardegna mia* (My Sardinia), which has about two hundred ten thousand followers, publishes photos of many enchanting beaches from around the whole of Sardinia, but when they represent Costa Smeralda, the comments about the past are more than those regarding the present. An image of the beach of Capriccioli, for example, again produces memories from the 1970s and 1980s, young loves and adolescent memories occurring in those decades (Facebook 2024b).

As regards the second group that debates whether Costa Smeralda belongs to Sardinia, the writer and blogger Claudia Zedda (2024) serenely explains in a post why Costa Smeralda is not to be considered as a part of Sardinia. She delves into the fact that nothing is spontaneous and authentic there and confesses that the two times she was there, she simply did not feel at home. Zedda is a writer who bases her books on Sardinia and thus is an expert and lover of the island. For this reason, her words assume great importance and explain the sentiment of many Sardinians who write similar things on social media (TripAdvisor 2011).

I could go on reporting posts assuming this view, but it is probably more interesting to refer to a post written on Facebook by the most famous Italian children's writer, Bianca Pitzorno, who is also Sardinian. On her page, Pitzorno published the cover of a book on Costa Smeralda, also writing: "This is not Sardinia. This is not enchanting. It is a nightmare, what a shame" (Zasso 2022).

A 30-year-old woman, Federica Ulliana, replied to the post: "I grew up in Porto Cervo. Since I have had memory, in Sardinia this is a stigma that you have to keep with you for your entire life. An original sin as you are not enough an island person to be considered Sardinian and at the same time you are not enough alien to be considered a mainland person" (Zasso 2022). Ulliana showed her disappointment, as she loved Pitzorno as a writer. Despite this, she goes on.

> I am really sorry that many Sardinians can only see the shining part of Summer luxury, and incidentally, everyone is free to spend their money as they want. However, how simplistic to judge a place, an object, or a person, just for one of their many facets is. To me, Porto Cervo is many things: it is Summer, Winter,

chaos and silence, total solitude, the trees bending to the wind and touching the land, the rocks you can lie on to see the stars while humidity emerges from the sea. The scent of the Mediterranean scrub, sun, mold and wetland. It is home. So, I ask: what kind of good things will this fury against Porto Cervo, my home, take to your lives?

The comment became viral and the discussion went on for months, but without any actual change in the two standpoints.

Relevantly, both the post and the comment perfectly summarize the spirit of this feeling and the real problem that Costa Smeralda has brought to Sardinia in general: the fracture between the island and the island on an island. This should be added to the first problem discussed in this section about social media—nostalgia. It is evident that the scenario is static and does not allow for change and innovation.

Despite all of this, some small signals are emerging and thus this chapter wants to briefly analyze what could happen to Costa Smeralda according to the new trends that tourism has shown all over the world in the last few years.

As a result, what I will do below is match what Costa Smeralda can offer to tourists and these trends. Can these matches produce something interesting? May Costa Smeralda find a new way, without betraying its history of being an exclusive destination and at the same time adjourning its identity? If there are positive questions, we might see in them the future of this tourist destination.

To start this last part of the chapter, in the next section, I will develop the main new trends in terms of tourism that can be of interest to "the island on an island." We will start from the three broad tourism categories that are gradually becoming of paramount relevance when it comes to talking about the future of hospitality and leisure: cultural, experiential, and sustainable tourism.

The New Trends in Tourism

The Big Umbrella: Cultural, Experiential and Sustainable Tourism

Many scholars agree that if we want to understand the new trends in tourism, we must look at the categories of cultural, experiential, and sustainable tourism. These are three big containers where it is possible to find many things. However, before focusing on something more specific, it is worth briefly reviewing these three concepts.

Cultural tourism is broadly meant as a form of tourism where visitors learn something. According to Trono (2014), it may be included in the broader category of active tourism, a type of tourism where those who travel want to be active. This activity can be physical, with the tourists asking for sport, adventures, etc.; but it may also be mental, with people requiring trips where they learn something about the history, culture, religion, or other aspects of a specific place. Fjagesund and Symes (2002) find that cultural tourism starts with the *Grand Tour*, the tourist experience of the Nordic elites visiting southern Europe in the nineteenth century. Picard (1996) points out that this model became massive in the twentieth century but mostly lost its cultural aims.

Richards (2001) explains how this kind of tourism has returned as a protagonist in the twenty-first century. He relies on Urry's (1992) seminal study on the postmodern tourist, to assume that "tourism is culture" (Richards 2001, 4), concluding that tourism in the postmodern era is gradually losing its massive character to become the result of individual choices.

The move of tourism from sightseeing to culture is also underlined by Burns and Holden (1995, 208), who focus on the new aim of tourism: "Giving new meaning and values to social order." All of this, added to globalization, leads to the fact that people "travel to cultural centers in many parts of the world. These social narratives may be expressed through diverse typologies of culture that reflect the consumptive trends of globalization and internationalization" (Griffin et al. 2014, 4).

In 2009, a report of the OECD (2009) found that about 40 percent of tourism choices were influenced by culture and that the phenomenon was growing. According to recent research, between 2023 and 2027, cultural tourism will grow by 17.32 percent (Technavio 2024). One of the major factors encouraging it is the search for identity and differentiation in times of globalization. Other factors are the rise of the importance of cultural capital, produced by higher levels of education; the higher age of tourists; postmodernity's focus on individual growth; the growing relevance of intangible culture and atmosphere, the rising awareness and interest in famous monuments; the ease of travel; and finally the importance of having experiences during a trip.

This last point has expanded in the 2000s, to the extent that today, experiential tourism is one of the major new trends in the field. Scott et al. (2010) see experiential tourism as a part of the broader experience economy, which according to Van Boven and Gilovich (2003, 1193), is the trend that gives "a considerable portion of our resources to the pursuit of the good life—one of contentment, pleasure, and happiness." Thus, experiences acquire great relevance in people's consumption (Erdly and Kesterson-Townes 2003), while the media create new desires and new technologies accelerate the process of purchasing.

If the entire economy encourages the consumption of "fantasies, feelings and fun" (Holbrook and Hirschman 1982, 132), it is evident that tourism may play a relevant role in it. Scott et al. (2010) see two degrees of experiential tours: the first is when tourists look for experiences while on a trip and find it in a quite spontaneous way; the second occurs when the experience is somehow marketed and staged, designed by the tourist and the organizer, who cooperate in a win-win situation.

Finally, implied in cultural and experiential tourism, there is the new trend of sustainable tourism. Sustainability is, in fact, connected to many cultural and experiential activities that we discuss here. Awareness of the environmental problems and a wish to solve them constitute a kind of background approach permeating curiosity, passion for activity, the will to know, and the other sentiments populating the new trends that we have mentioned above.

To conclude, cultural, experiential, and sustainable tourism are three good points from which to start. However, as mentioned at the beginning of this section, they are also three very broad concepts. Before entering the field of what Costa Smeralda can do to adapt to the new trends, it is necessary to examine more in depth and concretely what these new trends can produce in terms of practice, that is, itineraries, trips, activities, and so on.

A Deeper Insight

De Jong (2024) has summarized the most important new activities that will affect tourism in the next years. Some of them cannot be associated with Costa Smeralda, as the search for places having cool weather in summer, which today are considered valuable because of global warming. Other trends, conversely, could be of interest for the tourist destination we are analyzing in this book, because it seems that high quality is still popular among the higher-middle class and that Costa Smeralda may play a role in it. Even though salaries do not grow as the same level of inflation, people still like luxury and this can be a positive occurrence for a place that was originally designed to welcome exclusive tourists.

Increased growth for shoulder seasons: This is not a very new trend; however, De Jong (2024) points out that it is growing at a fast pace. Global warming, mounting expenses, and crowded destinations are serious issues that have threatened tourism for the last twenty years. De Jong (2024) advances that people traveling out of high season solve all of them successfully. What to do, for the interested entrepreneurs, is to find forms of attraction that can be appealing for the entire year. Adapting what one already has developed or creating new itineraries that present points of interest valid for twelve months a year is the main required effort.

Nature is seasonal. If people want to stay on the beach, they will certainly travel in summer. However, De Jong (2022) underlines that some assets can expand the tourist season of a destination: "Local heritage and traditions; cultural events or festivals; local cuisine connected to the various seasons; outdoor experiences in different periods." The strategy to adopt in this case is to make the tourist experience longer and to involve tourists even during months that are not traditionally considered mainstream by the tourist industry.

Moreover, new emerging targets such as digital nomads are changing the concept of tourism and should be considered, as they are not tourists in the traditional sense but also stay at the same destination out of high season. Children making school trips are another target group very often traveling outside of the standard season.

Low-carbon adventure travel: Many people, and thus tourists, are becoming more and more aware of the problems linked to carbon footprints, which menace the future of our planet. As a result, tourist experiences and activities that do not produce emissions are becoming popular among this target segment. Activities such as hiking, cycling, kayaking, trekking, rock climbing, scuba diving, and snorkeling may be considered the main options to offer to them.

For De Jong (2024), strategies in this field involve reducing carbon emissions in already existing itineraries, developing new low or no-emission experiences, and communicating it, to engage the more concerned. For an entrepreneur, there are various advantages: (1) offering a deeper experience to the tourists, as slow traveling helps in exploring and understanding the locals; (2) lowering expenses, as such activities mean lower or no costs of fuel and maintaining canoes and bikes is less expensive than maintaining cars or motorboats; (3) not disturbing wildlife and thus increasing the possibility of watching animals from further up close; (4) stimulating the local economy, as visitors can reach places off the traditional tourist path.

Food culture may be of help in this field. Walking food tours have no emissions, connect to the territory, and encourage relationships between tourists and locals, who also financially benefit from this kind of itinerary. Bike tours, in cities or countryside, silent whale watching voyages, and slow travel in general are other potential strategies that have the potential to fascinate tourists without polluting the planet.

Calmcation is a combination of the words "calm" and "vacation." According to research cited by De Jong (2024), about 70 percent of tourists travel to find relaxation and a slower rhythm in their everyday lives. The COVID-19 pandemic has stressed our lives more than any other emergence in the last ten years and has thus accelerated this process, encouraging serene vacations. Nature seems to be the context that helps people find this desired break, more than any other.

This form of tourism may occur with different variables. The first is the cost: there are extremely expensive campings with tents that are more organized and equipped than five-star hotels, but also cheaper forms of camping and solutions for tourists who cannot afford luxury holidays. What is important is to make tourists forget their lives, work, office, family issues, etc., and transport them to a calm, silent place where they can recharge their inner batteries.

Culinary tourism: According to various studies, in 2006, about 40 percent of the US population traveled because they were attracted by the food of a place abroad. In 2013, this rose to 60 percent and in 2020, almost 80 percent. People become tourists even to eat new foods, and this element cannot be ignored when we talk about experiential tourism.

Moreover, De Jong (2024) also highlights that tourists are interested today in experiencing not only the final stage of the food process, that is, eating, but also the production phase. Farms, fisheries, and other sites where food is produced are at the center of many tourist experiences throughout the world. Every place has connections to food production, and thus it is really easy to find something relevant for visitors coming from other food cultures. This strongly connects tourism to local cultures again, and this is a recurring theme when it comes to talking about new trends in tourism.

For De Jong (2024), new strategies such as traveling with a chef, wine tasting, and dining at locals' homes are growing significantly. Experiencing things may also mean learning to cook new dishes; kitchen courses organized by locals are very popular today. Foodie field trips are, for tourism experts, one of the solutions that will become more relevant in the next few years.

Another strategy is to facilitate the purchase of local food and its shipping to tourists' homes, without adding weight to the visitor's baggage or creating other issues. From the communicative point of view, a virtual way for tourists to be aware of local foods is to facilitate posts on social media, creating hashtags, social media pages and accounts, and other communication tools to save and share photos and promote local products. Again, local people here acquire decisive importance in creating new tourist experiences in a destination. Their involvement will also benefit them and their families, thus ensuring satisfaction for both parties.

Passion-focused niche travel: De Jong (2024) starts with culinary tourism to extend her discourse to every form of tourism based on niche passions. In this trend, the destination offers tourists a clear, distinguishable, and specific attraction. Certainly, tourists will not arrive in massive quantities, as the attraction only targets people passionate about that specific thing. However, many of the people passionate about it will come from all over the world, just because of the difficulty of finding that thing elsewhere.

Dinosaurs are extinct animals that stir the interest of many people of all ages around the world. Creating a museum of dinosaurs, for example, in a place where the remains of some of them have been rescued, could be a good idea to attract specific types of tourists.

In a recent study (Buscemi 2024), I have focused on film. Traditionally, film-induced tourism was the kind of tourism based in places where famous films were shot. In this sector, the new trend is instead what I have called tourism-induced film, that is, films only projected in a destination, connected to the territory, and adding more to the tourist experience. France is at the forefront here: the *Fête des Lumières* (the Festival of Lights) in Lyon and *Carrières de Lumières,* an entertainment artistic installation in the old quarry next to the medieval town of Les Baux-de-Provence, with the millions of tourists they attract along the entire year, are two illuminating examples.

The Ministry of Tourism and Creative Economy of the Republic of Indonesia (2024) finds that, in the near future, and differently from the past, people will prefer "mindful, memorable, meaningful, and quality trips." In short, they will pay major attention to the quality of the tourist experience, the details that will impact the journey, the stay, the offered experiences, etc. More specifically, the Ministry of Tourism and Creative Economy of the Republic of Indonesia (2024) finds four trends regarding the close future of tourism.

Bleasure, which is the combination of the words "business" and "pleasure." This category may, however, mean various things. First of all, the fact that especially after the COVID-19 pandemic many people have more flexible jobs and often organize short trips between one task and another. The post-pandemic work scenario has also increased the number of people having holidays over the entire year. While before the pandemic, many employees could take a vacation only in high season, now there is an array of tourists asking for winter or autumn vacations. Finally, people have also moved from the office to remote locations. Adding to what De Jong (2024) has already said about it, all of this must have a keyword: pleasure. Never has pleasure played a more relevant role than in this trend; people want to travel just to experience pleasant emotions and sensations.

Wellness experience: While the wellness experience related to tourism is not a novelty, the Ministry of Tourism and Creative Economy of the Republic of Indonesia (2024) points out that future trends will make mental health the most important element of wellness, which earlier was mainly based on physical health. The COVID-19 pandemic has made us understand the importance and the emergence of mental health issues, and tourism is one of the fields where people can cure them.

Deep and meaningful tourism: The Ministry of Tourism and Creative Economy of the Republic of Indonesia (2024) mentions a survey carried out by Booking.com where about 75 percent of the interviewees asked for meaningful tourism experiences. In other words, the old idea of a shallow vacation aiming to distract the traveler has been replaced by the new trend, according to which going on holiday should also signify something, not an empty and superficial break. People thus want to learn, understand, and realize something through travel. As a result, the travel experience does not finish when the tourist comes back home: its meaning, what it has taught to the tourist, continues to live in the existence of those who have experienced it.

Tourism storytelling: Last but not least, narrating the tourist promotion and experience is certainly another trend in tourism that experts include among the most successful in the near future. Campos and Almeida (2022) have given an insight into this very broad category, specifying the many things that, today, tourism storytelling means. Among other things, it is worth mentioning storytelling for cultural heritage, a field where tourists need a mediation between what they can learn and their disposition according to their different levels of acculturation, education, and so on. This mediation may be carried out by storytelling, a discipline that facilitates the understanding of complex realities and also requires cooperation between tourists and locals, who co-create the cultural heritage experience.

Another strategy is the creation of story-based tourist experiences. Locals develop itineraries, explaining them through stories. This also economically benefits them and improves their acceptance of tourists, who otherwise may be seen as extraneous presences invading their lands. Campos and Almeida (2022) touch upon forms of tourism storytelling applied to more traditional attractions, such as theme parks. These structures, sometimes perceived as surpassed, may find new life by adopting new forms of communication, for example, narration.

What is more, storytelling may be of help also before the tourist experience. Promoting destinations through storytelling has given satisfying results in many cases, demonstrating the powerful ability of this discipline to emotionally hit various targets. Finally, the new media are facilitating all of this: digital storytelling applied to social media results successfully before the experience (promotion), during it (accounts of trips), and later (telling something about the concluded experience) (Campos and Almeida 2022).

Waking up After the Dream

At first sight, it seems that the worst enemies of Costa Smeralda are today the new forms of tourism which were discussed in the previous sections: cultural, experiential, and sustainable tourism. The first one implies tourists who want to know, see holidays as a form of acculturation, and have the chance to change their minds even during vacations. Experiential tourists, on the other hand, like doing things, living like local people, mixing up work and holidays, and living not as tourists but as citizens. Sustainable tourism makes these traveling citizens aware; it needs tourists who are aware of the impact of their actions on the environment, climate change, the economy, and the exploitation of workers.

Costa Smeralda has nothing of this. It was designed for the traditional tourist, who wanted to see beautiful beaches, have a rest, and enjoy the passivity of the old-style holidays. In the beginning, Costa Smeralda was planned around a form of environmentalism, but firstly, the subsequent stages have canceled it, and secondly, it was an environmental concern based on dangers profoundly different from the present ones, which almost did not exist in the 1960s. Thus, is Costa Smeralda unfit to change? I am not sure about it.

What is sure is that all of this requires study and work. For the island on an island, today's age seems to be *the age of the big questions*. Big questions such as: What will Costa Smeralda become? Will other maps (in Baudrillard's sense) cover the previous ones? Is it possible to rescue the real territory? These are questions that are really difficult to answer. No one can say something certain about these concerns, at least today. However, we can start thinking about these issues. This is what the next sections want to do.

Importantly, what I write below is not because I want to see another Costa Smeralda, but only to see if there is a potential future development of the tourist destination that I have historically described over the rest of this book. For example, we cannot forget that Costa Smeralda was based on environmental respect for nature. Houses were built so as not to break the original landscape; the Costa Smeralda style adopted local materials and resulted in aesthetically unified buildings, avoiding the mix of various styles; beaches have been preserved more than in other areas in Sardinia or Italy. We must start from this, I believe, from the treasure that Costa Smeralda keeps with it, and try to integrate this scenario with novelties and updated adjustments.

Potential Cultural Tourism in Costa Smeralda

We have seen that one of the main topics in the field of cultural tourism is history, as tourists look for historical details about the places they visit. What they like is feeling a part of something bigger, knowing what those places were in the past, and understanding how what they see has developed in that way and not in another.

This book has demonstrated that Costa Smeralda has a very interesting history. It spans several decades, from the period well before it was a tourist destination to the years it was appreciated by visitors for the quality of holidays it offered. This history has precise locations where things happened: caves, nuraghes, towns, villas, beaches, hotels, etc. Many buildings have been refurbished and are thus unrecognizable; however, many other places have saved the features of the past. In this sense, projecting itineraries for tourists touching some of the sites where the history of Costa Smeralda took place, while "telling the history" of this tourist destination, may be a fruitful idea.

Tourism storytelling may be of help here. The history of Costa Smeralda is constituted by many compelling stories, from the medieval legends we have mentioned at the beginning of this book, to the Aga Khan's adventurous enterprise, to the failure of Phase 2, etc. These cultural activities could also happen in what has been called "shoulder seasons" (De Jong 2024). Clearly we are not referring to the entire year, as in winter there is little interest for a mainly marine destination. However, Sardinia has nice weather from April to September, and thus the holiday season could be expanded if tourists want to do something else apart from swimming and sunbathing.

Tourism storytelling could also involve the locals. This is a real issue in Costa Smeralda. The tourist destination has been, as the title of this book reminds the reader, an island on an island just because the locals have been continually ignored by the managers. Cultural tourism may be an opportunity to build a new relationship between the tourist destination and the people living just around it. This fracture between the destination and the locals is something that cannot continue, as it is out of any present conception of tourism. Involving the locals to tell the many fascinating stories revolving around Costa Smeralda could thus be the first sign of change.

What is more, even social media may play a role in it. At present, social media divides opinion when talking about Costa Smeralda: there are angry posts from people who do not recognize Costa Smeralda as a part of Sardinia; other posts are managed by the Consortium or by people who in the past worked in those places and are full of nostalgia for the good old days. Both approaches do not attract new tourists. Social media should instead adopt storytelling to explain what is in the destination that may result in interesting experiences for people who have never been there before.

Finally, culinary tourism is already developed in Costa Smeralda but perhaps in a way that should be adjourned. Restaurants and hotels inside the territory of the tourist destination offer dishes and ingredients that pertain to Sardinian food culture. However, they are parts of the international chains or are big enterprises; again, the locals are excluded, and there is not that feeling of authenticity that tourists today look for. There should be more information about places outside of the borders of Costa Smeralda that produce and sell Sardinian foods. Local restaurants should be promoted within the hotels and communication between Costa Smeralda and what is around it should be improved.

Potential Experiential Tourism in Costa Smeralda

Experiential tourism may first of all rely on wellness. Sardinia has a straightforward record: it is one of the five blue zones in the world where people live better and longer. The five zones in alphabetic order are: Ikaria (Greece), Loma Linda (California), Nicoya (Costa Rica), Okinawa (Japan), and Sardinia (Italy) (*Blue Zones* 2024). Why in these areas of the planet do people live longer is still debated. Certainly genetic factors play a role, but it seems that social and environmental conditions are equally relevant. Thus, if genetic characteristics cannot be transferred to tourists, breathing that air, eating that food, and sharing the same culture for a few days may make tourists learn something.

The fact that Sardinia is among the five places on the planet where people live better and longer is not sufficiently promoted in Costa Smeralda. Beyond this, what should be communicated to the tourists is why Sardinia has this record and the elements that help prolong people's lives. Having communicated this, tourists should be allowed access to these characteristics.

We have seen that wellness may refer to physical or mental health. Costa Smeralda thus should insist on both. At present, holidays in Costa Smeralda are designed for lazy tourists, and this has not been a mistake, as laziness is one of the main aims for many people who like going to the beach, having a rest under an umbrella at the seafront, etc. However, without canceling all of this, managers and operators should project wellness activities, because of the latest trends. For now, wellness in Costa Smeralda occurs principally in the luxury gyms of five-star hotels, and I am not saying that this has to be eliminated. Rather, given the latest trends, other opportunities for physical wellness should be added.

As regards mental health, and linking again to the five zones (Blue Zones 2024), Sardinia has many people who are more than 100 years of age and who are in perfect mental condition. Organizing meetings between them and the tourists could be useful for both: the elder Sardinians will have the opportunity to meet new people and understand new things; and visitors will enjoy knowing people who are to be taken as models, asking them how they live, what they eat and, who knows, some secrets explaining their good health. Incidentally, the tour operators could also commercially take advantage of these meetings.

Potential Sustainable Tourism in Costa Smeralda

Sustainability was born in Costa Smeralda, but as frequently happens, those who create things forget them briefly while others are more able to benefit from them. As reported by Magro (2022), the legendary Hotel Cala di Volpe, which has been one of the protagonists of this book, has saved its sustainable origins but has not been adjourned. technologically, as in the case of the few electric sockets available. Thus, the atmosphere is still rural-chic, but it needs some adjustment. Something has been done, as in the creation of the restaurant Matsuhisa, which is the surname of the Chef Nobu (Magro 2022) and which offers sushi on the beach. However, there is much work still to do, in this sense, and possibly in line with the concept of sustainability.

The already-seen categories of low-carbon adventure travel and calmcations may be of help. Thankfully, some trekking itineraries are, at the moment, available for tourists, but they are just a few and are not a consistent system able to involve tourists regularly. The territory of, and close to, Costa Smeralda is perfect for trekking. Plains, lowlands, and gentle hills end in beautiful beaches. Paths on high ground offer beautiful views of the sea, coves, bays, and sunny beaches.

Moreover, many parts of Costa Smeralda are perfect for exploring on horseback. Tourists concerned with the environment will certainly be attracted by horse-riding excursions. The same may be said for rock climbing, as that area of Sardinia has many zones where this activity is potentially possible.

Finally, there is the interesting matter of Sardinia's population density. Among the twenty Italian regions, Sardinia is the eighteenth most populated area, and so one with among the least number of people. It has 65 inhabitants per square kilometer, more than only Basilicata and Valle D'Aosta (*Tuttitalia* 2024). This means silence, and we have already seen that the absence of noise is one of the principal elements that is necessary for a calmcation. Again, as for the five blue zones, Sardinia has a record that has long been downsized. Perhaps, in the past, it was not seen as an upside, but we know that the new trends in tourism underline its relevance.

Today, the main activities in Costa Smeralda occur in the most noisy places with a high concentration of population: restaurants, hotels, beaches, etc. This was evidently requested by the tourists of the 1990s and early 2000s, and still is by those among them who continue to go to Costa Smeralda. However, if Costa Smeralda wants to come out of this present suspended existence and attract other types of tourists, silence should be promoted more. Calmcations could be one of the major trends in the future of this territory. In the end, if we go back to the Aga Khan's years, in Costa Smeralda, there was something similar, before the earthquake of the Berlusconian era. Adjourning that kind of tourism to the present might be the best way of taking advantage of existing strengths and paying tribute to the founder of the island on an island.

Conclusion

If the previous chapter talked about an earthquake, this conclusive one told the story of the uncertain atmosphere permeating a place after the telluric shock. People look at each other, say something, but do not see a future for themselves. The event has canceled the past, and now even the event has finished. What to do? Where we can start? How to go on? These and similar questions resonate around the place but no one finds the answers and, above all, nothing happens. This is the feeling in Costa Smeralda at present when I write these paragraphs. Tourism certainly goes on, and many of the hotels and restaurants continue to welcome visitors like in the past, but what is missing is identity, and thus a secure future.

Even the change in ownership of Costa Smeralda for the first time seems to be irrelevant. It has not instilled new meaning or aims in the destination. The Emir of Qatar entered the field in a moment of uncertainty and lack of identity, and left things as he found them. He did not follow any new direction and did not inform the territory with any new idea. Just go on, he seemed to say.

However, we know that culture changes, that it is always in a state of flux, and that nothing cultural remains still and unaltered. Everything is changing in terms of tourism around Costa Smeralda and pretending that change does not exist, in culture, usually does not end well. Nostalgic people dreaming of going back to the good old days are a normal phenomenon in these cases, but they are never those who will bring change and innovation; however, if the new owners do not want to change, that could be a bigger problem.

Even for the existence of this static scenario, in the last part of this chapter, I have "double-checked" the new trends in tourism and what Costa Smeralda may offer. The results are truly comforting. The first result that emerges is that Sardinia in general has two distinguishing characteristics that are not sufficiently communicated. Firstly, being one of the five places in the world where people live better and longer is a treasure that has not been discovered completely, and in tourism it can become a valuable asset; secondly, being the third to last Italian region for population density should be utilized to promote those new tourist trends linking to calmcations, slowness, silence, and serenity.

The second result is that many of the new tourist trends are based on concepts and ideas that Costa Smeralda has already operated on, be they linked to nature or the Aga Khan's first romantic conception. Rocks, beaches, and caves are not only suitable for lazy tourists wanting to stay under an umbrella in front of a beach; new types of tourists can also enjoy them, not eliminating the leisure and exclusive atmosphere that Prince Karim wanted for the place, which no one is calling into question.

The Aga Khan designed a place for high-level tourists and immersed them in an atmosphere based on what had no name in those times, but today is called "sustainability." In this sense, this frame may remain intact, with the understanding that the meaning of the concept of sustainability has in the meantime changed, and has been enriched with new things. First of all, this would imply building relationships with the locals. However, this is one of the topics of the general conclusion of this book, which follows below and concludes the trip.

CONCLUSION

The trip is over. In the space of a book, we have traveled across different eras, from prehistory to modernity, from postmodernity to the possible future. The temporal span we have walked has been wide, and the spatial one very little. We have remained in a space of 55 kilometers of coast, roughly from Cala Granu to Porto Rotondo. A really small area, scarcely populated, where in the last sixty-five years many things have happened, perhaps too many—some wonderful, others disputable. We have seen a strip of land where culture, commerce, history, and "story" have merged to create a fascinating cultural flux.

What is interesting in the history of Costa Smeralda is that in those 55 kilometers we have seen an abundant series of cultural changes that is rare to find in entire nations. Traveling through time but remaining still on that coast has allowed us to see what has passed in a small area in terms of changing cultures.

The last section of a book, especially when is called "Conclusion," very often contains answers. I do not know if what follows are answers, but they certainly are strands, lines that have gone through the entire trip, linking the various parts of this book around specific topics and, as ever in cultural tourism, helping us learn something. The island on an island has particularly been suitable to this end, as in ancient times it was rich in traditions and peculiarities that somehow returned when Monti di Mola became Costa Smeralda.

The first strand that has crossed the entire trip regards women. We have seen that Sardinia in antiquity was the land of matriarchy and of female heroines, such as Eleonora d'Arborea, who were in charge of society and used their power to defend themselves. Later, women lost this power and Sardinia became, even more than the rest of Italy, a patriarchal society. However, the women of Monti di Mola took their revenge when the land of the future Costa Smeralda was bought by the Aga Khan. Many women owned lots of the land by the sea by inheritance, as marine lands were considered less valuable than those inland, usually left to men. The rich investors, however, looked for the marine ones. As is said in that area, the rise of Costa Smeralda benefited a generation of women, even though the buyers abundantly speculated taking the land at a low price.

Moreover, we have got to know Gisele Podbielski. She was the only woman member of the group of adventurers who bought the land and constructed a tourist destination from scratch. Her account of those pioneering days is one of the most interesting documents I have studied to carry out this research. The Aga Khan did not leave us documents as profound as Gisele's account and less so his male collaborators. Probably obfuscated by the commercial aims, they centered on the practical side of the enterprise, while Gisele Podbielski opened her mind and talked about spirit, sentiments, and the stupor of a woman suddenly catapulted into one of the most beautiful and, at those times, savage places in the world.

The rest is male. Apart from this exception, Costa Smeralda has a male-led history. The Aga Khan, his architects and collaborators, the subsequent owners Tom Barrack and the Emir of Qatar, the Berlusconians, have all meant that there was the expression of a male point of view—so far, at least, as something new will certainly happen in Costa Smeralda in the near future. In the future, women, who are today more powerful than in the past, potentially could transform Costa Smeralda into a woman-led island on an island, based on cultural, experiential, and sustainable tourism.

Another interesting (and unexpected to me) thread crossing the entire temporal trip links bureaucracy, political economy, and culture. I wanted to write a book about cultural flux and not necessarily about ownership changes in Costa Smeralda. Only now, at the end of the writing process, I realize that I have devoted many pages to sales of land, hotel ownerships, deeds, notaries, financial agreements, conflicts of interest, regional policies, etc. I had not predicted this part, as my interest has always been in how cultures redesign themselves and mix and this usually does not happen in a notary's office, or on boring agreements written in bureaucratic language, or in the negotiation about the price at which a land is offered or sold. I know perfectly well that cultural studies and political economy have never gotten together, and I certainly prefer the former. However, never as in Costa Smeralda's history have the two fields gone so hand in hand; perhaps this has also happened elsewhere, so we should acknowledge it for future research.

Every change in Costa Smeralda's ownership, in fact, has coincided with a cultural change, or vice versa—any cultural change has anticipated a change in the people who have owned it. It is not clear what happened first. However, the two have been always present when new things have happened in those 55 kilometers.

Another surprising strand has regarded the Italian and Sardinian politicians. Italian politicians have never really gone down in history for the heroic defense of the Italian territory or the environment and the purity of the landscape. The entire territory of Ital is full of eco-monsters that have inexplicably been built with the permission of Italian national or local governments. The first stage of this story has confirmed this perception. It was the Aga Khan and his Consortium who set the rules not to destroy the Sardinian landscape in the part now called Costa Smeralda. Foreign investors did something to safeguard the environment, a concern that no Italian politicians had felt until then, as they had not planned any regulations about building a hotel next to a beach in Sardinia, not caring about these issues.

Surprisingly, when the owners, firstly the Aga Khan and secondly Tom Barrack, tried to realize Phase 2, which we can also call a concrete pour on a wonderful landscape, the Italian and Sardinian politicians turned into environmental advocates and said no. Both Prince Karim and Tom Barrack left Costa Smeralda for this reason, so we can imagine that the rejection by the politicians was neat and without room for negotiation.

Whatever we may think about the Italian political class (and I confess that I do not think well of it), we have to recognize that the Italian and Sardinian governors from the 1970s to the 2000s have saved the beauty of the place by rejecting Phase 2, a merit that is not so widespread in Italy and that perhaps should be taken as a model for today's governors.

This study has also concretely shown the straightforward ability of the media to create Baudrillard's maps of the territory. Monti di Mola, the Aga Khan's dream, Phase 2, Berlusconized Costa Smeralda, and the current state of suspension are different maps that have progressively covered each other in the same area; what is fascinating is to see how each of them has been drawn by a specific kind of society, ideology, and perspective. Monti di Mola was the idealized map of those who did not want the change to occur, the desire for a land destined to remain the same forever, and not betray their concept of purity. The Aga Khan's dream was the map of a savage society able to balance the consumerist and turbo-capitalist lives of a group of Western entrepreneurs, even though their leader was of Arab origins. Phase 2 was thus the map of consumerism and turbo-capital-ism. Berlusconized Costa Smeralda was the map of a certain way of conceiving politics as a mixture of power and entertainment, where they are not two sepa-rate components, but a whole in which it is impossible to distinguish one from another. The current state of suspension, finally, is the blank map to put over the previous, when no new map takes over the previous one, waiting for the next dominant group in the field.

All of them are certainly social constructions and media representations, places generated on TV or magazines and newspapers. However, the part of this book about architecture in Costa Smeralda has demonstrated that they are also material places. Exactly like Disneyland, the example taken by Baudrillard to explain hyperreality, Costa Smeralda has always had a material side that has reinforced its presence and role in the minds of its visitors and in the collective imagination, in general. In this sense, places are to be considered as material media, stronger than a TV program or a magazine just because of their concrete presence in the space. This might also be something to keep in mind in the case of future studies.

Continuing to link theory and practice, walking through the history of Costa Smeralda has also said something about Foucault's concepts of utopia and heterotopia. We have defined the first stage of Costa Smeralda, especially as it has been narrated by Gisele Podbielski, as an existing utopia, which is certainly an inherent contradiction. However, this group of rich investors and capitalists tried to do exactly that, to materialize a dream.

Can utopias be true? Certainly not. In fact, as Costa Smeralda became an existing utopia, it transformed into a heterotopia for tourists, a place where people stay in a suspended status, detaching from their everyday lives. Later, this heterotopia also became worrying, a place of crime, drugs, and kidnapping, as Foucault has described.

In conclusion, I would say that this temporal trip remaining within the spatial limit of 55 kilometers of coast has demonstrated how many things we may learn from tourism and tourist destinations. The places where people spend their holidays are increasingly becoming litmus papers capable of reflecting the illuminating cultural changes around us. Cultural values continually appear, mix up, fade, and disappear, being replaced by new ones, drawing on new conceptions and perspectives.

I hope that this book has transmitted all of this. If so, those who have been interested in it might continue to look at Costa Smeralda, as I will surely do. As has already happened in its whole history, what will occur in the next years to the island on an island will tell us something new and relevant about what we will be as a society and where we will go in the near future.

REFERENCES

Addis, Maria Cristina. 2016. *L'Isola che non c'è: Sulla Costa Smeralda, o di un'utopia che non c'è* [The Non-Existent Island: On Costa Smeralda, or a Utopia That Does Not Exist]. Società Editrice Esculapio.

Agus, Luigi. 2016. *La scuola di Stampace: Da Pietro a Michele Cavaro* [Stampece's School: From Pietro to Michele Cavaro]. Arkadia editore.

Aiello, Giorgia. 2020. "Visual Semiotics: Key Concepts and New Directions." In *The Sage Handbook of Visual Research Methods,* edited by Luc Pawels and Dawn Mannay. Sage.

Altichieri, Alessio. 2004. "Blair a Villa Certosa? Scelta di cattivo gusto" [Blair in Villa Certosa? A Tacky Choice]. *Corriere della Sera* [Evening Courier], July 30.

Anatra, Bruno, Antonello Mattone, and Raimondo Turtas. 1989. *Storia dei sardi e della Sardegna, Vol. III: L'Età moderna: Dagli Aragonesi alla fine del dominio spagnolo* [History of Sardinians and Sardinia: Vol. III: The Modern Age: From the Aragonese to the End of the Spanish Dominion]. Jaca Book.

Andovino, Paolo. 2021. "Luci su Porto Rafael, il borgo incantato del Conte di Berlanga" [Lights on Porto Rafael, the Enchanted Hamlet of the Count of Berlanga]. *La Nuova Sardegna* [New Sardinia] December 29. https://www.lanuovasardegna.it/olbia/cronaca/2021/12/29/news/luci -su-porto-rafael-il-borgo-incantato-del-conte-di-berlanga-1.41077425

Ansa. 2015. "Berlusconi, ultimo giorno di servizi sociali a Cesano Boscone" [Berlusconi, the Last Day at Social Services in Cesano Boscone]. March 8. https://www.ansa.it/sito/notizie/politica/2015/03/06/berlusconi-ultimo-giorno-di -servizi-sociali-a-cesano-boscone_60b290d1-beaf-49b1-8e91-75d58200b970.html

Archilli, Stefania. 2023. "Jacques Couelle, l'architetto che ha dato forma (organica) alla Costa Smeralda" [Jacques Couelle, the Architect Who Gave (Organic) Form to Costa Smeralda]. *Decor*, August 23. https://www.elledecor.com/it/people/a44863742 /jacques-couelle-larchitetto-che-ha-dato-forma-organica-alla-costa-smeralda/

Asunis, Antonio. 2014. *Elmas: Paese di Sardegna* [Elmas: A Town in Sardinia]. Logus Mondi interattivi editore.

Balducci, Dario. 2024. "Hotel Cala di Volpe." *Atlante Architettura Contemporanea* [Atlas of Contemporary Architecture]. https://atlantearchitetturacon temporanea.cultura.gov.it/hotel-cala-di-volpe/

Bandinu, Bachisio. 1980. *Costa Smeralda: Come nasce una favola turistica* [Costa Smeralda: How a Tourist Fairytale Was Born]. Rizzoli.

Bandinu, Banchisio. 1994. *Narciso in vacanza: Il turismo in Sardegna tra mito e storia* [Narcissus on Holyday: Tourism in Sardinia Between Myth and History]. AM&D Edizioni.

Bandinu, Banchisio. 2011. *L'amore del figlio meraviglioso* [The Love of the Wonderful Son]. Il maestrale.

Barbieri, Marcello. 2008. "The Challenge of Biosemiotics." In *Introduction to Biosemiotics: The New Biological Synthesis*, edited by Marcello Barbieri. Springer.

Barone, Dario, and Anna Di Francisca. 2015. "Memorie: Costa Smeralda" [Memories: Costa Smeralda]. *RAI*, Documentary. https://www.sardegnadigitallibrary .it/detail/6499b8a6e487374c8f8019d0

Barthes, Roland. 1977. *Image, Music, Text*. Translated by Stephen Heath. Fontana Press.

Barthes, Roland. 2013. *Mythologies: The Complete Edition in a New Translation*. Translated by Richard Howard and Annette Lavers. Farrar, Straus and Giroux.

Battista, Pierluigi. 2008. "La mai appagata fame di linciaggio" [The Never Sated Hunger for Lynching]. *Corriere della Sera* [Evening Courier], May 5.

Baudrillard, Jean. 1994. *Simulacra and Simulation*. Translated by Sheila Faria Glaser. The University of Michigan Press.

Bezemer, Jeff. 2012. "What Is Multimodality?" University College London, February 16. https://mode.ioe.ac.uk/2012/02/16/what-is-multimodality/

Blue Zones. 2024. "Our Story." https://www.bluezones.com/

Bocchi, Lorenzo. 1964. "De Gaulle ha già potuto alzarsi per qualche momento" [De Gaulle Could Get Up for Some Moments]. *Corriere della Sera* [Evening Courier], April 19.

Bonu, Giada. 2021. "Le parole per dirlo: Uno sguardo femminista e decoloniale sulla Sardegna" [The Words to Say It: A Feminist and De-Colonial Sight on Sardinia]. In *Filosofia De Logu: Decolonizzare il pensiero e la ricerca in Sardegna* [Decolonizing Sardinia's Thought and Research], edited by Sebastiano Ghisu e Alessandro Mongili. Meltemi.

Booking. 2024. "Hotel Cala di Volpe: A Luxury Collection Hotel, Costa Smeralda." https://www.booking.com/hotel/it/cala-di-volpe.it.html

Bua, Francesca. 2013. "L'insediamento storico della Sardegna" [The Historical Settlement in Sardinia]. In *Sardegna: La Nuova e l'Antica Felicità* [Sardinia: New and Ancient Happiness], edited by Erika Buonacucina, Francesca Bua, Sonia Borsato, Cristian Cannaos, Alessandra Cappai, Paola Idini, Miriam Mastinu, Giuseppe Onni, Sabrina Scalas, Valentina Talu. Franco Angeli.

Burns, Peter M., and Andrew Holden. 1995. *Tourism: A New Perspective.* Prentice Hall.

Buscemi, Francesco. 2018. "The Ancestral Room of the State? Scotland and the UK on *Jamie's Great Britain.*" *Journal of Communication Inquiry* 42 (3): 258–274. https://doi.org/10.1177/0196859918766880

Buscemi, Francesco. 2024. **"From Film-induced Tourism to Tourism-induced Film"**. In *Tourisme, arts et territoires. Impacts réciproques à travers des études de cas*, edited by Nathalie Dupont and Laetitia Garcia. Peter Lang Verlag.

Cagliari Magazine. 2020. "La Sardegna e De André: Storia di un legame unico" [Sardinia and De André: History of a Unique Tie]. March 9. https://www.cagliarimag.com/sardegna/de-andre-sardegna-storia/

Camillo, Lorenzo. 2000. "Rafael Neville, creatore di Porto Rafael" [Rafael Neville, the Creator of Porto Rafael]. *1-Camillo.* https://www.l-camillo.com/activity/Articles/rafael.htm

Camillo, Lorenzo. 2023. "L'Aga Kahn e la Costa Smeralda: I miei 50 anni in Costa Smeralda" [The Aga Khan and Costa Smeralda: My 50 Years in Costa Smeralda]. *Gallura Tour*, April 27. https://www.galluratour.it/aga-khan-e-costa-smeralda-di-lorenzo-camillo/

Campos, Claudia, and Sofia Almeida. 2022. *Global Perspectives in Strategic Storytelling in Destination Marketing*. IGI Global.

Cannaos, Cristian. 2013. "L'insediamento e la rete di città in Sardegna" [The Settlement and the City Net in Sardinia]. In *Sardegna: La Nuova e l'Antica Felicità* [Sardinia: New and Ancient Happiness], edited by Erika Buonacucina, Francesca Bua, Sonia Borsato, Cristian Cannaos, Alessandra Cappai, Paola Idini, Miriam Mastinu, Giuseppe Onni, Sabrina Scalas, Valentina Talu. Franco Angeli.

Cannas, Rita. 2018. "Case Study Italy: The Tourism Management of Climate Change in the Mediterranean Region: Adaptation Strategies in Sardinia and Sicily." In *Global Climate Change and Coastal Tourism: Recognizing Problems, Managing Solutions and Future Expectations*, edited by Andrew Jones and Michael Philips. Cabi Books.

Cannas, Rita, and Ernestina Giudici. 2015. "Tourism Relationships Between Sardinia and Its Islands: Collaborative or Conflicting?" In *Archipelago Tourism: Policies and Practices,* edited by Godfrey Baldacchino. Ashgate.

Cappai, Alessandra. 2014. "Dal nerorealismo italiano al landscape planning americano: la fondazione del paesaggio turistico della Costa Smeralda" [From Italian Neorealism to American Landscape Planning: The Foundation of Tourist Landscape in Costa Smeralda]. PhD diss., Universitat Politècnica de Catalunya.

Cappai, Alessandra. 2015. "La costruzione dello spazio turistico nella Costa Smeralda: Neorealismo o banalizzazione dell'architettura vernacolare?" [The Construction of the Tourist Space in Costa Smeralda: Neorealism or Banalization of Vernacular Architecture?] *QRU: Quaderns de Recerca en Urbanisme* [Notebooks of Urban Research] 5/6: 176–187. https://doi.org/10.5821/qru.9587.

Casula, Francesco C. 1998. *La storia di Sardegna* [History of Sardinia]. Carlo Delfino Editore.

Cerasarda. 2024. "Cerasarda Website." https://www.cerasarda.it/

Cerruti, Alberto. 2013. "Riva, 50 anni di Sardegna: 'E dire che non ci volevo venire'" [Riva, 50 Years in Sardinia: "And I Did Not Want to Come"]. *La Gazzetta dello Sport* [Sport Gazzette], April 4. https://www.gazzetta.it/Calcio/Squadre/Cagliari/03-04-2013/riva-50-anni-sardegna-scoprii-isola-che-mi-ama-92810622006.shtml

Coast Magazine. 2021a. "Storia di un aeroporto" [History of an Airport]. https://live.coastmagazine.it/it/turismo/storie/storia-di-un-aeroporto-1430.html/

Coast Magazine. 2021b. Instagram, August 28. https://www.instagram.com/p
/CTHoBr3tv4W/?next=%2Forbis_jp%2F&img_index=2 x

Colavitti, Anna Maria. 2018. *Urban Heritage Management: Planning with
History.* Springer.

Colavitti, Anna Maria. 2022. "Sardinia in Hard Changing Times: Reflections
on Territory and New Development Models." In *Building the Urban Bioregion:
Governance Scenarios for Urban and Territorial Planning,* edited by Anna Maria
Colavitti and Sergio Serra. SDT edizioni.

Colosimo, Valentina. 2023. "I 60 anni di Cala di Volpe, l'albergo che 'in-
ventò' la Costa Smeralda" [60 Years of Cala di Volpe, the Hotel That "Invented"
Costa Smeralda]. *Vanity Fair*, August 11. https://www.vanityfair.it/gallery
/cala-di-volpe-albergo-costa-smeralda

Consorzio Costa Smeralda. 2019a. "60 anni fa a oggi furono venduti i ter-
reni di Porto Cervo." [60 years ago today, Porto Cervo's plots of land were
sold]. Facebook, June 14. https://www.facebook.com/consorziocostasmeralda
/posts/2193540160906932

Consorzio Costa Smeralda. 2019b. "In memoria di René Podbielski" [In
Memory of René Podbielski]. Facebook, September 29. https://www.facebook
.com/consorziocostasmeralda/posts/in-memoria-di-ren%C3%A9-podbielskioggi
-%C3%A8-una-data-importante-per-il-consorzio-costa-s/2266007940326820/

Consorzio Costa Smeralda. 2020. "La nostra storia" [Our History]. https://
www.consorziocostasmeralda.com/la-nostra-storia/

Consorzio Costa Smeralda. 2021. "Porto Cervo il 15 agosto 1964, giorno
della sua inaugurazione." [Porto Cervo on August 15, 1964, the inauguration
day]. Facebook, August 15. https://www.facebook.com/consorziocostasmeralda
/posts/porto-cervo-il-15-agosto-1964-giorno-della-sua-inaugurazione/2821682451426030/

Corriere della Sera [Evening Courier]. 1961a. "L'Aga Khan in Sardegna"
[The Aga Khan in Sardinia]. September 28.

Corriere della Sera [Evening Courier]. 1961b. "L'Aga Khan inaugura l'inverno"
[The Aga Khan Inaugurates the Winter]. November 26.

Corriere della Sera [Evening Courier]. 1962. "L'Aga Khan investe quarantasei
miliardi in Sardegna" [The Aga Khan Invests 46 Billion in Sardinia]. January 23.

Corriere della Sera [Evening Courier]. 1964a. "L'incontro col Ministro Pastore dell'Aga Khan in Sardegna" [The Aga Khan's Meeting in Sardinia with Ministry Pastore]. April 19.

Corriere della Sera [Evening Courier]. 1964b. "Vogliono vendere la Valtellina all'Aga Khan" [They Want to Sell Valtellina to the Aga Khan]. October 30.

Corriere della Sera [Evening Courier]. 1965a. "La Principessa Margaret sulla Costa Smeralda" [Princess Margaret in Costa Smeralda]. August 14.

Corriere della Sera [Evening Courier]. 1965b. "L'Aga Khan in visita alla FIAT" [The Aga Khan Visited FIAT]. October 20.

Corriere della Sera [Evening Courier]. 1966a. "Margaret in Sardegna" [Margaret in Sardinia]. August 12.

Corriere della Sera [Evening Courier]. 1966b. "La Bardot e Gunther Sachs sulla Costa Smeralda" [Bardot and Gunther Sachs in Costa Smeralda]. August 29.

Corriere della Sera [Evening Courier]. 1967a. "Fallito rapimento di un tedesco in Sardegna" [Failed Kidnapping of a German Man in Sardinia]. March 8.

Corriere della Sera [Evening Courier]. 1967b. "I banditi sparano sulla Costa Smeralda" [Bandits Shoot in Costa Smeralda]. August 10.

Corriere della Sera [Evening Courier]. 1969. "Manette a due fidanzati nella villa di Baby Pignatari" [Engaged Couple Arrested in Baby Pignatari's Villa]. September 1.

Corriere della Sera [Evening Courier]. 1977a. "Leone Concato sarebbe stato rapito vicino alla sua villa di Cala di Volpe" [Leone Concato Could Have Been Kidnapped Close to His Villa in Cala di Volpe]. May 30.

Corriere della Sera [Evening Courier]. 1977b. "Leone Concato è ancora vivo: Nuovo appello della famiglia" [Leone Concato Is Still Alive: A New Appeal from His Family]. September 16.

Corriere della Sera [Evening Courier]. 1977c. "Interrotto in contatto con i rapitori: Si teme il peggio per la sorte di Concato" [The Contacts with the Kidnappers Is Interrupted: The Worst Is Feared for Concato's Sort]. October 5.

Corriere della Sera [Evening Courier]. 1980. "Nuovo Centro Sanitario a Porto Cervo" [A New Health Center in Porto Cervo]. June 1.

Corriere della Sera [Evening Courier]. 2002. "Vacanze da Berlusconi: Ma Blair smentisce" [Holidays at Berlusconi's: But Blair Denies]. April 15.

Corriere della Sera [Evening Courier]. 2005. "Il Senatur in Sardegna" [The Senator in Sardinia]. August 11.

Corriere d'Informazione [Information Courier]. 1961. "L'Agha Khan dovrà sposare una principessa mussulmana?" [Shall the Aga Khan Marry a Muslim Princess?]. January 6–7.

Corriere d'Informazione [Information Courier]. 1964. "Aga Khan e Margaret naufraghi in Sardegna" [The Aga Khan and Margaret Castaways in Sardinia]. August 27–28.

Corriere d'Informazione [Information Courier]. 1967. "Meg e Tony in vacanza sulla Costa Smeralda" [Meg and Tony on Holiday in Costa Smeralda]. August 18–19.

Corriere d'Informazione [Information Courier]. 1969. "Nelle mani della polizia l'uomo della droga" [The Drug Man in the Hands of the Police]. August 21–22.

Corriere d'Informazione [Information Courier]. 1971a. "Sardegna, in contatto con i banditi per liberare il bimbo rapito col padre" [Sardinia, in Contact with Bandits to Free the Child Who Was Kidnapped with His Father]. April 9–10.

Corriere d'Informazione [Information Courier]. 1971b. "E' la gemella della miss" [She Is Miss's Twin]. August 25.

Corriere d'Informazione [Information Courier]. 1972. "Pace o armistizio fra Jackie e Ari?" [Peace or Armistice Between Jackie and Ari?]. August 8.

Costa Smeralda. 2019. "Busiri Vici, l'architetto alla corte del Principe" [Busiri Vici, the Architect of the Prince's Court]. August 19. https://www.costasmeralda.it/articolo/busiri-vici-larchitetto-alla-corte-del-principe/

Counihan, Carole. 1984. "Bread as World: Food Habits and Social Relations in Modernizing Sardinia." *Anthropological Quarterly* 57 (2): 47–59. https://doi.org/10.2307/3317579.

Curtin, Philip D. 1984. *Cross Cultural Trade in World History*. Cambridge University Press.

Decandia, Lidia. 2017. "L'invenzione della Costa Smeralda: la costruzione di un simulacro come embrione di un'inedita realtà urbana" [The Invention of Costa

Smeralda: The Construction of a Simulacrum as an Embryo of an Unprecedented Urban Reality]. *Archivio di studi urbani e regionali* [Archives of Urban and Regional Studies] 118 (1): 5–26. https://doi.org/10.3280/ASUR2017-118001

De Jong, Anne. 2022. "How to Develop Low Season Travel Experiences." Good Tourism Institute, October 28. https://goodtourisminstitute.com/library /low-season-travel-experiences/

De Jong, Anne. 2024. "8 Good Tourism Trends for 2024." Good Tourism Institute, January 2. https://goodtourisminstitute.com/library/good-tourism-trends-2024/

Del Chiappa, Giacomo, Marcello Atzeni, and Vahid Ghasemi. 2018. "Community-Based Collaborative Tourism Planning in Islands: A Cluster Analysis in the Context of Costa Smeralda." *Journal of Destination Marketing & Management* 8: 41–48. https://doi.org/10.1016/j.jdmm.2016.10.005

Del Chiappa, Giacomo, and Giacomo Presenza. 2013. "The Use of Network Analysis to Assess Relationships Among Stakeholders Within a Tourism Destination: An Empirical Investigation on Costa Smeralda-Gallura, Italy." *Tourism Analysis* 18 (1): 1–13. https://doi.org/10.3727/108354213X13613720283520

Di Caro, Paola. 2004. "Calzoni di lino e bandana: Silvio spinge Tony al bagno di folla" [Linen Trousers and a Bandana: Silvio Pushes Tony into a Huge Crowd]. *Corriere della Sera* [Evening Courier], August 17.

Domus Web. 2024. "Villa Nido d'uccello." [Bird Nest Villa]. https://www.domusweb.it/it /architettura/gallery/2023/07/04/villa-nido-duccello-savin-couelle.html

Ducci, Carlo. 2021. "Estate Italiana" (Italian Summer). *Conde Nast Traveller*, 1 June. https://www.pressreader.com/

Durkheim, Emile. 1982. *The Rules of Sociological Method*. Translated by Wilfred Douglas Halls. The Free Press.

Erdly, Marvin, and Lynn Kesterson-Townes. 2003. "Experience Rules: A Scenario for the Hospitality and Leisure Industry circa 2010 Envisions Transformation." *Strategy and Leadership* 31 (3): 12–18. https://doi.org/10.1108/10878570310698250

Facebook. 2024a. "I Professionisti della Costa Smeralda di ieri e di oggi" [Yesterday and Today's Professionals in Costa Smeralda]. https://www.facebook .com/groups/506860454336942

Facebook. 2024b. "Sardegna mia" [My Sardinia]. https://www.facebook.com /instagramsardinia

Fantozzi, Matteo. 2023. "Francesco Arca e la foto con Lele Mora del massaggio ai piedi: I retroscena e le dichiarazioni" [Francesco Arca and the Photo with Lele Mora of the Foot Massage: The Background and the Statements]. *Cultweb*, February 19. https://cultweb.it/spettacolo/francesco-arca-e-la-foto-con-lele -mora-del-massaggio-ai-piedi-i-retroscena-e-le-dichiarazioni/

Ferraino, Giuliana. 2012. "La Costa Smeralda cambia padrone: Hotel e Golf all'Emiro del Qatar" [Costa Smeralda Changes Its Owner: Hotel and Golf to the Emir of Qatar]. *Corriere della Sera* [Evening Courier], April 3.

Fiocchetto, Rossana. 2003. "Viaggio nella Sardegna matriarcale: Dee, deinas, janas, fadas, donni di fuora" [A Journey to Matriarchal Sardinia: Goddesses, Sacred Women, Heroc Women]. Università delle donne [Women University]. http://www.universitadelledonne.it/sardegna.htm

Fiori, Rossella. 2015. "La Costa Smeralda: la storia, lo sviluppo economico, il modello di sistema turistico territoriale" [Costa Smeralda: History, Economic Development, the Model of Territorial Tourist System]. First degree diss., Università di Pisa.

Fjagesund, Peter, and Ruth A. Symes. 2002. *The Northern Utopia: British Perceptions of Norway in the Nineteenth Century*. Rodopi.

Fludernik, Monika. 2009. *An Introduction to Narratology*. Routledge.

Foucault, Michel. 1966. *The Order of Things: An Archeology of the Human Sciences*. Translated by Alan Sheridan. Vintage Books.

Foucault, Michel. 1986. "Of Other Spaces." *Diacritics* 16 (1): 22–27. https:// doi.org/10.2307/464648

F.P. 1968. "Sei morti su un aereo precipitato in Sardegna" [Six Dead People on an Airplane That Precipitated in Sardinia]. *Corriere della Sera* [Evening Courier], July 24.

F.P. 1969a. "Hashish sulla Costa Smeralda" [Hash in Costa Smeralda]. *Corriere della Sera* [Evening Courier], August 21.

F.P. 1969b. "Nove ordini di cattura per la droga sulla Costa Smeralda" [Nine Arrest Warrants for Drugs in Costa Smeralda]. *Corriere della Sera* [Evening Courier], August 31.

F.P. 1969c. "Nobildonna milanese coinvolta nel traffico di droga" [Milan Noblewoman Involved in Drug Traffiking]. *Corriere della Sera* [Evening Courier], September 8.

F.P. 1971. "Karim rimane in Sardegna" [Karim Remains in Sardinia]. *Corriere della Sera* [Evening Courier], October 29.

Fuccaro, Lorenzo. 2004a. "Berlusconi-Blair cena con fuochi artificiali" [Berlusconi-Blair, Dinner with Fireworks]. *Corriere della Sera* [Evening Courier], August 15.

Fuccaro, Lorenzo. 2004b. "Berlusconi-Blair, prove di mediazione con gli USA" [Berlusconi-Blair, Rehearsal of Mediation with the US]. *Corriere della Sera* [Evening Courier], August 17.

Funedda, Antonio, and Fabrizio Cocco. 2019. "La geologia: Una storia di 500 milioni di anni" [Geology: A History of 500 Billion Years]. In *Sardegna: Geografie di un'isola* [Sardinia: Geographies of an Island], edited by Andrea Corsale and Giovanni Sistu. Franco Angeli.

Galleria Francesca Antonacci. 2006. *Milton Gendel: Fotografie*. Trinity Fine Art. https://www.fondazioneprimoli.it/wp-content/uploads/2022/10/2006 _Galleria_Francesca_Antonacci.pdf

Galluzzo, Marco. 2008a. "Putin va in Sardegna e Berlusconi gli regala lo show del Bagaglino" [Putin Goes to Sardinia and Berlusconi Gives Him as a Present the Bagaglino Show]. *Corriere della Sera*, [Evening Courier], April 18.

Galluzzo, Marco. 2008b. "Domanda sull'amante, Vladimir in imbarazzo e Silvio mima il mitra" [A Question About His Lover, Vladimir Is Embarrassed and Silvio Mimics a Machine Gun]. *Corriere della Sera* [Evening Courier], April 19.

Ghislanzoni, Giancarlo. 1967. "Sparatoria in Sardegna presso la Costa Smeralda" [Shooting in Sardinia Close to Costa Smeralda]. *Corriere d'Informazione* [Information Courier], August 10–11.

Gòmez, John M. 2017. *A Macat Analysis: Roland Barthes's Mythologies*. Macat-Routledge.

Gordin, Giancarlo, and Giuliana Bianchi. 1999. *Case di Sardegna: Le ville esclusive della Costa Smeralda* [Houses in Sardinia: The Exclusive Villas in Costa Smeralda]. Archideos Libri.

Grasso, Aldo. 2011. "L'ex parrucchiere diventato il re della TV" (tra risse e tronisti) [The Ex-Hairstylist Who Became the King of TV (Among Fights and False Kings]. *Corriere della Sera* [Evening Courier], June 21.

Grasso, Aldo. 2018. "Il mondo di Lucci, la perfidia mista a una travolgente ilarità" [Lucci's World, Perfidy Combined with an Overwhelming Hilarity]. *Corriere della Sera* [Evening Courier], September 13.

Griffin, Kevin A., Raj Razaq, and Nigel D. Morpeth, eds. 2014. "Introduction to Cultural Tourism: Philosophy and Management." In *Cultural Tourism*. CABI.

Guerin Sportivo [Sports Guerino Blog]. 2011. "Lo scudetto cagliaritano dei Moratti" [Moratti's Cagliari Scudetto]. March 5. https://www.guerinsportivo.it /news/altro/2011/03/05-1138902/lo_scudetto_cagliaritano_dei_moratti.

G.Z. 1979. "Scomparsa una famiglia di tre inglesi: Forse è un nuovo sequestro in Sardegna" [A Family of Three English People Is Missing: Perhaps It Is a New Kidnapping in Sardinia]. *Corriere della Sera* [Evening Courier], August 24.

G.Z. 1980. "Daphne Schild fu prigioniera nelle campagne verso Oruni" [Daphne Schild Was Trapped in the Countryside Around Orune]. *Corriere della sera* [Evening Courier], March 18.

Holbrook, Morris B., and Elizabeth C. Hirschman. 1982. "The Experiential Aspects of Consumption: Consumer Fantasies, Feelings and Fun." *Journal of Consumer Research* 9 (2): 132–140. https://doi.org/10.1086/208906

Idea Sardegna. 2013. "Donne di Sardegna: Dal matriarcato del neolitico alle minatrici del Sulcis" [Sardinian Women: From Neolithic Matriarchy to Sulcis's Miners]. July 25. https:// ideasardegna.it/donne-di-sardegna-dal-matriarcato-del-neolitico-alle-minatrici-del-sulcis/

Il Post. 2020. "Chi è l'Aga Khan" [Who the Aga Khan Is]. February 12. https:// www.ilpost.it/2020/02/12/aga-khan/

Inside Sardinia. 2020. "La nascita della Costa Smeralda" [Costa Smeralda's Birth]. June 8. https://blog.insidesardiniaguide.it/blog/la-nascita-della-costa-smeralda/

Italia Oggi. 1994. "L'Aga Khan lascia la Costa Smeralda" [The Aga Khan Leaves Costa Smeralda]. April 9.

Izzo, Enrica. 2021. "Grazia Deledda, la donna che non mise limiti alle donne" [Grazia Deledda, the Woman Who Did Not put Limits to Women]. *Radio Radicale*, October 29. https://www.radioradicale.it/scheda/651444 /grazia-deledda-la-donna-che-non-mise-limiti-alle-donne

Jattoni Dall'Asen, Massimiliano. 2024. "Feste, scandali e vertici politici: La storia controversa di Villa Certosa messa in vendita dai figli di Berlusconi" [Parties, Scandals and Political Meetings: The Controversial History of Villa Certosa, put on Sale by Berlusconi's Sons and Daughters]. *Corriere della Sera* [Evening Courier], February 1. https://www.corriere.it/economia/finanza/24_febbraio_01 /feste-scandali-e-vertici-politici-la-storia-controversa-di-villa-certosa-messa-in -vendita-dai-figli-di-berlusconi-1154f468-4bb4-4ec7-8831-9224990bfxlk.shtml

Jenks, Chris. 1998. *Core Sociological Dichotomies.* Sage.

Jovane, Paolo. 1977. "La Signora Zoff è Lady Sardegna" [Lady Zoff Is Lady Sardinia]. *Corriere dell'Informazione* [Information Courier], July 11.

Lahusen, Christian. 1996. *The Rhetoric of Moral Protest: Public Campaigns, Celebrity Endorsement, and Political Mobilization.* Walter de Gruiter.

La Nuova Sardegna [New Sardinia]. 2012a. "Il pastore che voleva milioni, non miliardi: una leggenda" [The Shepherd Who Wanted Millions, not Billions: A Legend]. *La Nuova Sardegna* [New Sardinia]. March 14. https://www.lanuovasardegna.it /regione/2012/03/14/news/il-pastore-che-voleva-milioni-non-miliardi-una-leggenda-1.3689333

La Nuova Sardegna [New Sardinia]. 2012b. "E' morto Jean Paul De Marchi, geniale architetto della Costa" [Jean-Paul De Marchi Died, He Was the Genius Architect of the Costa]. October 17. https://www.lanuovasardegna.it/olbia/cronaca/2012/10/17 /news/e-morto-jean-paul-de-marchi-geniale-architetto-della-costa-1.5879198

La Nuova Sardegna [New Sardinia]. 2016. "Addio all'avvocato André Ardoin, uno dei fondatori della Costa Smeralda" [Farewell to Lawyer André Ardoin, One of the Founders of Costa Smeralda]. November 25. https://www.lanuovasardegna.it /olbia/cronaca/2016/11/25/news/addio-all-avvocato-andre-ardoin-uno-dei -fondatori-della-costa-smeralda-1.14467615

La Stampa [The Press]. 2022. "Così nacque il mito della Costa Smeralda: Marzo 1962, l'Aga Khan dà vita a un sogno che tutt'ora resiste" [The Myth of Costa Smeralda Was Born in This Way: March 1962, the Aga Khan Gives Birth to a Dream That Still Resists]. March 17. https://www.lastampa.it/viaggi /italia/2022/03/17/news/cosi_nacque_il_mito_della_costa_smeralda_marzo _1962_l_aga_khan_da_vita_a_un_sogno_che_tutt_ora_resiste-2875950/

Ledda, Massimo. 2019. "L'esercito degli scomparsi in Sardegna, Vite sospese e spesso dimenticate" [The Army of the Missing People in Sardinia: Suspended Lives Very Often Forgotten]. *L'Unione Sarda*, November 15. https://www.unionesarda.it/news-sardegna /cagliari/l-esercito-degli-scomparsi-in-sardegna-vite-sospese-e-spesso-dimenticate-ige66dz8

Lilliu, Giovanni, 2006. *Sardegna nuragica* [Nuracich Sardinia]. Il Maestrale.

Lisai, Gianmichele. 2013. *Sardegna giallo e nera: Omicidi, sequestri, fatti di sangue e serial killer, trent'anni di criminalità nell'isola più misteriosa d'Italia* [Yellow and Black Sardinia: Homicides, Kidnapping, Crimes and Serial Killers, Thirty Years of Crime in the Most Mysterious Italian Island]. Newton Compton editori.

Lisai, Gianmichele, and Antonio Maccioni. 2021. *Breve storia della Sardegna: La lunga e affascinante storia dell'isola più affascinante del Mediterraneo* [Brief History of Sardinia: The Long and Fascinating History of the Most Appealing Island of the Mediterranean Sea]. Newton Compton.

Longhi Javarini, Giuseppe. 1992. *In Costa Smeralda: Il segno dell'architetto* [In Costa Smeralda: The Architect's Sign]. Di Baio

Lullia, Serena. 2012. "Morto a 51 anni l'ex sequestrato Ghilardi" [The Ex-Kidnapped Ghilardi Died at 51]. *La Nuova Sardegna* [New Sardinia], November 29. https://www.lanuovasardegna.it/olbia/cronaca/2012/11/29/news /morto-a-51-anni-l-ex-sequestrato-ghilardi-1.6111247

Madeo, Alfonso. 1965a. "Il successo della Costa Smeralda si misura in centinaia di panfili" [Costa Smeralda's Success Is Measured by the Hundreds of Yachts]. *Corriere della Sera* [Evening Courier], August 31.

Madeo, Alfonso. 1965b. "Virna Lisi coinvolta in una scena da Western" [Virna Lisi Involved in a Western Film Scene]. *Corriere della Sera* [Evening Courier], August 17.

Magro, Sara. 2022. "Costa Smeralda, la sostenibilità ante litteram immaginata 60 anni fa dall'Aga Khan" [Costa Smeralda, Sustainability in Advance Imagined 60 Years Ago by the Aga Khan]. *Il Sole 24 Ore*, July 25. https://www.ilsole24ore.com/art/costa -smeralda-sostenibilita-ante-litteram-immaginata-60-anni-fa-dall-aga-khan-AE0ijQmB

Maiorani, Arianna, and Christine Christie. 2014. "Introduction." In *Multimodal Epistemologies: Towards an Integrated Framework*, edited by Arianna Maiorani and Christine Christie. Routledge.

Marestelle. 2024. "Donne" [Women]. https://marestelle.wordpress.com/blog /sardegnacord/donne/

Marrocu, Luciano. 2021. *Storia popolare del sardi e della Sardegna* [Popular History of Sardinians and Sardinia]. Laterza.

Marshall, Catherine, and Gretchen B. Rossman. 2011. *Designing Qualitative Research*. 5th ed. Sage.

Martinelli, Dario. 2010. *A Critical Companion to Zoosemiotics.* Springer.

Masneri, Michele. 2022. "Sessant'anni di Costa Smeralda, il mare dei potenti" [Sixty Years of Costa Smeralda, the Sea of the Powerful People]. *Il Foglio*, September 26. https://www.ilfoglio.it/terrazzo/2022/09/26/news /sessant-anni-di-costa-smeralda-il-mare-dei-potenti-4484461/

Mauss, Marcel. 1990. *The Gift: The Form and Reason for Exchange in Archaic Society*. Translated by Wilfred Douglas Halls. Routledge.

Mazza, Giovanni. 2006. *Storia di un'isola: La Sardegna dalle origini al duemila* [History of an Island: Sardinia from the Origins to 2000]. Scuola Sarda editore.

Mediobanca. 2024. "John Duncan Miller—Cuccia." *Archivio Storico Mediobanca* [Mediobanca Historical Archive]. https://archiviostorico.mediobanca.com /patrimonio/documenti/john-duncan-miller-cuccia-de6fee0a.html

Melo. 2021. "Cos'era l'Anonima Sarda?" [What the Sardinian Anonymous Banditry Was?] *Sardegna Sud*, July 16. https://www.sardegnasud.it/cosera-lanonima-sarda/

Ministry of Tourism and Creative Economy of the Republic of Indonesia. 2024. "4 Tourism Trends in 2024, Bleisure Is Predicted to Continue Growing." March 14. https://kemenparekraf .go.id/en/articles/4-tourism-trends-in-2024-bleisure-is-predicted-to-continue-growing

Monoscoppio TV. 2018a. "Realiti Sciò, Enrico Lucci intervista Emilio Fede" [Reality Show, Enrico Lucci Interviews Emilio Fede]. You Tube, September 14. https://www.youtube.com/watch?v=J0_pYh9s3tU

Monoscoppio TV. 2018b. "Realiti Sciò, Lele Mora intervistato da Enrico Lucci" [Lele Mora Interviewed by Enrico Lucci]. You Tube, September 14. https://www .youtube.com/watch?v=gvhnv0ObZS0

Monoscoppio TV. 2018c. "Realiti Sciò: Emilio Fede e Lele Mora si riabbrac-ciano" [Reality Show: Emilio Fede and Lele Mora Hug Each Other Again]. You Tube, September 14. https://www.youtube.com/watch?v=3FBYp7z0oTM

Motroni, Andrea. 2019. "Clima, cambiamenti climatici e desertificazioni" [Weather, Climate Changes and Desertification]. In *Sardegna: Geografie di un'isola* [Sardinia: Geographies of an Island], edited by Andrea Corsale and Giovanni Sistu. Franco Angeli.

Muresu, Giada. 2023. "Silvio Berlusconi è morto: Il suo legame indissolubile con Olbia" [Silvio Berlusconi Died: His Indissoluble Tie with Olbia]. *Olbiapuntoit*, June 12. https://www.olbia.it/silvio-berlusconi-e-morto-il-suo-legame-indissolubile-con-la-sardegna

Noonan, Theresa C. 1999. *Document-Based Assessment Activity for Global History Classes*. Weston Walch.

OECD. 2009. *The Impact of Culture on Tourism*. OECD.

Onni, Giuseppe. 2013. "La città del turismo: Processi e forme del turismo sulle coste della Sardegna" [The City of Tourism: Processes and Forms of Tourism on the Sardinian Coasts]. In *Sardegna: La Nuova e l'Antica Felicità* [Sardinia: New and Ancient Happiness], edited by Erika Buonacucina, Francesca Bua, Sonia Borsato, Cristian Cannaos, Alessandra Cappai, Paola Idini, Miriam Mastinu, Giuseppe Onni, Sabrina Scalas, Valentina Talu. Franco Angeli.

Oriolo, Giovanni. 2023. "Gigi Riva si racconta: Dal trasferimento in Sarde-gna al leggendario 4-3 tra Italia e Germania" [Gigi Riva Talks About Himself: From His Move to Sardinia to the Legendary 4-3 Between Italy and Germany]. *Vita Sportiva*, August 7. https://www.vita-sportiva.it/gigi-riva-si-racconta-dal-trasferimento-in-sardegna-al-leggendario-4-3-tra-italia-e-germania/

Ottone, Lorenzo. 2023. "Porto Cervo, la spiaggia del jet-set internazionale dove nacque l'architettura pan-moderna" [Porto Cervo, the Beach of the International Jet-Set Where the Architecture Pan-Modern Was Born]. *Domus*, August 1. https://www.domusweb.it/it/architettura/2023/08/01/porto-cervo.html

Oviglia, Maurizio. 1987. *Sardegna* [Sardinia]. Club Alpino Italiano and Touring Club Italiano editori.

Paolinelli, Patrizio, and Giulio Salierno. 1988. *La carcassa del tempo: Inchiesta sulla Costa Smeralda* [Time's Carcass: Investigation on Costa Smer-alda]. Pellicani Editore.

Paracchini, Gian Luigi. 1999. "Naomi accende la notte di Porto Cervo" [Naomi Lights Up Porto Cervo's Night]. *Corriere della Sera* [Evening Courier], July 8.

Parsons, Craig. 2022. "Constructivism and Interpretive Theory." In *Theory and Methods in Political Science.* 4th ed. Edited by Vivien Lowndes, David Marsh, and Gerry Stoker. Bloomsbury.

Pasqualetto, Andrea. 2019. "Gianmaria Deriu: 'Io, ultimo custode sull'isola del diavolo' " [Gianmaria Deriu: I Am the Last Guardian on the Devil's Island]. *Corriere della sera 7* [Evening Courier, 7], August 30. https://www.corriere.it /sette/incontri/19_agosto_30/gianmaria-deriu-io-ultimo-custode-sull-isola-diavolo -aa1e13d4-c9b3-11e9-89f2-27d7028d49f0.shtml

Peirce, Charles S. 1960. *Collected Papers. Vol. II: Elements of Logic.* Harvard University Press.

Picard, Michael. 1996. *Bali: Cultural Tourism and Touristic Culture.* Archipelago.

Piga, Guido. 2012a. "Così 50 anni fa nacque la Costa Smeralda" [Costa Smeralda 50 Years Ago Was Generated This Way]. *La Nuova Sardegna* [New Sardinia], March 14. https://www.lanuovasardegna.it/regione/2012/03/14/news /cosi-50-anni-fa-nacque-la-costa-smeralda-1.3690312

Piga, Guido. 2012b. *La Principessa: Storia della Costa Smeralda, 1959–2013* [The Princess: History of Costa Smeralda]. Servizi Didattici

Piga, Guido. 2014. "Costa Smeralda, Diventa una villa lo stazzo di Karim" [Costa Smeralda, Karim's Stazzo Becomes a Villa]. *La Nuova Sardegna* [New Sardinia], September 21. https://www.lanuovasardegna.it/regione/2014/09/21 /news/costa-smeralda-diventa-una-villa-lo-stazzo-di-karim-1.9971111

Piga, Guido. 2016. "Ghinami e quel No del 1971 che cancellò la Costa Smeralda" [Ginami and That No in 1971 That Cancelled Costa Smeralda]. *La Nuova Sardegna* [New Sardinia], January 9. https://www.lanuovasardegna.it/olbia/cronaca/2016/01/09/news /ghinami-e-quel-no-del-1971-che-cancello-la-costa-smeralda-1.12747466

Piga, Guido. 2019. *Il grande Principe: La vera storia della Costa Smeralda* [The Great Prince: The True History of Costa Smeralda]. Guido Piga.

Pinna, Alberto. 2006. "Porto Cervo, Berlusconi balla con Lippi alla festa dello sceicco" [Porto Cervo, Berlusconi Dances with Lippi at the Sheik's Party]. *Corriere della Sera* [Evening Courier], August 7.

Pinna, Alberto. 2007. "Veline e karaoke: La dolce estate di Fiorani" [Showgirls and Karaoke: Fiorani's Sweet Summer]. *Corriere della Sera* [Evening Courier], July 4.

Pinna, Alberto. 2008. "E i bagnanti contestano Briatore: Via dalla baia" [Bathers Contest Briatore: Go Away from the Bay]. *Corriere della Sera* [Evening Courier], August 9.

Pinna, Alberto. 2012. "Dal Principe ai nuovi saraceni: Le stagioni della Costa Smeralda" [From the Prince to the New Saracens: Costa Smeralda's Seasons]. *Corriere della Sera* [Evening Courier], April 5.

Pinna, Alberto. 2013. "Costa Smeralda: La Finanza in casa degli Emiri" [Costa Smeralda: The Financial Police at Emirs's House]. *Corriere della Sera* [Evening Courier], October 14.

Pinna, Alessandro. 1981. "Sardegna: Sulla Costa Smeralda è arrivata la stagione dei dollari" [Sardinia: In Costa Smeralda the Dollars's Season Has Arrived]. *Corriere della Sera* [Evening Courier], July 13.

Pinna, Alessandro. 1985. "L'Aga Kahn non lascia le attività in Sardegna" [The Aga Khan Does Not Leave His Activities in Costa Smeralda]. *Corriere della Sera* [Evening Courier], April 3.

Pinna, Alessandro. 2003. "La Costa Smeralda cambia proprietario: Barrack ha offerto 300 milioni di Euro" [Costa Smeralda Changes Its Owner: Barrack Has Offered 300 Million Euro]. *Corriere della Sera* [Evening Courier], January 13.

Pinna, Alessandro. 2005. "Il sogno di Berlusconi: George e Laura a luglio a Villa Certosa" [Berlusconi's Dream: George and Laura in July at Villa Certosa]. *Corriere della Sera* [Evening Courier], June 25.

Pinna, Alessandro. 2022. "Putin e i vertici in Sardegna, tra bagni, feste e lanciamissili" [Putin and the Sardinia's Meetings, Among Swimming, Parties and Missile Launchers]. *La Nuova Sardegna* [New Sardinia], March 3. https://www.lanuovasardegna.it/regione/2022/03/03/news/putin-e-i-vertici-in-sardegna-tra-bagni-feste-e-lanciamissili-1.41271127

Pinna, Piergiorgio. 2011. "Folli notti dei figli di Gheddafi in Sardegna" [The Crazy Nights of Gaddafi's Sons in Sardinia]. *La Nuova Sardegna* [New Sardinia], March 2. https://www.lanuovasardegna.it/regione/2011/03/02/news/folli-notti-dei-figli-di-gheddafi-in-sardegna-1.3375067

Pittau, Massimo. 2018. *Luoghi e toponimi della Sardegna* [Places and Toponyms of Sardinia]. Ipazia Books.

Pitzorno, Bianca. 2013. *Vita di Eleonora d'Arborea, principessa medievale di Sardegna* [The Life of Eleonora D'Arborea, the Medieval Princess of Sardinia]. Mondadori.

Podbielski, Gisele. 1993. *Two European Lives*. Book Guild.

Porru, Franco. 1970. "Persino sull'esclusiva Costa Smeralda sboccia, discreto, il turismo di massa" [Even in the Exclusive Costa Smeralda Discretely the Mass Tourism Blooms]. *Corriere d'Informazione* [Information Courier], July 11.

Posocco, Pisana. 2017. *Progettare la vacanza. Studi sull'architettura balneare del secondo dopoguerra* [Projecting Holidays: Studies on Bath Architecture in the Second Postwar Years]. Quodlibet.

Posocco, Pisana. 2018. "La difficile scelta tra modernità e tradizione. Simon Mossa nel panorama italiano ed internazionale" [The Difficult Choice Between Modernity and Tradition. Simon Massa in the Italian and International Scenario]. In *Antonio Simon Mossa a Nuoro. L'architettura, il cinema, la politica* [Antonio Simon Mossa in Nuoro: Architecture, Cinema, and Politics], edited by Antonello Nasone. ISRE.

Posocco, Pisana, 2019. "Luigi Vietti e l'avventura della Costa Smeralda" [Luigi Vietti and the Adventure of Costa Smeralda]. *FAM: Festival dell'Architettura Magazine* 48/49: 59–72. https://doi.org/10.1283/fam/issn2039-0491/n48-2019/287

Rai News. 2018. "Berlusconi, l'unica condanna definitiva nel processo Mediaset. Portò all'espulsione dal Parlamento" [Berlusconi, His Only Definitive Condemnation in the Mediaset Trial, It Led to His Expulsion from the Parliament]. November 27. https://www.rainews.it/archivio-rainews/articoli/Berlusconi-unica-condanna-nel-processo-Mediaset-e-espulsione-dal-Parlamento-3e0b47ad-3cc7-4411-84bd-ce6a9c74eaeb.html?refresh_ce

Real Estate Costa Smeralda. 2024. "La Storia" [History]. https://www.realestate-costasmeralda.com/la-storia/

Riccardi, Paolo. 2010. *Alla corte dell'Aga Khan: Memorie della Costa Smeralda* [At the Aga Khan's Court: Memories of Costa Smeralda]. Antonio Delfino Editore.

Richards, Greg. 2001. *Cultural Attractions and European Tourism*. CAB International.

Rodwell, Mary. 1998. *Social Work Constructivist Research*. Garland Publishing.

Roggeri, Vanessa. 2022. " 'Ti mando in Sardegna': Un tempo era una minaccia, oggi è un regalo. tutti vogliono venire qui da noi" [I'll Send You to Sardinia: Once It Was a Threat, Today Is a Gift, Everybody Wants to Come Here]. *La Nuova Sardegna* [New Sardinia], August 13. https://www.lanuovasardegna.it /opinioni/2022/08/13/news/ora-tutti-dicono-mi-mando-in-sardegna-1.100070429

Sanna, Emanuele. 2006. *Il popolamento dell'isola e l'origine dei sardi* [The Island's Population and the Sardinians' Origins]. CUEC Editrice.

Sanna, Maria Vittoria. 2007. *Diaspore mercantili e regia azienda nella Sardegna Sabauda: Commercio e imprese dal passaggio dell'isola ai Savoia alle riforme degli anni venti dell'ottocento* [Merchant Diasporas and Regal Company in Savoy Sardinia: Trade and Enterprise from the Island's Passage to the Savoy to the Reformations of the 1800s]. PhD diss., Università di Cagliari.

Sardegna Abbandonata. 2015. "Ex aeroporto di Olbia-Venafiorita" [The Olbia-Villafiorita Ex-Airport]. September 5. https://www.sardegnaabbandonata.it/ ex-aeroporto-abbandonato-di-olbia-venafiorita/

Sardegna Statistiche. 2023. "Carta d'identità" [Identity Card]. https://www .sardegnastatistiche.it/

Scano, Daniela. 1986. "Palau, l'amaro prezzo del successo" [Palau, the Sour Price of Success]. *La Nuova Sardegna* [New Sardinia], August 17.

Scarpellini, Laura. 2019. "Porto Cervo: Ecco la villa da cui tutto ebbe inizio" [Porto Cervo: Here Is the Villa Where Everything Started]. *Olbia.it*, April 18. https://www.olbia.it/porto-cervo-ecco-la-villa-da-cui-tutto-ebbe-inizio

Sconocchia, Adriano. 2020. *Banditi e Briganti d'Italia: La storia, le imprese e la vita violenta dei fuorilegge più famosi tra leggenda e realtà* [Italy's Bandits and Brigants: History, Deeds and Violent Lives of the Most Famous Outlaws Between Legend and Reality]. Newton Compton editori.

Scott, Noel, Eric Laws, and Philipp Boksberger. 2010. *Marketing of Tourism Experiences*. Routledge.

Sebeok, Thomas Albert. 1977. *How Animals Communicate*. Indiana University Press.

Sebeok, Thomas Albert. 1991. *A Sign Is Just a Sign*. Indiana University Press.

Sebeok, Thomas Albert. 2001. "Biosemiotics: Its Roots, Proliferation, and Prospects." *Semiotica* 134 (1–4): 61–78. https://doi.org/10.1515/semi.2001.014

Sechi, Antonello. 2020a. "L'Aga Khan vende Geasar. Il Costa Smeralda va a F2i" [The Aga Khan Sells Geasar. The Costa Smeralda Airport Goes to F2i]. *La Nuova Sardegna* [New Sardinia], October 24. https://www.lanuovasardegna.it /regione/2020/10/24/news/l-aga-khan-vende-geasar-il-costa-smeralda-va-a-f2i-1.39459059

Sechi, Antonello. 2020b. "Finisce l'era dell'Aga Khan, ma lui non lascia la Costa" [The Aga Khan's Era Ends, but He Does Not Leave the Costa]. *La Nuova Sardegna* [New Sardinia], October 25. https://www.lanuovasardegna.it/regione/2020/10/25 /news/finisce-l-era-dell-aga-khan-ma-lui-non-lascia-la-costa-1.39462619

Sella, Quintino. 1871. *Relazione del deputato Sella alla Commissione d'inchiesta composta dai deputati Depretis, Ferracciù, Macchi, Mantegazza, Sella, Tenani sulle condizioni dell'industria mineraria nell'isola di Sardegna* [MP Sella's Relation to the Committee of Inquiry Composed of MPs Depretis, Ferracciù, Macchi, Mantegazza, Sella, Tenani on the Conditions of the Mining Industry in the Island of Sardinia]. May 3. Edizioni del Parlamento Italiano.

Sirigu, Paola. 2007. *Il codice barbaricino* [The Barbaricino Codex]. La Riflessione editore.

Sorge, Antonio. 2015. *Legacies of Violence: History, Society, and the State in Sardinia.* University of Toronto Press.

Stella, Gianantonio. 2004. "Camicia aperta e sorrisi, il Cavaliere lancia il bagnino style" [Open Shirt and Smiles, Berlusconi Launches the Lifeguard Style]. *Corriere della Sera* [Evening Courier], August 18.

Stewart, Alex. 1998. *The Ethnographer's Method.* Sage.

Stringfellow, Lindsay, Andrew MacLaren, Mairi Maclean, and Kevin O'Gorman. 2013. "Conceptualizing Taste: Food, Culture, and Celebrity." *Tourism Management* 37: 77–85. https://doi.org/10.1016/j.tourman.2012.12.016

Taylor, Roberta. 2014. "Multimodal Analysis of the Textual Function in Children's Face-to-Face Classroom Interaction." In *Multimodal Epistemologies: Towards an Integrated Framework*, edited by Arianna Maiorani and Christine Christie. Routledge.

Technavio. 2024. "Cultural Tourism Market Analysis Europe, APAC, North America, South America, Middle East and Africa—China, Japan, Italy, France,

Spain—Size and Forecast 2024–2028." https://www.technavio.com/report/cultural-tourism-market-industry-analysis

Tgcom24. 2013. "Lele Mora: 'Mi pento di certe cose' " [Lele Mora: "I Regret of Some Things"]. February 22. https://www.tgcom24.mediaset.it/spettacolo/articoli/1082750/lele-mora-mi-pento-di-certe-cose-.shtml

Tolu, Francesca. 2023. "Storia della Sardegna" [History of Sardinia]. *Sardegna Natura.* https://www.sardegnanatura.com/sardegna/storia-sardegna.html

Touring Club. 2013. *Sardegna : Cagliari e La Maddalena, le spiagge dal sud alla Gallura, nuraghi, tradizioni, natura* [Sardinia: Cagliari and La Maddalena, the Beaches from South to Gallura, Nuraghes, Traditions, Nature]. Touring Club Editore.

Trillo, Claudia. 2003. *Territori del Turismo tra Utopia e Atopia* [Tourism Territories Between Utopia and Atopia]. Alinea editrice.

TripAdvisor. 2011. "Costa Smeralda... Sardegna?" [Costa Smeralda... Sardinia?] https://www.tripadvisor.it/ShowTopic-g1-i11064-k4034176-Costa_smeralda_sardegna-General_Discussion.html

Trono, Anna. 2014. "Cultural and Religious Routes: A New Opportunity for Regional Development." In *New Tourism in the 21st Century: Culture, the City, Nature and Spirituality,* edited by Rubén Lois Gonzàles, Xosé Santos-Solla, and Pilar Taboada de Zuniga. Cambridge Scholar.

Tuttitalia. 2024. "Regioni italiane per densità" [Italian Regions According to Population Density]. https://www.tuttitalia.it/regioni/densita/

Urry, John Richard. 1992. *The Tourist Gaze: Leisure and Travel in Contemporary Societies.* Sage.

Vacca, Andrea. 2019. "I suoli della Sardegna: Caratteristiche principali e fattori e processo di degradazione" [Sardinia's Soil: Principal Characteristics and Factors and Degradation Processes]. In *Sardegna: Geografie di un'isola* [Sardinia: Geographies of an Island], edited by Andrea Corsale and Giovanni Sistu. Franco Angeli.

Vacca, Bruno F. 1990. *Gli antichi sardi dei bronzetti nuragici* [The Ancient Sardinians of the Nuraghic Bronzes]. Edizioni V.I.S. Visioni Informative Sarde.

Van Boven, Leaf, and Thomas Gilovich. 2003. "To Do or to Have: That Is the Question." *Journal of Personality and Social Psychology* 85 (6): 1193–1202. https://doi.org/10.1037/0022-3514.85.6.1193

Van Leeuwen, Theo. 2005. *Introducing Social Semiotics*. Routledge.

Vasconi, Marcella. 1998. *Sardegna: l'orgoglio, la cultura, il mistero di un popolo* [Sardinia: The Pride, Culture, Mystery of a People]. Giunti Demetra edizioni.

Weber, Max. 2012. *The Protestant Ethic and the Spirit of Capitalism*. Translated by Stephen Kalberg. Routledge.

World Bank. 1955. "For Release." https://documents1.worldbank.org/curated /en/375871592963206922/pdf/Announcement-of-Appointment-of-John -Duncan-Miller-to-Act-as-the-World-Bank-s-Special-Representative-in-Europe-on -January-24-1955.pdf

Zasso, di Marcello. 2022. " 'Questa non è la Sardegna': Bianca Pitzorno infiamma il dibattito sulla Costa Smeralda" [This Is Not Sardinia: Bianca Pitzorno Inflames the Debate on Costa Smeralda]. *Gallura Oggi*, August 3. https://www.galluraoggi.it /costa-smeralda/bianca-pitzorno-sardegna-costa-smeralda-post-porto-cervo-3-agosto-2022/

Zasso, Gino. 1980. "Anche l'industria turistica in Sardegna scricchiola, sono diminuiti gli arrivi nella zona dei sequestri" [Even the Tourism Industry Creaks in Sardinia, in the Areas of Kidnapping the Arrivals Decrease]. *Corriere della Sera* [Evening Courier], July 11.

Zasso, Gino. 1981. "La Costa Smeralda vuole difendere il suo marchio dalle imitazioni" [Costa Smeralda Wants to Defend Its Brand from Imitations]. *Corriere della Sera* [Evening Courier], July 25.

Zasso, Gino. 1984. "L'Aga Khan voleva investire mille miliardi nella Costa Smeralda, ma un decreto dell'assessore regionale riduce il piano urbanistico" [The Aga Khan Wanted to Invest 1000 Billions on Costa Smeralda, but a Regional Councilor's Decree Limits the Urban Plan]. *Corriere della Sera* [Evening Courier], February 20.

Zasso, Gino. 1997. "Distrutta la tartaruga di pietra: Nuova e definitiva decapitazione della roccia simbolo delle bellezze sarde" [The Stone Tartle Has Been Destroyed: A New and Definitive Beheading of the Stone That Is the Symbol of Sardinian Beauties]. *Corriere della Sera* [Evening Courier], February 22.

Zedda, Claudia. 2024. "Costa Smeralda: La Sardegna che non è più Sardegna" [Costa Smeralda: Sardinia That Is Not Sardinia Anymore]. *Claudiazedda.it*. https://www .claudiazedda.it/costa-smeralda-la-sardegna-che-non-e-piu-sardegna/